Evangelism Is...

How to Share Jesus with Passion and Confidence

DAVE EARLEY & DAVID WHEELER

ACADEMIC

Nashville, Tennessee

Published by B & H Academic Publishing Group
Nashville, Tennessee

ISBN: 978–0–8054–4959–4

Dewey Decimal Classification: 248.5

Subject Heading: WITNESSING \ EVANGELISTIC WORK

Printed in the United States of America

1 2 3 4 5 6 7 8 9 10 11 12 • 18 17 16 15 14 13 12 11 10

BP

Contents

Part 3. Manner

Evangelism Is . . .

Part 4. Methods

Evangelism Is . . .

APPENDIXES

Preface

This is more than just another book; it is your guide to the great adventure of doing your part to change the world for Jesus Christ. Let us warn you: these 40 chapters are dangerous. They will transform your life. They will set you on a course that will cause you to see and treat people differently than you have ever seen them before. They will make you a spiritual change agent, a difference maker, an impact player for Jesus Christ. They can even make your name known in hell.

We have given our adult lives to fulfilling the Great Commission. Our journey has led us to state universities, steaming inner cities, rural churches, South American mission fields, megachurches, denominational positions, church planting ventures, and a Christian university and seminary campus. In attempting to fulfill the Great Commission, we have tried anything we thought might help. We have made plenty of mistakes and won many victories. We have read the books and attended the conferences. We have trained thousands of students, laypersons, and pastors across America and in many foreign nations. As a result we have culled our combined 60 years of personal evangelism experience to give you what we believe are the 40 most important lessons to grasp in order to share Jesus with passion and confidence.

We deeply desire to help you. We are incredibly proud of you. Anybody who has the guts to read a book with the word *Evangelism* in the title is our kind of person. Effective personal evangelism can be one of the hardest yet most fulfilling challenges you can accept. Often it demands immense patience and perseverance. Continuing to work and wait for a harvest that seems slow in coming is extremely hard. At times the enemy seems to be fighting you every step of the way. You need encouragement in strong doses. That's why we wrote this book.

You can easily get in a routine and a rut. You find yourself doing what you have always done. Your spiritual life quickly becomes stagnant and monotonous. You need some fresh ideas, some practical suggestions, and a new perspective. That's also why we wrote this book.

Learning to share Jesus with passion and confidence can seem a little like eating an elephant. You don't get it all at once. You have to "eat it one bite at a time," learning a little more each week.

This book contains 40 chapters of high-octane equipment, empowerment, and encouragement for anyone who wants to make a difference. We cover personal evangelism from almost every conceivable angle possible. Great for beginners, it also offers practical guidance for the most seasoned veteran. Each of the 40 chapters was written as a stand-alone article, yet they tie together to train, teach, and encourage any potential difference maker.

This book was not designed to be rapidly read and quickly forgotten. It was prayerfully put together with the goal of changing your life. It will explain the what, why, and how of personal evangelism. Read it with a pen in hand to mark it up and make notes in the margin. Personalize it. Let it mark your life by making it *your* book.

Before we begin to explain what *Evangelism Is*, David Wheeler will express some thoughts about what it is not.

What Evangelism Is Not

A few years ago I had the misfortune of discussing the idea of evangelism with a high ranking administrator at a major Christian institution in the Midwest. While he was appreciative of the many ways that our organization was willing to serve and assist his students by providing motivational speakers and opportunities for outreach, he was perplexed by the use of the word *evangelism* in reference to promoting our ministry to his student body. He even went as far as to state, "Evangelism is a negative term for our students!" I recall thinking, "Wow . . . when did Evangelicals become offended by the concept of evangelism?"

Unfortunately, I have had similar experiences working with pastors and other church leaders. In fact, it is common to meet Christians like this college administrator who place a low value on the concept of evangelism. The question is . . . why?

Much of the reason is because the church has believed a series of false assumptions related to evangelism. So here are some things that *Evangelism is not . . .*

1. A choice. It is generally accepted in Christian circles that the majority of believers rarely share their faith with another unsaved person. I have noticed this in my graduate-level evangelism classes. By a simple show of hands, well over half of the students will admit that they rarely share their faith with an unsaved person. One of the contributing factors is that evangelism is taught as an individual *choice* rather than a biblical *command*. This is misleading and dangerous in reference to the Great Commission. Consider what Jesus says in Acts 1:8: "But you shall receive power when the Holy Spirit has come upon you; and you shall be witnesses to Me in Jerusalem, and in all Judea and Samaria, and to the end of the earth." The phrase "you shall be witnesses" is written as a direct *command* of Christ. The aim is to mobilize His disciples into the world to fulfill His earlier promise as recorded in Mark 1:17: "Follow Me, and I will make you become fishers of men."

2. Just passing on information. There are hundreds of ways to effectively share Christ with an unbeliever. However, in doing so, one must remember that evangelism is *not* just sharing the right biblical information. As I always tell my classes, "You cannot divorce Jesus' message from the life He lived." This simply means that Jesus not only shared the truth in word; He also embodied that same truth through a consistent lifestyle. While it is very important to share the correct biblical knowledge related to salvation, always remember that the knowledge you share is validated to the world through a consistent testimony of a changed life.

3. A spiritual gift. Contrary to what many people believe in the church, evangelism is *not* listed as a spiritual gift in Scripture. While some people may have talents that aid in becoming more natural at evangelism, the call to evangelize is meant for the entire church. It is *not* reserved for a selected few soldiers.

As we discuss in chapter 7, the word for evangelism literally means "good news" or the "message." The problem is that most people define evangelism as merely *sharing* the good news (a verb), when actually evangelism *is* the good news (a noun). Our problem with evangelism is that we define it by the action, not the nature or essence of the action. At the core, evangelism is the "good news" of Christ and therefore must be embraced as a lifestyle by every Christ follower.

4. Just something you do. Evangelism must never be minimized to something you perform as a duty to God. Rather, like breathing it should be an involuntary response to naturally share Christ whenever possible. In short, evangelism is the essence of who you are as you walk through daily life. It is the consistent and natural overflow of a deep and abiding relationship with Christ.

5. In competition with discipleship. I often hear people espousing the tenets of discipleship over the call to evangelize. These people often minimize evangelism and use phrases like "I am a disciple maker, not an evangelist." This may sound good, but it is biblically incorrect. The truth is, evangelism and discipleship are uniquely dependent on each other. While intentional evangelism that leads to a spiritual conversion always precedes the process of discipleship, neither process is complete until the one who is being discipled learns to multiply their witness through sharing Christ with unsaved people. Possessing a genuine passion for biblical multiplication through evangelism is a key indicator when evaluating spiritual maturity.

6. Based on your personality. Some people believe that evangelism is only reserved for "A" type personalities. Nothing could be further from the truth. Evangelism *is* a biblical *command* to be fulfilled through all types of people. Regardless if you are shy or outgoing, remember that every Christian is responsible to the call of evangelism.

7. The same as "missions." The word *evangelism* has lost its distinctiveness and importance to the church over the past 25 years, as many people have replaced it with the concept of "missions." The essential nature and expression of evangelism is the passionate proclamation of the message of the gospel to the end that people will be redeemed as they trust Christ and his saving work at the cross to receive forgiveness and eternal life. On the other hand, missions is a transcultural enterprise in which the gospel message is taken into another culture at home or overseas (Acts 1:8). Therefore, it always has evangelism at its heart. If the pursuit of missions drives evangelism to the point that sharing the gospel message is secondary, then both expressions lose their biblical focus. Evangelism must be the purpose and driving force of all missions. It is impossible to do real missions without intentionally doing evangelism.

8. Acting arrogant or superior. First Peter 5:6 says, "Humble yourselves, therefore, under God's mighty hand, that he may lift you up in due time" (NIV). The key to effective evangelism is a well-prepared, obedient, loving, and humble heart for God. A "know it all" and "cocky" attitude will always hinder the effectiveness of evangelism.

9. Meant to be silenced by fear. In 2 Tim 1:7–8, the apostle Paul states, "For God did not give us a spirit of timidity [fear], but a spirit of power, of love and of self-discipline. So do not be ashamed to testify about our Lord" (NIV). While appropriate fear is rational in certain situations, according to Scripture, this should not apply to the task of evangelism.

10. **A theological dilemma.** Some people try to use theological constructs to ignore the Great Commission. Because of extreme viewpoints related to the doctrine of election, more contemporary ministers are ignoring their responsibility to be active in evangelism. The same is true when liberal theologians compromise the authority of Scripture. In many cases humility and obedience are replaced by theological superiority and a critical spirit that is detrimental to evangelism. In short, theology without evangelism is not Christian theology at all.

Conclusion

At the end of each chapter in this book, you will find challenges to apply what you have just read. You will also find a few big truths to learn, a verse to remember, and often some quotes to consider.

Because we have experienced the amazing joy and fulfillment that come from sharing Jesus with passion and confidence, we want to encourage you to read all 40 chapters. You may want to read one a day for the next 40 days. You will want to make your daily reading a regular appointment in your schedule.

So get a cup of coffee, grab your Bible, and dive in. We pray that this little book will become a big book in your life. May it become your coach, equipping encourager, and idea catalyst for a lifetime of making a difference.

Part 1
Motive

1

Joyfully Intoxicating

Dave Earley

*There is no escape: if we, by God's grace,
are successful in evangelism we will be happier.
Our joy in God will be increased.*

—JOHN PIPER[1]

The thought of talking to anyone about Jesus made me break out in a sweat and get all queasy inside. I am an introvert, and talking to people about anything, let alone something controversial like Jesus, was light-years beyond my comfort zone. But after several years of wild living, I had recently given myself 100 percent to God. Plus I did care about the present life and eternal destiny of my best friend, Scott. Scott needed Jesus. He could curse better than anyone I had ever met. When he got mad, he would enthusiastically weave a web of profanity that could impress a sailor. Deeper than that, I knew he was empty inside.

Lee, our youth pastor, had asked us to pair up and prayerfully attempt to share the gospel with a friend within a week. I felt a little better knowing that my partner, Roy, had been witnessing for years and had even led some people to Christ. Unlike me, he knew all the right verses and where to find them. He also was pretty good friends with Scott. So that night we prayed about sharing Jesus with Scott.

For several reasons that prayer was possibly the hardest I had ever prayed. First, Lee's teaching the last few weeks on evangelism gave me a deep concern for Scott. I realized that he was empty and his wicked mouth was merely the reflection of his aching heart. He was lost and needed God.

Second, Scott's dad was certainly no fan of real Christianity. I was afraid of what he might think, say, or even do.

Third, Scott was my best friend. I did not want him to think we were sissies, religious weirdos, or worst of all, "Jesus salesmen." I did not want to lose a friend.

Fourth, like I said, Scott was my best friend. He knew me as well as anyone. If anyone knew I was not perfect, it was Scott.

Fifth, I was flat-out scared. I had never talked with anyone about Jesus. I did not know all the verses or what to say. Lee had taught us some opening questions, but I was worried that I would say something stupid and mess it all up. What if something I said drove Scott farther away from God? What if he asked something I did not know how to answer?

Roy was more confident than I was. He said something about us doing our part and the Holy Spirit doing His.

The next night Roy came to my house. Again we prayed for Scott and what we had to share with him. Then we walked over to Scott's house.

I had told Scott that Roy and I were coming by and had something important to talk to him about, but I had not told him what it was. Scott was understandably curious when he answered the door. We went in and made some small talk with his parents, then looked for an excuse to go up to Scott's room.

Scott Hears the Good News

Scott is both a sports fan and an artist. Even back then the walls of his room were covered with pictures he had drawn or painted and posters of his favorite athletes. With the Cincinnati Reds' own Johnny Bench gazing down on us, we pulled the pocket New Testaments out of our back pockets and dove in.

"Scott, we have come to tell you about Jesus," I said resolutely.

"No kidding," he smirked, looking down at our New Testaments.

"We all know you need Jesus, and Roy is going to show you why," I offered looking over at Roy for help.

Fortunately Roy was ready. "This is Romans 3:23," he said, pointing down at his KJV New Testament. "Would you read that verse out loud for us?"

Scott stared down at the page and quietly read, "For all have sinned, and come short of the glory of God."

"That's right," I said. "We have all sinned—me, you, and even Roy. We are not perfect. We have fallen short. We have sinned." Then I didn't know what else to say, so looking over at Roy I said, "Show him another one."

"This is Romans 3:10–12," Roy said calmly pointing down at his New Testament. "Would you read those verses for us?"

Scott peered down on the page and began to read: "As it is written, There is none righteous, no, not one: There is none that understandeth, there is none that seeketh after God. They are all gone out of the way, they are together become unprofitable; there is none that doeth good, no, not one."

"Yeah," I said, trying to think of what to say.

Fortunately Roy was ready. "You see, Scott," he said, "because we have all sinned, in the eyes of God we are not righteous. We are corrupt. In fact we tend to mess everything up."

"Yeah," I said. "Show him another one Roy."

"This is Romans 6:23," he said. "Please read it for us."

"For the wages of sin is death; but the gift of God is eternal life through Jesus Christ our Lord."

"Sin has consequences," I said.

"The punishment we have earned for our sins is death," Roy added. "Not just physical death but eternal death."

"That's hell," I said. "This is serious."

Scott sighed.

"Show him another one, Roy," I said.

"Before we go on," Roy said, "would you please read the last part of that verse again, Scott?"

"But the gift of God is eternal life through Jesus Christ our Lord," Scott read.

"That's the good news," Roy said. "The bad news is that we have all sinned and deserve death. The good news is that Jesus died for our sins."

"Yeah," I said sounding intelligent.

"Scott, please read this verse for us," Roy said, pointing to Romans 5:8.

Slowly Scott read the verse, "But God commendeth his great love for us, in that, while we were yet sinners, Christ died for us."

"God loves you so much, Scott, that He sent Jesus to die for you," Roy said.

"We love you, too, Scott," I added. "That's why we are here tonight." I could not believe I had said that. What had gotten into me? Scott would definitely think we were sissies or worse now. "Show him another verse," I said quickly.

"This is Romans 10:9," Roy said. "Please read it for us."

Scott looked down seriously. Slowly he read, "That if thou shalt confess with thy mouth the Lord Jesus, and shalt believe in thine heart that God hath raised him from the dead, thou shalt be saved."

"Because of Jesus' death on our behalf," Roy said, "all we have to do is believe in Him, trusting His death as the payment for our sins; and if we are willing to let Him be Lord of our lives, we will be saved! Look at this verse," he said, pointing down at Romans 10:13.

Well trained by now, Scott read, "For whosoever shall call upon the name of the Lord shall be saved."

"Scott, let me ask you a few questions," Roy began. "Do you believe that you are a sinner?"

I was silently praying as hard as I could.

"We all know I am," Scott said as he stared into Roy's eyes.

"Do you believe Jesus died to pay for your sins?"

Surprisingly, Scott said, "Yes."

"Are you willing to call Jesus Lord of your life?"

Again Scott said, "Yes."

"Would you like to be saved right now?" Roy asked.

"Yes," Scott said weakly.

Unable to be quiet another moment, I piped up, "What you have to do is pray and mean it. If you really believe it when you call on the Lord, you will be saved." Roy shot a pleasantly surprised glance. I was shocked myself. That actually sounded pretty good and made sense. Where did that come from?

"Do you want to pray right now?" Roy asked.

"Yes," Scott gulped. "I have to. But I have never prayed out loud before."

"OK," Roy said. "Let's try this. We will all get down on our knees. I am going to say a phrase out loud. If you agree with it, Scott, you can pray it out loud to God."

"OK," Scott said dropping quietly to his knees.

"Dear God," Roy said.

"Dear . . . uh . . . Dear God," Scott gulped. I opened my eyes and peeked over at Scott. I could not believe what I saw. A tear was racing down his cheek. Scott never cried. Wow!

"I admit that I have sinned," Roy said.

"I have sinned," Scott said.

Roy continued, "I believe that Jesus died to pay for all of my sins."

"I believe that Jesus died to pay for all of my sins," Scott repeated.

"I believe that He rose from the dead," Roy said.

"I believe that He rose from the dead," Scott prayed.

I could not believe it. My foul-mouthed best friend was actually praying to God and calling on Jesus to save him. Wow!

"Dear God, please forgive my sins," Roy said.

Scott was really breathing heavy by now, "Dear God, please forgive my sins," he gasped.

"Please come into my life and change me."

"Please come into my life and change me," Scott prayed.

"I want You to be Lord of the rest of my life," Roy said.

"I want You to be Lord of the rest of my life," Scott repeated.

"I believe that You heard me and that I now am saved," Roy said.

"I believe that You heard me and that I now am saved," Scott said firmly.

"Amen," Roy stated.

"Amen," Scott and I said at the same time.

The next few minutes Roy shared with Scott some other verses, and we made an appointment to get together and study the Bible later in the week. Scott also agreed to go to church with us.

The next thing I knew we were out on the street. Those two hours had flown by.

Scott Got Saved!

I walked out of Scott's house tingling all over. It felt like I was in a dream, a really good dream. When we got down to the corner, sufficiently out of sight and earshot, I pumped my fist. "Yes!" I said.

"Yes!" Roy followed, pumping his fist.

"I cannot believe it," I laughed. "Scott got saved."

"Believe it, my friend," Roy chuckled. "Scott got saved."

Then Roy did something that I will never forget. A funny look came over his face. "I heard an evangelist at a youth camp last summer," he said, bending down and taking off his shoes. "He said that whenever he got happy in Jesus, he took his shoes off and pounded them together."

Then Roy jumped up with a shoe in each hand. He began to pogo stick up and down, pounding his shoes together, shouting, "Scott got saved! Scott got saved!"

Within seconds I had my shoes off and had joined him, slapping them together, shouting in unison, "Scott got saved! Scott got saved!"

Reading this must seem pretty bizarre, but I assure you, it was real. We just could not help it. Scott was our friend, and we had been concerned about him. On top of that, we had experienced what it felt like to have the Lord use us to share Jesus effectively. It was so much fun. It was one of the best highs I had ever or have ever known.

I did not realize it at the time, but I now know that we were not alone in our rejoicing.

Luke 15:10 gives us a staggering glimpse beyond the veil when it says, "I tell you, there is rejoicing in the presence of the angels of God over one sinner who repents" (NIV). Think of it, maybe the angels who witnessed Scott's conversion had their sandals off and pounded them together the night Scott got saved. Maybe the Lord Jesus Himself had His sandals off pounding them together. Maybe some of Scott's relatives who had gone on to heaven were jumping around heaven rejoicing.

Although I have been privileged to lead many people to Jesus (usually I keep my shoes on now but not always), nothing has surpassed the incredible adrenaline rush of the night Scott got saved. It launched me on a journey I would never trade. It is an addiction I hope I won't kick until I get to heaven.

We wanted to write this book to help you know what it is like to see one of your friends give his or her life to Jesus Christ. We can tell you, it is amazing! Nothing is more fulfilling or fun! We also wrote this book because we know that you can do it. If God could use me to help my friend get saved, He certainly can use you. And He will if you let Him.

By the way, the last time I spoke with Scott, he was active in his church. He is married to a lovely Christian lady and has two great kids. He now uses his artistic skills to design book covers for Christian publishers.

Over the years I have found that evangelism brings me joy simply because God commanded it and obedience is always a joy producer. It also brings me joy because when I evangelize, I am making the name of Jesus famous. It especially brings joy when the person I share with says, "Yes."

∼ Evangelism Is . . . ∼

1. Friends telling friends about Jesus. Roy and I were able to get away with showing up at Scott's house and sharing the gospel because we had already earned his friendship.
2. Powerful! Scott got saved and his life was changed.
3. An intoxicating increaser of the joy for everyone involved. The person sharing the gospel, the person receiving the gospel, and heaven itself erupt in joy.
4. Joyfully addictive. Since that first time God used me to help someone find Jesus, I have been doing evangelism.

∼ Key Verse ∼

"Likewise, I say to you, there is joy in the presence of the angels of God over one sinner who repents." (Luke 15:10)

∼ Good Quotes ∼

Something happened to me—I got a taste of what it was like to be used by God. I knew that no matter what I did in life, I wanted to continue to share the gospel.

—GREG LURIE[2]

Therefore, under God, our goal in evangelism is to be his instruments in creating new people who delight in God through Jesus Christ and who thus bring us great joy.

—JOHN PIPER[3]

Even if I were utterly selfish, and had no care for anything but my own happiness, I would choose, if I might, under God, to be a soul-winner; for never did I know perfect, overflowing, utterable happiness of the purest and most ennobling order till I first heard of one who had sought and found the Saviour through my means. No young mother ever so rejoiced over her firstborn child, no warrior was so exultant over a hard-won victory.

—C. H. SPURGEON[4]

— Application —

List the names of a few of your friends or acquaintances who do not yet know Jesus. Make it a daily habit to ask God to use you to share Jesus with them.

Notes

1. J. Piper, "How Does Christian Hedonism Relate to Evangelism?" (January 1, 1978), http://www.desiringGod.org, accessed April 1, 2009.

2. G. Laurie, *New Believer's Guide to How to Share Your Faith* (Wheaton, IL: Tyndale, 1999), 3.

3. Piper, "How Does Christian Hedonism Relate to Evangelism?" 3.

4. C. H. Spurgeon, quoted in J. Oswald Sanders, *The Divine Art of Soul-Winning* (Chicago: IL: Moody Press, 1980), 11.

2

The Real Business of Life

Dave Earley

The glory of God, and, as our only means of glorifying Him,
the salvation of souls is the real business of life.

—C. S. Lewis[1]

The Hamburger and Ice Cream Business

When I was in high school, I entered the business world by taking a job at a local hamburger and ice cream restaurant. During my shifts I dipped ice cream; made milkshakes, malts, and sodas; created ice cream sundaes; and produced banana splits. I also ran the cash register, washed the dishes, bused the tables clean, acted as the host, did meal prep, and occasionally waited on tables. I liked the job for several reasons: they gave me a paycheck every week, the restaurant was usually busy so the time flew by, and most of the waitresses were pretty cute. I was really enjoying it.

Yet after a few weeks of late-night weekend shifts, the thrill was gone. A dark truth crashed into my idealistic head. I was in the hamburger and ice cream business. I was working my tail off night after night so people could feed their faces. The only lasting value of the food we prepared was the pounds of fat it might create on the customers.

At that time a friend challenged me to read through the writings of Christian thinker and author C. S. Lewis. One sentence jumped off the page and changed everything about my job. Lewis said, "The glory of God, and, as our only means of glorifying Him, the salvation of souls is the real business of life."

The Salvation of Souls Business

On that day I made a glorious transition out of the hamburger and ice cream business into "the salvation of souls" business. My job at the restaurant took on new meaning as I began to go to work with an eternal purpose. I wanted to glorify God by cooperating in His plan to bring salvation to my coworkers. Every time I went to work I tried to work as hard and efficiently as I could. I also tried to build relationships with the other employees. And I began to pray for their souls every morning.

When I went into the restaurant with the attitude of glorifying God by seeing people come to know Him, an interesting phenomenon occurred: work became more fulfilling and challenging. It was no longer about ice cream or hamburgers, getting a paycheck, or flirting with a waitress. It was about something much bigger than all of that. It was about the glory of God. It was about eternity.

As I went into work with a new attitude, I quickly saw clearly why I was there. The chief cook was a broken, alcoholic Vietnam vet. The head manager was an unhappy, overworked husband. The head waitress was an attractive young lady who was more than willing to use her sexual charms to sleep her way out of the life she had known. Another waitress was a scared, single mom. Yet another waitress was a lonely single girl whose only friends were the people who worked in the restaurant. The assistant managers were empty young men trying to find happiness in the age-old temptations of money, sex, and power.

I began to work out with the assistant managers on our days off or in the mornings when we worked the late shift. We became friends. As a result of my efforts and prayers, one of my assistant managers started to come to church with me. One Sunday after church he and I were eating lunch in the city park. The pastor had clearly shared the gospel in the sermon that morning, and I was discussing it with my assistant manager. I reviewed the gospel with him, and he gave his life to Christ. That moment was more exciting than getting my first paycheck.

When I made the real business of life the real business of *my* life, my life became more fulfilling and work became more fun.

It's Not About You

A common myth of our culture is that we need to make ourselves the center of our universe in order to be fulfilled. We live with the lie that God exists to make us happy. Yet the truth is that it's not about you, and it's not about me. The real business of life is far greater than your own personal fulfillment, your peace of mind, or even your happiness. It's far greater than your family, your career, or even your wildest dreams and ambitions. The real business of life is glorifying God and being used by Him to transform unbelievers into people whose great delight in life is to know and trust Him.

Deep happiness never comes through focusing on yourself. It is the result of living a life centered on God and directed toward others. True joy does not reach its climax in a private communion with God. Rather it reaches its fullest extent only when it is compounded by the joy of seeing others share in it with us.

Why Are We Here?

What is life about? What is it for? Why do I exist? Why am I here?

Sooner or later every thinking person asks those questions. The Bible is crystal clear: God created us for His glory. He said: "Bring my sons from afar and my daughters from the ends of the earth—everyone who is called by my name, whom I created for my glory" (Isa 43:6–7 NIV).

Notice those last four words: "created for my glory." The meaning of life is found in glorifying God. God knows that the best thing for us is Himself. As we focus our lives on Him—or in other words, as we glorify Him—doing so gives us fulfillment. This is because He truly is the best thing that could ever happen to us.

The Westminster Shorter Catechism opens with this foundational question:

Q. 1. What is the chief end of man?
A. Man's chief end is to glorify God, and to enjoy him forever.

Our primary purpose is to glorify God and derive our greatest joy from Him. Yet there is more. Not only were we created for God's glory, but we were saved to live for God's glory: "For you were bought at a price; therefore glorify God in your body and in your spirit, which are God's" (1 Cor 6:20).

How to Glorify God

We are created for God's glory (Isa 43:7) and saved to glorify God (1 Cor 6:20). The next logical question is this: *How* do I best glorify God? Lewis answered that for us in his *Reflections:* "The glory of God, and, as our only means of glorifying Him, *the salvation of souls* is the real business of life."

Ultimately God gets the most glory, and we find the deepest fulfillment when our lives are concentrated on "the salvation of souls." God is glorified as we lead others to also become God glorifiers. In other words God gets glory when we help others get saved. The apostle Paul tells us that God's glory through the salvation of others should be the driving motivation behind everything we do, even what we eat or drink: "Therefore, whether you eat or drink, or whatever you do, do all to the glory of God. Give no offense, either to the Jews or to the Greeks or to the church of God, just as I also please all men in all things, not seeking my own profit, but the profit of many, that they may be saved" (1 Cor 10:31–33).

Notice the first sentence: "Whatever you do, do all to the glory of God." Now notice those last five words, "that they may be saved." Evangelism, helping people get saved, is deeply rewarding because it fulfills the reason for our existence. Evangelism is why you are here. You will never be fulfilled until you live for the glory of God. You can't glorify God unless you live a lifestyle of evangelism.

You must make the real business of life, the salvation of souls, the real business of *your* life. Don't waste your life living for yourself. Don't waste it pursuing pleasure, position, or possessions. Don't waste it merely collecting experiences and adventures. Don't waste it at all. Instead use it for that which will bring you the most fulfillment on Earth and the most joy in eternity. Invest your life in glorifying God by the salvation of souls.

God may lead you to be a schoolteacher, a homemaker, a missionary, an artist, a doctor, or a musician. You may sense God's directing you to be a businessperson, an engineer, a laborer, a lawyer, a farmer, a church planter, or a technician. Whatever career God guides you into, let it be a platform by which you help cultivate the salvation of souls.

Ambassadors

No matter where you may be employed at the time, the real business of life is glorifying God through the salvation of souls. It is being on mission with

God. It is serving as His representative to the people needing Him in that store, office, restaurant, or factory. It is living and telling His message to the people who need to see and hear it.

> Therefore, if anyone is in Christ, he is a new creation; old things have passed away; behold, all things have become new. Now all things are of God, who has reconciled us to Himself through Jesus Christ, and has given us the ministry of reconciliation, that is, that God was in Christ reconciling the world to Himself, not imputing their trespasses to them, and has committed to us the word of reconciliation.
> Now then, we are ambassadors for Christ. (2 Cor 5:17–20)

Notice that once we have been made new by Christ, we are given "the ministry of reconciliation." Notice also the statement, "We are ambassadors for Christ." The term "ambassador" is described in the dictionary in three ways:

1. A diplomatic official of the highest rank appointed and accredited as *representative in residence* by one government or sovereign to another;
2. A diplomatic official heading his or her country's *permanent mission* to certain international organizations, such as the United Nations;
3. An *authorized messenger* or representative.

We are ambassadors for Christ. As ones who have experienced the new life of forgiveness of our sins through faith in Jesus Christ, we must not keep it to ourselves. We are obligated to serve as His "representatives in residence" sent from the kingdom of God into the kingdom of darkness. We are part of His "permanent mission" to mankind. We are His "authorized messengers" sent to tell others about Him.

⇁ Evangelism Is . . . ⇁

1. The real business of life.
2. Refusing to be quickly and easily distracted away from the real business of life.
3. Serving as Christ's ambassadors. We are His "representatives in residence" sent from the kingdom of God into the kingdom of darkness, His "authorized messengers" sent to tell others about Him.

➤ Key Verse ➤

Therefore, whether you eat or drink, or whatever you do, do all to the glory of God. Give no offense, either to the Jews or to the Greeks or to the church of God, just as I also please all men in all things, not seeking my own profit, but the profit of many, that they may be saved. (1 Cor 10:31–33)

➤ Good Quotes ➤

Our English word "mission" comes from the Latin word for "sending." Being a Christian includes being sent *into the world as a representative of Jesus Christ. . . . What is that mission? Introducing people to Jesus. . . . Once we are his, God uses us to reach others. He saved us then sends us out.*

—Rick Warren[2]

Christian people; your one business in life is to lead men to believe in Jesus Christ by the power of the Holy Spirit, and every other thing should be made subservient to this one object; if you can but get them saved, everything else will come right in due time.

—Charles Spurgeon[3]

➤ Application ➤

Ask God to help you see yourself as His ambassador in every setting of your life. Whether on the job, sitting in a class, or living in your apartment, ask the Lord to use you to glorify Him by helping others be saved.

Notes

1. C. S. Lewis, *Reflections* (Grand Rapids, MI: Eerdmans, 1967), 14.
2. R. Warren, *The Purpose Driven Life* (Grand Rapids, MI: Zondervan, 2007), 282 (emphasis his).
3. Charles H. Spurgeon, *The Soul Winner* (New Kensington, PA: Whitaker House, 2001), 272.

3

Obedience to the Great Commission

Dave Earley

The last words and deeds of anyone's life are usually significant as they are an indication of that person's values and priorities. For example, one of the last things my father did was to have me sit down and write checks to the 20 church, ministry, and mission organizations he and my mother supported. They had a special account for some of these above their tithe gifts, and I was told to clean it out. As my father lay in the bed dying of cancer, he gave me detailed directions on how to invest for eternity every last penny in that account. He said, "Give it all away." A few days later he passed into glory.

A few days before Jesus ascended into glory, He gave some final instructions. Of all the words Jesus gave, these words are especially important because of *when* He gave them: they were the last words He gave. They were also important because of *who* gave them—Jesus Christ—and *who He gave them to*—His followers. Today we call these statements, these detailed instructions, the Great Commission:

> Go therefore and make disciples of all the nations, baptizing them in the name of the Father and of the Son and of the Holy Spirit, teaching them to observe all things that I have commanded you; and lo, I am with you always, even to the end of the age. (Matt 28:19–20)

> And He said to them, "Go into all the world and preach the gospel to every creature." (Mark 16:15)

Then He said to them, "Thus it is written, and thus it was necessary
for the Christ to suffer and to rise from the dead the third day, and that
repentance and remission of sins should be preached in His name to all
nations, beginning at Jerusalem." (Luke 24:46–47)

But you shall receive power when the Holy Spirit has come upon you;
and you shall be witnesses to Me in Jerusalem, and in all Judea and
Samaria, and to the end of the earth. (Acts 1:8)

These four statements are variations of the same mandate, each issued by
Jesus, each emphasizing a slightly different aspect of what it means to obey
Him. The operative verbs in these NT commissions are: *make disciples, preach,*
and *witness.* The scope of fulfilling these commands is *all the nations, all the
world, every creature, all nations,* and *to the end of the earth.* If you isolate
the essence of each passage and add them all together, you get one imperative:
Evangelize the world!

Go therefore and make disciples of all the nations. (Matt 28:19)
+ Go into all the world and preach the gospel. (Mark 16:15)
+ Repentance and remission of sins should be preached in His name to all
   nations. (Luke 24:47)
+ You shall be witnesses to Me in Jerusalem, and in all Judea and Samaria,
   and to the end of the earth. (Acts 1:8)
_____

= Evangelize the world!

The Great Commission Has Always Been the Heart of God

Some argue that the Great Commission was only binding on the handful of
disciples who originally heard it, but this is not possible. God has been evange-
listically interested in all nations since the beginning of time.

Readers of the Old Testament note that God's dealings with people prior
to the time of Jesus were primarily dealings with the Hebrews. Yet clearly the
message of the OT was/is both universal in its scope and international in its
range. This is clear from the start when God promised to Abraham that in him
"all the families of the earth shall be blessed."

I will make you a great nation;
I will bless you
And make your name great;

And you shall be a blessing.
I will bless those who bless you,
And I will curse him who curses you;
And in you all the families of the earth shall be blessed. (Gen 12:2–3)

God's heart for and mission to all the peoples of the Earth is evident as one notes the number of non-Hebrews touched by God as described in the OT. Think of Melchizedek, Jethro, the mixed multitude of Egyptians that went up out of Egypt with the Israelites, Balaam, Rahab, Ruth, the widow at Zarephath, and many others like them who responded through the preaching of prophets like Jonah, Jeremiah, and Isaiah. Also consider the vast number of "sermons" given by the major writing prophets (Isaiah, Jeremiah, and Ezekiel) who addressed 25 chapters of their prophecies to the Gentile nations of their day (Isaiah 13–23; Jeremiah 46–51; Ezekiel 25–32). Scholar Walter Kaiser notes: "There are more verses dedicated to the foreign nations in those twenty-five chapters of the three major prophets alone than are found in all of the Pauline prison epistles in the N.T. There can be little doubt that God was more than mildly interested in winning the nations outside of Israel."[1]

God's heart is and has always been pounding for all peoples of all nations. As you read through the following verses, notice God's passion for His salvation to extend to the entire Earth. If we have the heart of God, we will yearn to take His message to every single person without limit.

Ask of Me,
and I will make the nations Your inheritance
and the ends of the earth Your possession. (Ps 2:8 HCSB)

All the ends of the earth
will remember and turn to the LORD,
and all families of the nations
will bow down before him. (Ps 22:27 NIV)

Be still, and know that I am God;
I will be exalted among the nations,
I will be exalted in the earth. (Ps 46:10 NIV)

Be exalted, O God, above the heavens;
let your glory be over all the earth. (Ps 57:5 NIV)

May your ways be known throughout the earth,
your saving power among people everywhere. (Ps 67:2 NLT)

All the nations you have made
will come and worship before you, O Lord. (Ps 86:9 NIV)

I will also make you a light for the Gentiles,
that you may bring my salvation to the ends of the earth. (Isa 49:6 NIV)

The LORD will bare his holy arm
in the sight of all the nations,
and all the ends of the earth will see
the salvation of our God. (Isa 52:10 NIV)

For the earth will be filled with the knowledge of the glory of the LORD,
as the waters cover the sea. (Hab 2:14 NIV)

The Great Commission Is for All Followers of Jesus

Jesus' followers took seriously the responsibility to fulfill the Great Commission. After hearing Jesus give the commission for the last time and seeing Him ascend to heaven in the clouds (Acts 1:1–11), they immediately convened a weeklong prayer meeting (Acts 1:12–14) asking God for power to fulfill the command. God answered by giving them the Holy Spirit, and they immediately began to preach the gospel and plant a church (Acts 2). They were repeatedly thrown in jail because they refused to stop preaching the gospel. But you probably know all of this.

Maybe you are thinking, *Yeah, but that's the apostles. I'm just a regular person. God does not really expect me to evangelize, does He?*

While the first evangelists were the apostles, they certainly weren't the only ones. A nonapostle named Stephen had a powerful ministry speaking the Word with wisdom and the Holy Spirit (Acts 6:8–10). He was so effective that the Jews decided the only way to shut him up was to kill him, so they did (Acts 7:54–60).

Notice what happened next: "Now Saul was consenting to his [Stephen's] death. At that time a great persecution arose against the church which was at Jerusalem; and they were all scattered throughout the regions of Judea and Samaria, except the apostles. . . . Therefore those who were scattered went everywhere preaching the word" (Acts 8:1,4).

Notice *who* had been scattered by the persecution: "They were all scattered throughout the regions of Judea and Samaria, *except the apostles.*" Notice *what* they did: "Therefore those who were scattered *went everywhere preaching* the word."

The gospel spread to the entire world when normal, obedient, nonapostles shared Jesus. Now notice how God blessed this ministry of the obedient Christ followers: "Now those who were scattered after the persecution that arose over Stephen traveled as far as Phoenicia, Cyprus, and Antioch, preaching the word to no one but the Jews only. But some of them were men from Cyprus and Cyrene, who, when they had come to Antioch, spoke to the Hellenists, preaching the Lord Jesus. And the hand of the Lord was with them, and a great number believed and turned to the Lord" (Acts 11:19–21).

The Great Commission Is Not the Great "Suggestion"

The word *commission* is a military term meaning "an authoritative order, charge, or direction." It is used for a document conferring authority issued by the president of the U.S. to officers in the army, navy, and other military services. As an authoritative order, obedience is not an option. To disobey would be considered an act of treason. The one disobeying the commission would be subject to court martial.

No one can call himself a follower of Jesus who is refusing to obey His orders. Since this order to evangelize the world was clearly and repeatedly given, it must be obeyed. Jesus' commission to evangelize the world was not a suggestion to be considered but a command to be obeyed. Jesus' followers did not consider this Great Commission to evangelize the world as an option to entertain but rather saw it as a mandate to fulfill whatever the cost.

The Great Commission Must Be Obeyed at All Costs

The last words anyone speaks are considered of utmost significance. The last words of the principal person in history are of such significance they must be taken with grave and total seriousness. The last words of Jesus Christ, the most important person ever to walk the Earth should stir, drive, inspire, instruct, and implore everyone who is His follower. Jesus' last words were these: "But you shall receive power when the Holy Spirit has come upon you; and you shall be witnesses to Me in Jerusalem, and in all Judea and Samaria, and to the end of the earth" (Acts 1:8).

Interestingly, in this final giving of the Great Commission, Jesus does not tell them what to do (evangelize) but what to be (witnesses). Sharing the message of the death, burial, and resurrection of Jesus should so consume His followers that they literally become it.

In a legal sense the word *witness* means "telling what you have seen and heard with consuming passion." It is the Greek word *martus,* from which we get our term *martyr.* Therefore, we should be so consumed with telling people all over the world about Jesus that we will die doing so. That is exactly what serious followers of Jesus have been doing the last 2,000 years!

Stephen was stoned to death about AD 34. James, the brother of John, was beheaded about AD 44. Philip was scourged, thrown into prison, and afterwards crucified about AD 54. Matthew suffered martyrdom by the sword about AD 60. James, the brother of Jesus, was beaten, stoned, and had his brains bashed out with a club. Matthias was stoned at Jerusalem and then beheaded. Andrew was arrested and crucified on a cross, two ends of which were fixed transversely in the ground (thus the term, St. Andrew's cross). Mark was dragged to pieces by the people of Alexandria in front of Serapis, their pagan idol. Peter was crucified upside down, at his own request, because he said he was unworthy to be crucified in the same manner as his Lord. Paul gave his neck to the sword. Bartholomew was beaten and crucified in India. Thomas was thrust through with a spear by pagan priests. Luke was hanged on an olive tree in Greece. Jude, the half brother of Jesus, was crucified at Edessa in about AD 72.

"No Reserve, No Retreat, No Regret"

In 1904 William Borden graduated from a Chicago high school. As heir to the Borden family fortune, he was already a millionaire. For his high school graduation present, his parents gave 16-year-old Borden a trip around the world. As the young man traveled through Asia, the Middle East, and Europe, he felt a growing burden for the world's hurting people. Finally, Bill Borden wrote home about his "desire to be a missionary."

One friend expressed surprise that he was "throwing himself away as a missionary."

In response Bill wrote two words in the back of his Bible: "No reserves."

Even though Bill was wealthy, he arrived on the campus of Yale University in 1905 trying to look like just one more freshman. Quickly, however, Borden's classmates noticed something unusual about him, and it wasn't his money. One of them wrote, "He came to college far ahead, spiritually, of any of us. He had already given his heart in full surrender to Christ and had really done it. We who were his classmates learned to lean on him and find in him a strength that was solid as a rock, just because of this settled purpose and consecration."[2]

During his college years Bill Borden made one entry in his personal journal that defined what his classmates were seeing in him. That entry said, "Say 'no' to self and 'yes' to Jesus every time."[3]

During his first semester at Yale, Borden started something that would transform campus life. One of his friends described how it happened:

> It was well on in the first term when Bill and I began to pray together in the morning before breakfast. I cannot say positively whose suggestion it was, but I feel sure it must have originated with Bill. We had been meeting only a short time when a third student joined us and soon after a fourth. The time was spent in prayer after a brief reading of Scripture. Bill's handling of Scripture was helpful. . . . He would read to us from the Bible, show us something that God had promised and then proceed to claim the promise with assurance.[4]

Borden's small morning prayer group gave birth to a movement that spread across the campus. By the end of his first year, 150 freshman were meeting for weekly Bible study and prayer. By the time Bill Borden was a senior, 1,000 of Yale's 1,300 students were meeting in such groups!

Borden made it his habit to seek out the most incorrigible students and try to bring them to salvation.

> In his sophomore year we organized Bible study groups and divided up the class of 300 or more, each man interested taking a certain number, so that all might, if possible, be reached. The names were gone over one by one, and the question asked, "Who will take this person?" When it came to someone thought to be a hard proposition, there would be an ominous pause. Nobody wanted the responsibility. Then Bill's voice would be heard, "Put him down to me."[5]

Borden's outreach ministry was not confined to the Yale campus. He cared about widows and orphans and people with handicaps. He rescued drunks from the streets of New Haven. To rehabilitate them he founded the Yale Hope Mission. One of his friends wrote that he "might often be found in the lower parts of the city at night, on the street, in a cheap lodging house or some restaurant to which he had taken a poor hungry fellow to feed him, seeking to lead men to Christ."[6]

Borden's missionary call narrowed to the Muslim Kansu people in China. Once that goal was in sight, Borden never wavered. He also inspired his classmates to consider missionary service. One of them said, "He certainly was one of the strongest characters I have ever known, and he put backbone into the rest of us at college. There was real iron in him, and I always felt he was of the stuff martyrs were made of, and heroic missionaries of more modern times."[7]

Although he was a millionaire, Bill seemed to "realize always that he must be about his Father's business, and not wasting time in the pursuit of amusement."[8] Upon graduation from Yale, Borden turned down some high-paying job offers. In his Bible he wrote two more words: "No retreats."

William Borden went on to graduate work at Princeton Seminary in New Jersey. When he finished his studies at Princeton, he sailed for China. Because he was hoping to work with Muslims, he stopped first in Egypt to study Arabic. While there he contracted spinal meningitis. Within a month 25-year-old William Borden was dead.

When news of William Whiting Borden's death was cabled back to the U.S., the story was carried by nearly every American newspaper. His biographer wrote, "A wave of sorrow went round the world. . . . Borden not only gave (away) his wealth, but himself, in a way so joyous and natural that it (seemed) a privilege rather than a sacrifice."[9]

Was Borden's untimely death a waste? Not in God's plan. Prior to his death, Borden had written two more words in his Bible. Underneath the words "No reserves" and "No retreats," he had written, "No regrets."

⚊ Evangelism Is . . . ⚊

1. All-out obedience to the Great Commission.
2. Sharing the gospel to the ends of the Earth whatever the cost.

⚊ Key Verse ⚊

*"But you shall receive power when the Holy Spirit
has come upon you; and you shall be witnesses to Me
in Jerusalem, and in all Judea and Samaria, and to
the end of the earth." (Acts 1:8)*

⚊ Good Quotes ⚊

*The earliest churches obeyed the Great Commission by
planting new congregations to carry out the assignments
of discipling, baptizing, and teaching that would begin the*

multiplication process of planting more and more churches.
You notice that the process begins and ends in obedience.

—ED STETZER[10]

Being an extrovert isn't essential to evangelism. . . .
Obedience and love are.

—REBECCA MANLEY PIPPERT[11]

Notes

1. W. C. Kaiser Jr., "The Great Commission in the Old Testament," *International Journal of Frontier Missions*, 13, no. 1 (January–March 1996): 3.

2. Mrs. H. Taylor, *Borden of Yale '09* (Philadelphia: China Inland Mission, 1926), 98.

3. Ibid., 122.

4. Ibid., 97.

5. Ibid., 150.

6. Ibid., 148.

7. Ibid., 149.

8. Ibid.

9. Ibid., ix.

10. E. Stetzer, *Planting Missional Churches* (Nashville, TN: B&H, 2006), 38.

11. R. M. Pippert, *Out of the Saltshaker into the World* (Downers Grove, IL: IVP, 1979), 113.

4

The Supreme Challenge of This Generation

Dave Earley and David Wheeler

The Bad News

In his sobering book *The Last Christian Generation*, Josh McDowell grabbed our attention when he wrote, "Over the last generation the number of students who say that the church will play a part in their lives when they leave home has dropped from 66% to 55% down to 33%!" He further points out that "between 69% to 94% of young people are leaving the traditional church after High School and few are returning!!!"[1]

The Good News

On the positive side, McDowell notes that "65% of this generation wants a close relationship with God; and 49% want to make a difference in the world!"[2] In fact, most will say that "God is still important to them," but "they just believe some different things from you and I [sic]."[3]

The Not Exactly Good News

When McDowell mentioned that this generation proclaims that God is still important to them but they have beliefs different from ours, that sounded better. But is it? How does the concept of "different things" factor into this generation's belief system?

- 63% don't believe that Jesus is the Son of the one true God.
- 58% believe all faiths teach equally valid truths.
- 51% don't believe Jesus rose from the dead.
- 68% don't believe that the Holy Spirit is a real entity.
- 65% don't believe Satan is a real entity.[4]

The Problem

Furthermore, studies from the Nehemiah Institute show that there is no real belief difference between students at Christian and public schools. Eighty-five percent of public school students from Christian homes do not embrace a biblical worldview. At the same time, while Christian school students scored slightly higher, only 6 percent embraced a biblical theism worldview.[5]

On the positive side McDowell observes, "Today's youth seem to be just as interested in God and just as passionate about spiritual things as any generation. . . . For more than a decade, young people have been the most spiritually interested individuals in America. . . . Their interest is not in question at all."[6]

So what is the problem? McDowell responds:

> The fundamental question is: "How are they forming their view of God?" And what brand of religion are they adopting? In other words, our kids are departing from the faith of their fathers . . . and mothers. They are believing "some different things from you and me." Much of what they believe about Christianity, truth, reality, and the church comes from a distorted view they have gleaned from the world around them. It's not that they haven't embraced a version of Christianity; it's simply that the version they believe in is not built on the true foundation of what biblical Christianity is all about.[7]

Beliefs Affect Future Behavior

Beliefs always affect the way people behave. Our approach to life comes from our view of the world around us. If we have faulty beliefs, we will develop negative attitudes. In fact, research reveals that the failure of a young person to adopt a Christian belief system negatively impacts their overall *attitude* toward life. The young people surveyed are . . .

- 225% more likely to be angry with life.
- 216% more likely to be resentful.
- 210% more likely to lack purpose in life.
- 200% more likely to be disappointed in life.[8]

In addition, a failure to embrace an authentic Christian worldview and belief system as a foundation for life will negatively impact *future behavior*. For example, they are . . .

- 48% more likely to cheat on an exam.
- 200% more likely to steal.
- 200% more likely to hurt someone physically.
- 300% more likely to use illegal drugs.
- 600% more likely to attempt suicide.[9]

The sad part is that, according to the Josephson Institute on Ethics, "There is no more than 4% difference between the attitudes and actions of professing Christian youth and non-Christian young people."[10]

George Barna led a revealing study that divided "so-called born-again" Christians into two categories: (1) those who believe in Christ but their lives don't reflect Christlikeness, and (2) those who believe in Christ and live a Christlike life. Barna discovered that "ninety-eight percent (98%) of professed born-again young people do 'believe in Christ,' *but they do not reflect Christlike attitudes or actions!*"[11]

Faulty Beliefs Negatively Impact the Effectiveness of the Church

The decay of American society and our foundational belief system is not because the Church lacks creative ideas and resources for education and basic ministries.[12] It is that these ideas and resources have lacked effectiveness. Pollster George Barna concluded:

> Nothing is more numbing to the church than the fact that it is mired in a rut of seemingly unfathomable depths. The various creative approaches attempted over the course of this decade have drawn much attention but produces little if any, transformational impact. . . . Although many people attend a church, few Americans are committed to *being* the Church."[13]

The idea of *being* the Church is nothing new. It is, in fact, the organic call of all Christians as they multiply through evangelism and participate in the

Great Commission. Unfortunately, too often evangelism has been the least of our concerns.

For instance, just as the core belief system of American Christianity has declined, so have the negative results on the North American church. As unbelievable as it may seem, recent research indicates that there are now more than 200 million nonchurched people in America, making our nation one of the largest unchurched countries in the world. Author Justice Anderson has stated, "The American church is in the midst of one of the largest mission fields in the world today. Only three other nations—China, India and Indonesia—have more lost people."[14]

Did you know that in 1987 the number of evangelicals in Asia surpassed the number of evangelicals in North America? And did you know that in 1991 the number of evangelicals in Asia surpassed the number of evangelicals in the entire Western world?[15]

In spite of the rise of American megachurches, no county in our nation has a greater churched population than it did 10 years ago.[16] During the last 10 years, combined communicant membership of all Protestant denominations declined by 9.5 percent (4,498,242), while the national population increased by 11.4 percent (24,153,000).[17]

In 1990 20.4 percent of Americans attended church on any given Sunday. By 2000 only 18.7 percent attended church. This percentage is still in decline, and if this trend is not turned around, it will not be long before only 6 percent of Americans attend church each week. According to Dave Olson's research, the recent increase in the number of churches is only about one-eighth of what is needed to keep up with population growth.[18]

As a result, even though America has more people, it has fewer churches per person than at any time in its history. And while the number of churches in America has increased by 50 percent in the last century, the population has increased a staggering 300 percent.[19] There are now nearly 60 percent fewer churches per 10,000 Americans than there were in 1920!

Table 1: Number of Churches per Americans

1920	27 churches existed for every 10,000 Americans.
1950	17 churches existed for every 10,000 Americans.
1996	11 churches existed for every 10,000 Americans.[20]

How Does This Impact Evangelism?

It is easy to understand why the church is in decline. After all, if Jesus is only one of many ways to God, then evangelism is not essential. If the Holy Spirit, Satan, and the resurrection are mythical characterizations of delirious Christian zealots who were naïve and misguided, then Christianity becomes merely a cultural expression with no inherent validity or urgency of message.

In a day of tolerance and religious pluralism, the concept of evangelism smacks against acceptable behavior. The presumption that Christianity is the one and only true belief system is considered hate speech in some cultural circles.

The problem is that in many cases it is not unbelievers who object to evangelizing. While the culture of modern society can discourage Christians from sharing their faith, it is often the church culture that inflicts the most harm. The church's preoccupation with maintaining the status quo and making sure members are happy is contrary to the Great Commission of Christ to "go" and "be My witnesses."

The fruit of maintaining the status quo and making sure church members are happy is few (true) disciples and almost no spiritual fruit! Therefore, without a mammoth change in the culture of the contemporary church that prioritizes fervent evangelism, Christ-centered discipleship, and biblical truth over personal comfort and individual preferences, the Church will continue to decline, and Christianity will lose its influence and identity.

A New Generation

If current trends continue, the younger generation could be the last Christian generation in America. We believe, however, that God wants to raise up a new generation of Christian warriors. We further believe, regardless of the statistics, that God is still actively at work calling young men and women who will go against the grain and will turn the tide. With God's help they will make a stand and change the spiritual destiny of American.

"The Few, the Proud"

The Marine Corps is a branch of the United States armed forces. There motto is "First to Fight: Ready to win on land and at sea." Their stated mission is to be first on the scene, first to help, and first to fight. For this they have earned the reputation as "America's 911 Force," our nation's first line of defense. The

Marine Corps is ready to respond on the ground, in the air, and by sea. This integrated approach distinguishes the Marine Corps as the premier U.S. expeditionary force.

Marines pride themselves in upholding core values of honor, courage, and commitment. The marine motto is *Semper Fidelis,* Latin for "always faithful." Marines are to remain faithful to the mission at hand, to one another, to the Corps, and to country. In boot camp marines are taught that becoming a marine is a transformation that cannot be undone. Once made, a marine should be forever faithful to live by the ethics and values of the Corps. There is no such thing as an ex-marine.

Marines swear an oath to uphold the U. S. Constitution against all enemies and to obey the orders of the president of the United States. Their symbol includes a globe signifying worldwide presence. When in their dress blues, they wear a scarlet "blood stripe" down the leg of each trouser in honor of fallen comrades.

Spiritual Marines

The reason we have dedicated ourselves to training young adults is that we believe God is calling out a new generation of Christian marines, sold-out followers of Jesus who are the church's first line of defense. They are willing to be first on the scene, first to help, and first to fight. They are ready to respond to the need of the hour by spreading the gospel by land, air, sea, or any other means available. They are young men and women of honor, courage, and commitment.

This army of young adults must be dedicated and always faithful to the Word of God, passionately dedicated to the orders of Christ to fulfill the Great Commission. They are committed to the mission at hand, to one another, and to the church. Jesus has transformed their lives with a metamorphosis that cannot be undone. They refuse to give up, give in, or go back.

They wear the "blood stripes" of Jesus Christ on their hearts and in their lifestyles. They are willing to put their lives on the line for the cause of Christ. They are spiritual marines.

Good Soldiers of the Lord Jesus Christ

Paul also had the privilege of investing in champions such as Titus, Silas, Luke, and Timothy. Timothy served as lead pastor for the strategic church in Ephesus.

Ephesus was the sending center for spreading the gospel through Asia Minor. In his correspondence with Timothy and his church, the Ephesians, Paul encouraged Timothy to remember that he was a spiritual warrior:

> Put on the whole armor of God, that you may be able to stand against the wiles of the devil. For we do not wrestle against flesh and blood, but against principalities, against powers, against the rulers of the darkness of this age, against spiritual hosts of wickedness in the heavenly places. (Eph 6:11–12)

> You therefore must endure hardship as a good soldier of Jesus Christ. No one engaged in warfare entangles himself with the affairs of this life, that he may please him who enlisted him as a soldier. (2 Tim 2:3–4)

In order to make a difference in the murky spiritual waters of the first century, Paul told Timothy that he needed to see himself as a spiritual change agent. If you and I are to make a spiritual difference in a culture where Christianity is on a steep decline, we must also adopt the mind-set of spiritual warriors. We must become spiritual marines.

"Served His Generation"

Over 3,000 years ago a young man was watching sheep in the Judean wilderness. During David's lonely times in the wilderness, God put a passion in his heart to make a difference. David adopted the personality and values of a spiritual marine.

A few years later, when no one else would stand against the pagan Philistines and their giant champion, Goliath, David did. He alone stood up against the grain, against the scorn of his brother, and faced Goliath. Crying, "Is there not a cause?" he ran into battle. God joined him in his courageous endeavor, and together they brought down the giant and won the battle.

After many more successful campaigns against the enemy, David inadvertently was given the favor of the people. When the jealous envy of King Saul consumed him, he turned against David, running him out into the wilderness. David became a fugitive fleeing for his life. Yet David remained faithful to God and to God's people.

After Saul's death David became the king of Israel and Judea. As the king, David led his entire nation back to worship God. He set the stage for Israel to build the temple and be a people dedicated to God. In summarizing David's life, Paul said that David "had served his own generation by the will of God" (Acts 13:36).

Our desire is that God will raise up an army from this generation who will adopt the mind-set and values of spiritual marines. They will be ready to serve. They will not be afraid of bringing down giants. They will serve God in their generation.

A Few Good Men and Women

In 1779 in Boston, Captain William Jones, of the USMC, advertised for "a few good men" to enlist in the Corps for naval duty against the English. In a culture rapidly moving into the moral vacuum of post-Christian secularism, a few good men and women can make a difference. Our deep desire is that God will use us to recruit and train an army of men and women who will stand up and say, "I will be a spiritual marine. I will serve my generation."

— Evangelism Is . . . —

1. Standing up for your faith even if everyone else remains seated.
2. Going against the grain of culture.
3. Becoming a spiritual marine.
4. The supreme challenge of this generation.

— Key Verse —

You therefore must endure hardship as a good soldier
of Jesus Christ. (2 Tim 2:3)

— Good Quotes —

We are convinced that once a person really knows God—and
we mean really knows Him for who He is and what He
means to us—the kind of response to Him that we want our
kids to have will be inevitable. If we can reintroduce Christ
to our young people regarding who He is, what He has done
for us, how much He loves us, and how He yearns to restore
all things to His original design, we won't have to cajole them
to respond to Him. There will be no holding them back!

—Josh McDowell[21]

Christians have nothing to fear. The gates of hell will
not prevail against us. We have nothing to fear,
but in Christ's name, we have much to offer.

—Thom Rainer[22]

Notes

1. J. McDowell, *The Last Christian Generation* (Holiday, FL: Green Key Books, 2006), 13.

2. Ibid., 14.

3. Ibid., 15.

4. Ibid.

5. Ibid., 14.

6. Ibid., 15.

7. Ibid.

8. Ibid. 16.

9. Ibid.

10. Ibid., 17.

11. Ibid., 18.

12. Ibid., 18–19.

13. Ibid., 19.

14. J. Anderson, in *Missiology: An Introduction to the Foundations, History and Strategies of World Missions*, ed. J. M. Terry, E. Smith, and J. Anderson (Nashville: B&H, 1998), 243.

15. W. Craig, *Reasonable Faith*, "Subject: Molinism, the Unevangelized, and Cultural Chauvinism," http://www.reasonablefaith.org/site/News2?page=News Article&id=5681, accessed January 21, 2008.

16. R. Sylvia, *High Definition Church Planting* (Ocala, FL: High Definition Resources, 2004), 26.

17. T. Clegg, "How to Plant a Church for the 21st Century," seminar materials, 1997, author's collection, Gahanna, Ohio.

18. D. Olson, http://www.theamericanchurch.org.

19. B. Easum, "The Easum Report," March 2003, http://www.easum.com/church.htm.

20. T. Clegg and T. Bird, *Lost in America* (Loveland, CO: Group Publishing, 2001), 30.

21. McDowell, *The Last Christian Generation*, 83.

22. T. Rainer, *The Unexpected Journey* (Grand Rapids, MI: Zondervan, 2005), 202.

5

Pursuing Lost People

Dave Earley

In his book *The Coming Revival*, Bill Bright reported that "only *two* percent of believers in America regularly share their faith in Christ with others." According to research by Dr. D. James Kennedy, a popular pastor and Christian author, only 5 percent of all Christians have ever led anybody to Christ.

The George Barna research group did a survey in 2007 asking Catholic and Protestant believers if they felt a responsibility to share their faith with others. Eighty-one percent of Catholics said no; 53 percent of Protestants said no. Barna also found that 75 percent of American adults who said that they were "born again" could not even define the Great Commission.

Every minute around the world, 102 people die. Every hour 6,098 people die. Every day 146,357 people die. If we were to line up the people who are without Christ in the world today and give each non-Christian two feet of space, the line would be approximately 1,734,848 miles long. This line would reach around the earth's equator 70 times![1]

I don't know about you, but information like that given above makes me uncomfortable.

Why Did Jesus Come?

As a boy in Sunday school my favorite story was about a guy named Zacchaeus. I liked it because we always sang a catchy little song about him. I also liked it because I was fairly short (and still am) as was Zacchaeus. But my favorite part was that this story has a happy ending.

Zacchaeus had the reputation as a sinner. He was curious about Jesus and had a hunger to meet God. Jesus ended up going to his house for dinner. Zacchaeus ended up being saved. Luke's Gospel records the story. In it we find the secret to understanding the heart and mission of Jesus.

> Now behold, there was a man named Zacchaeus who was a chief tax collector, and he was rich. And he sought to see who Jesus was, but could not because of the crowd, for he was of short stature. So he ran ahead and climbed up into a sycamore tree to see Him, for He was going to pass that way. And when Jesus came to the place, He looked up and saw him, and said to him, "Zacchaeus, make haste and come down, for today I must stay at your house." So he made haste and came down, and received Him joyfully. But when they saw it, they all complained, saying, "He has gone to be a guest with a man who is a sinner."
>
> Then Zacchaeus stood and said to the Lord, "Look, Lord, I give half of my goods to the poor; and if I have taken anything from anyone by false accusation, I restore fourfold."
>
> And Jesus said to him, "Today salvation has come to this house, because he also is a son of Abraham; *for the Son of Man has come to seek and to save that which was lost.*" (Luke 19:2–10, italics added).

Why did Jesus come to Earth? What was His life mission?

Was it to set a good example? Was it to teach great lessons? Was it to heal the sick, feed the hungry, and raise the dead?

Jesus said that His primary purpose in coming to Earth was more than all of these. He came "to seek and to save that which was *lost.*" He came to retrieve *lost* people.

Which raises a good question: What does it mean to be lost?

Lost

What does it mean to be "lost"? A word study of "lost" (*apollymi* in the original) is sobering. The root word means "destroy."

In the passage we read about Zacchaeus, the word "lost" describes a man who was clearly "missing out." Those outside the kingdom of God like the wealthy yet corrupt tax collector, Zacchaeus, are *missing out on real life.*

In Luke 5:37 "lost" is used to describe something that is "*ruined.*" The verse is talking about a brittle old wineskin that is ruined by the influx and expansion of new wine. In Luke 15:4–6, "lost" speaks of something that is "*disoriented,*" as it is used for a sheep that is in serious danger because of having wandered from the shepherd. In Luke 15:17, "lost" is used for the son *"wasting his life and potential"* because he was not in fellowship with his father. In Luke 4:34 the word is used for *"eternal destruction"* as "lost" describes the state of destruction a demon wants to avoid at all costs.

Putting these usages of the term together paints a chilling picture of those who are spiritually lost. They are "missing out" on the life God has for them, "ruining" what could be a beautiful life, "wasting" their potential, are "disoriented and confused" in darkness, and face ultimate "destruction." No wonder Jesus said that He came to save the "lost."

Jesus Loves Lost People

God is invincible. He is omnipotent, omniscient, and omnipresent. When Satan wants to get at God, he knows that attacking God directly is futile. God is too powerful. So what does Satan do? He attacks God at His only point of "weakness." God's only "weakness" is that He loves people. To attack God, Satan attacks people. He accuses, tempts, and deceives people.

In Luke 15:1–2 we see an interchange between Jesus and the Pharisees. They were upset because Jesus associated with "sinners." They accused Him of receiving and eating with "sinners." In this passage we clearly see the heart of Jesus toward the lost. "Then all the tax collectors and the sinners drew near to Him to hear Him. And the Pharisees and scribes complained, saying, 'This Man receives sinners and eats with them'" (Luke 15:1–2).

What's the problem here? The core of the controversy was this. People—all people, even sinners—were important to Jesus. But people didn't matter to the Pharisees. Rules mattered to the Pharisees, appearances mattered to the Pharisees, traditions mattered to the Pharisees, but lost people didn't matter to the Pharisees.

To Pharisees lost people were not important, especially tax collectors and sinners. It's easy to become like the Pharisees in our evaluations of people. We can compile little unpublished lists of people we don't think are important. The criteria of the list may be personality, looks, income, race, gender, social status, education, marital status, age, size, political preference, or religion. God carries no such list.

To Jesus lost people are important. Jesus loves all people. But Jesus especially loves lost people. His response to the Pharisees was to tell the story of the lost coin to teach us that lost people merit an all-out search. God actively loves everyone in the world (John 3:16). Jesus' stories of Luke 15 tell us that you have never locked eyes with another human being who isn't valuable to God.

God doesn't limit His love to the people on His team. In fact He carries a special place in His heart for those who are not on His team. He has an immense love for them. Bill Hybels and Mark Mittelberg described the massive love of God for the lost when they wrote:

> [God's] love [is] so large that it could look beyond sins and treasure the wayward people behind them; a love so powerful that it could patiently endure years of resistance, selfish pleasure-seeking, money chasing, and power-wielding. In the face of all this, God's love says, "Even though you are way off the track, you still matter to Me! You really do!"[2]

Some of us need to realize that lost people are not the enemy. They are victims of the enemy. We have been called to set them free.

Sometimes we think that there are people who really do not need Jesus. When I was a college student, another student and I wanted to do some evangelizing. We were sent to an affluent neighborhood to pass out some literature about Jesus Christ. The guy I was with was completely blown away by the huge houses and manicured lawns. He was complaining about our assignment and blurted out, "I doubt that any of these people need Jesus." He mistakenly assumed that because the people living in the nice homes appeared to have it all together and were financially well off, they didn't need Jesus. He was wrong.

Everybody needs Jesus. There has never been a person born on this planet who did not have a gaping, God-shaped void in his heart. All of us are alienated from God by sin. All of us have a need for the gospel. All of us need a life-changing dose of Jesus Christ.

Sometimes we think that some people are too messed up to be candidates for Christianity. We tend to forget that those who are looking for love, meaning, happiness, and fulfillment in all the wrong places are people who are actually searching for Jesus. They just don't realize it yet. Rebecca Manley Pippert writes:

> Everywhere I look I see people frantically looking for the right things in all the wrong places. The tragedy is that so often my initial response is to withdraw and assume they will never become Christians. We must ask ourselves, "How do I interpret the needs and lifestyles of my friends? Do I look at their drinking and sleeping around and say, 'That's wrong' and walk away? Or do I penetrate their mask and discover why they do this in the first place? And then do I try to love them where they are?"[3]

No one is too lost to be a candidate for the love of Jesus. The church I started in Ohio had alcoholics, drugs addicts, and ex-criminals in our membership.

One of our best members came out of 20 years of living a lesbian lifestyle. The day she joined the church, she told me that she had never been more excited. She wanted to tell her friends how Jesus could set them free and give them real love.

To the follower of Jesus, lost people are of utmost importance. Jesus had a heart for lost people. If we are to be His followers, we too need to have a heart for lost people. The eighteenth-century pastor Charles Spurgeon once stated, "Have you no wish for others to be saved? Then you are not saved yourself. Be sure of that."[4] Jesus had a heart for lost people, and so will His followers.

Jesus Believed Lost People Merited an All-out Search

"What man of you, having a hundred sheep, if he loses one of them, does not leave the ninety-nine in the wilderness, and go after the one which is lost until he finds it?" (Luke 15:4)

Importance: Retrieving Lost People Is of Highest Priority

God views lost people as being of such great value that they deserve an all-out effort. In the verse quoted above, Jesus is saying, "If a sheep is worth pursuing, *how much more* is a human soul worth seeking?" Jesus always taught that following God was a matter of not only doing what God wants but also valuing what God values.

Notice the great importance of the lost sheep. It was so important that the shepherd was willing to leave the 99 "found" sheep in order to retrieve the one lost sheep. This speaks volumes to us. So often we spend all our time, energy, and effort with the 99 who are found that we neglect the one who is lost. Notice the ratio here: one lost person takes precedence over 99 found ones. In the United States the ratio is more like 30 found and 70 lost. So, if one lost sheep could command a search that left the 99 behind, how much more should 70 lost sheep command our energies and efforts over the 30 who are found?

We will have all of eternity to rest and hang out with the found. We need to be consumed with going after the lost. Can't you get out of bed on a Saturday morning to go out to try and rescue some lost people?

Initiative: Retrieving Lost People Requires Costly Initiative

It is highly insightful to recognize that Luke 15 comes after chapter 14. Look carefully at what Jesus said in Luke 14 before He launched into this discussion about reaching lost people that is recorded in Luke 15.

> "If anyone comes to Me and does not hate his father and mother, wife and children, brothers and sisters, yes, and his own life also, he cannot be My disciple. And whoever does not bear his cross and come after Me cannot be My disciple. For which of you, intending to build a tower, does not sit down first and count the cost, whether he has enough to finish it—lest, after he has laid the foundation, and is not able to finish, all who see it begin to mock him, saying, "This man began to build and was not able to finish"? Or what king, going to make war against another king, does not sit down first and consider whether he is able with ten thousand to meet him who comes against him with twenty thousand? Or else, while the other is still a great way off, he sends a delegation and asks conditions of peace. So likewise, whoever of you does not forsake all that he has cannot be My disciple." (Luke 14:26–33)

In Luke 14:26–33 Jesus explained the cost of discipleship. The point Jesus was making is that to reach lost people we will have to put our relationship with God above our human relationships and above our own selves. Certainly reaching out to lost people might not be as easy or as fun as hanging out with your "found" friends. But we should count the cost and put the priorities of Jesus ahead of our selfish pursuits.

Identification: Retrieving Lost People Won't Happen Without Active Identification with Them

The Pharisees were upset with Jesus because they saw Him identifying with sinners. For Him this involved loving people where they are and for who they are. We are not to look down on people. Jesus was the only human who ever really had the right to look down on another person, but He never did. He identified with people as fully as possible. Apart from sin He was fully one of us. "We must live with the tension of being called to identify with others without being identical to them."[5]

It is often easier to build walls than bridges, but God calls us to be bridge builders. My kids are Christian kids. As Christians, especially as they got older, they were not allowed to particpate in some activities the unsaved kids their age did. We did not want them to be *identical* with non-Christian kids, but we did want them to be able to *identify* with lost kids. That is one reason we encouraged them to play sports. Sports can be a neutral bridge of identification. One reason I often got involved with my kids' sports teams as a coach was because it is an area where I could easily identify with lost people.

Christians and non-Christians alike have many common points of identification. We wrestle with our relationships, our jobs, our kids, our marriages, our dreams, our desires. We are not all that different. Rebecca Manley Pippert notes, "Our message is not that we have it all together. Our message is that we know the One who does!"[6]

When I started coaching sports, I was really nervous about blowing my testimony. I am highly competitive, and I didn't want to get upset as a coach and mess up as an evangelist. But God taught me a lesson when it comes to evangelism: God did not call us to be passively perfect but rather to be transparently real. He wants us to live with and love lost people, and He uses us to touch them and bring them to Himself.

Two of the finest evangelists I know are Sandy and Scott. Sandy has a boatload of health problems, and Scott has had a lifelong battle with obesity. Both will be the first to tell you that they do not have it all together. Yet they definitely love and value people. God is so good that He uses their weaknesses as points of strength in their witness.

Inside we all know that we do not have it all together. So when someone sees Scott, whose battle he cannot hide, that person sees that God does not love perfect people but real people. Scott will be the first to tell you that he is trying to cooperate with God and lose weight, and I believe that will be a great testimony as well. But until then Scott is useful as is because he is willing to get out of his comfort zone and love lost people.

Following Jesus Means Actively Loving Lost People

Don't sit back and view yourself as a follower of Jesus if you are not actively going out to find and retrieve lost people. You can do it. He will help you.

— Evangelism Is . . . —

1. Loving those whom Jesus loves, lost people.
2. Actively pursuing and retrieving lost people for God.
3. Identifying with lost people where they are and where we are.

— Key Verse —

"For the Son of Man came to seek and to save what was lost."
(Luke 19:10 NIV)

~ Good Quotes ~

*We invalidate the message of God's love for men when
we do not love men for God.*

—Howard Hendricks[7]

*The essence of God's mission is extravagant love. . . . The
essence of God's love is to make a difference, by God's power,
in the lives of other people, for now and for eternity.*

—Tom Clegg and Warren Bird[8]

*You tell me the depth of a Christian's compassion
and I will tell you the measure of His usefulness.*

—Alexander Maclaren[9]

*A man will work harder to recover diamonds than gravel.
Why? Because they are of so much greater value.
And so with the souls of men. Christ conceived the human
soul to be of such transcendent value that He gladly
exchanged the shining courts of glory for a life of poverty,
suffering, shame and death, rather than that it should perish.
He placed the world and all it could offer in the one scale and
a human soul in the other, and declared that the scale went
down on the side of the soul.*

—J. Oswald Sanders[10]

*If we had to preach to thousands year after year, and never
rescued but one soul, that one soul would be full reward for
all our labor, for a soul is of countless price.*

—C. H. Spurgeon

Notes

1. Information gleaned by C. Campbell, "Evangelism Help," The Always Be Ready Apologetics Ministries, http://www.alwaysbeready.com/index.php?option=com_content&task=view&id=110&Itemid=97, accessed April 15, 2009.

2. B. Hybels and M. Mittelberg, *Becoming a Contagious Christian* (Grand Rapids, MI: Zondervan, 1994), 19.

3. R. M. Pippert, *Out of the Saltshaker into the World* (Downers Grove, IL: IVP, 1979), 119–20.

4. C. H. Spurgeon, *The Soul Winner* (New Kensington, PA: Whitaker House, 2001), 245.

5. Pippert, *Out of the Saltshaker into the World*, 120.

6. Ibid., 121.

7. H. G. Hendricks, *Say It with Love* (Wheaton, IL: Victor Books, 1979), Preface.

8. T. Clegg and T. Bird, *Lost in America* (Loveland, CO: Group Publishing, 2001), 20.

9. A. Maclaren quoted in G. Laurie, *New Believer's Guide to How to Share Your Faith* (Wheaton, IL: Tyndale House Publishers, 1999).

10. J. O. Sanders, *The Divine Art of Soul-Winning* (Chicago: IL: Moody Press, 1980), 19.

6

Shaking and Shining

Dave Earley

One Sunday at my church, the Bible passage we were teaching addressed the privilege and responsibility of evangelism. A Christian lady came up to me afterward and said, "Would you pray that God would send some Christians to work in my office and witness to my coworkers? I am the only Christian who works there; the rest of the people are lost."

"I certainly will not," I smiled and said.

She looked at me as if I was an absolute nut.

"But I just heard you say that God loves lost people." Her mouth dropped open. She gulped and blinked a few times. Then she stammered. "I thought you would be happy to pray that God would send a Christian to witness to the people in my office."

"I definitely will *not* pray that God will send a Christian to witness to the people in your office," I repeated.

"But why not?" she gasped.

"Because God already has sent a Christian to witness to the people in your office."

Her eyes got large. "Who?" she asked.

"You!" I said.

Jesus

One day Jesus was teaching a large crowd of His followers. In their minds spiritual ministry was reserved for professionals—priests, scribes, and rabbis. Yet Jesus made a statement that changed everything.

You are the salt of the earth; but if the salt loses its flavor, how shall it be seasoned? It is then good for nothing but to be thrown out and trampled underfoot by men.

You are the light of the world. A city that is set on a hill cannot be hidden. Nor do they light a lamp and put it under a basket, but on a lampstand, and it gives light to all who are in the house. Let your light so shine before men, that they may see your good works and glorify your Father in heaven. (Matt 5:13–16, italics added)

You!

Often we look at the needs of lost people and ask, "God, who are You going to send? What are You going to do?"

In Matt 5:13–16 God has already answered that question. He said, "*You* are the salt of the earth. . . . *You* are the light of the world." God's answer to this hurting, lost world is you!

God will do what we cannot do, but God will not do what we can do. God's method is mankind. His plan is people. His strategy is you and I. We are the only Jesus the world will ever see. Making a difference is up to you and me. If we do not do it, it will not get done. If it is not getting done, it is because we are not doing it.

Salt and Light

Jesus chose to use the word pictures of salt and light partly because they were absolutely necessary in every home of His day. No family tried to do without them.

Then as now salt preserved and flavored. In a world without refrigeration, salt was an absolute necessity. Meat of any type—fish, poultry, or beef—quickly rotted in the Mediterranean heat. The only way to preserve it was salt.

Yet salt had another benefit in that it not only preserved meat but also seasoned all types of food. I have been to Israel, and in 2,000 years the food has not changed all that much. They have some fairly bland meat and vegetable dishes. Thank God for salt to season it.

Light has a single, striking, powerful ability. Light alone has the power to dispel darkness. In fact darkness by definition is the absence of light. Because it dispels darkness, light has the resulting benefits of giving direction and lifting spirits. It dispels fear and creates a climate for fellowship. Life is sad and miserable when there is no light.

I suppose that it was possible to get by without salt and light, but who would want to? Just as salt and light were necessary then for improving the physical quality of life in the first century, salt and light are also necessary now for improving the spiritual quality of life today. This world is rotten without the salty nature of the people of God. It is tasteless without the seasoning of Christianity. It is a dark and depressing place without the light of God's truth. It thirsts for everything other than God if we are not causing it to thirst for God.

Different from the World

The distinction is drawn in these verses between *us*—the salt of the earth and light of the world—and *the world*, the place needing salt and light. That is because we not only are *needed by* the world but we are *different from* the world.

"The world," as it is used in this passage, is speaking of the system of people apart from God. As such, it is rotten and tasteless. It has no thirst for God. It is dark. It is in great need. Non-Christians are spiritually lost and dead. They need direction and life.

As Christians we have the ability to be exactly what the world needs. We can be like salt preserving a rotting society and bringing taste to a tasteless culture. We can be like light giving hope and direction to those stumbling in darkness. As light we can attract people to *the* Light of the world. As salt we can cause people to thirst after the Water of life.

Our usefulness depends on our distinctiveness. We must not lose our distinctiveness, or we will lose our usefulness. Notice what Jesus said: "You are the salt of the earth; but if the salt loses its flavor, how shall it be seasoned? It is then good for nothing but to be thrown out and trampled underfoot by men" (Matt 5:13).

I find these words to be sobering. When He says "good for nothing," He's not talking about God's not loving us anymore. He is talking about our no longer being useful in impacting the world.

The question is, How does salt lose its saltiness? The answer is that it loses saltiness by gaining other stuff. Every other chemical added to salt weakens its saltiness. Salt alone is more powerful than salt *and* something else. The same is true of light. Anything other than light added to light weakens the power of light.

What makes us spiritually salty? What makes us spiritual light? What makes us useful for the world and different from the world?

We are not different just because we have a holy book called the Bible; other religions have a holy book. We are not different because we regularly attend religious services; adherents of other religions attend religious services regularly. We are not different because we do not smoke, drink, or chew; other religions have stricter rules than we do. The only true difference is Jesus. The more we have of Jesus in our lives, the more salty we become. The more Jesus is allowed to govern our lives, the more His light shines through us. When our lives become full of things other than Jesus, we will lose our saltiness. We will lose our light and will never make much of an impact.

Go Public

I like the way Eugene Peterson renders Matt 5:14–16:

Here's another way to put it: You're here to be light, bringing out the God-colors in the world. God is not a secret to be kept. We're *going public* with this, as public as a city on a hill. If I make you light-bearers, you don't think I'm going to hide you under a bucket, do you? I'm putting you on a light stand. Now that I've put you there on a hilltop, on a light stand—shine! Keep open house; be generous with your lives. By opening up to others, you'll prompt people to open up with God, this generous Father in heaven. (Matt 5:14–16 *The Message*, italics added)

Fire, and the light it gave, was a precious commodity in Jesus' day. In order always to have a flame, people often kept a small flame burning 24 hours a day so they would be ready when night came. To keep the flame burning slowly, so as to use little oil, they kept it under a basket or bowl during the day. This also kept it out of the way until it was needed when night fell.

Jesus pointed out that if you kept the flame under the bowl or basket when darkness came, then the light did you no good. It was useless. The house would remain dark until the darkness came in contact with the light. His point is making a difference requires involvement not isolation.

Useless Until . . .

Light is useless until it comes in contact with darkness. In speaking of our light, Jesus said, "Do not hide it under a bowl. Let it shine!" Put it on a stand, get it out of its isolation and into direct contact with the darkness. Then light is useful but not until then.

In the same way salt is useless until it gets out of the shaker and makes contact As long as salt is isolated in its shaker with the other salt, it does no one any good. Yet get it out of the shaker and in direct contact with the meat, and the impact is immediate and lasting.

The Value Comes from Going Public

We can be Christians who are spiritually salty and full of light but still make little or no impact on the world if we are hiding under a bowl or sitting in our Christian saltshaker. We must not become undercover Christians or rabbit-hole Christians. Rabbit-hole Christians pop their heads out only when they must. Their only contacts with the world are mad dashes to and from Christian activities. They live with the unspoken motto, The less contact with non-Christians the better the day. They pop out to get in the car to run their Christian kids to the Christian school. They listen to their Christian radio station, run off to their Christian Bible study, then go to lunch with their Christian friend. After dinner they pop out to visit their Christian friends for Christian fellowship.

When that is a description of our lives, Jesus is not impressed. People can be as salty and contagious as possible, but if they never come into contact with a lost person, what good do their lives accomplish?

What Did Jesus Do?

I had a discussion with a Christian couple who so strongly believed in separation from the world that they truly tried to avoid ever having themselves or anyone in their family ever have contact with non-Christians. They looked at me and said, "But Pastor Dave, aren't we to stay separate from that dark, nasty world? Isn't that what a good Christian would do? What would Jesus think of us if we did not stay separate from the world?"

Well, what would a good Christian do? An ever better question is, What would Jesus do? Let's take a walk through the Gospels asking how Jesus dealt with nonbelievers. Did He hide in the shaker? Did He hide under the basket? What does the Bible say?

What Would Jesus Do?

1. Jesus was a friend of sinners (Luke 7:34).
2. Jesus went into the homes of sinners (Luke 19:10).
3. Jesus invited sinners to eat with Him (Matt 9:9–11).
4. Jesus came to seek and save the lost (Luke 19:10).
5. Jesus sent us to do the same (John 20:21).

I wonder how many of us could really be called "friends of sinners"? Do we have any non-Christian friends? Do we ever eat with sinners? Do we ever have sinners in our homes? Is our mission to impact the lost, or is it to please and preserve ourselves?

What did Jesus do? He got involved with the world.

You say, "Yes, but that's Jesus. What would He have *us* do?"

The answer is that He would have us do the same.

What Would Jesus Have *Us* Do?

Note carefully what Jesus prayed for His followers.

"I have given them Your word; and the world has hated them because they are not of the world, just as I am not of the world. *I do not pray that You should take them out of the world,* but that You should keep them from the evil one. They are not of the world, just as I am not of the world. Sanctify them by Your truth. Your word is truth. As You sent Me into the world, *I also have sent them into the world.*" (John 17:14–18, italics added)

Note carefully that Jesus said, "I do not pray that You should take them out of the world, but that You should keep them from the evil one. . . . As You sent Me into the world, I also have sent them into the world." Jesus is praying that the Father would not take us from the world but send us into the world.

If you are saved, you are salt and light. Right now! Get out of your shaker. Shine your light. Lost people in the darkness of the world will see it. That is what glorifies our Father. "Let your light so shine before men, that they may see your good works and glorify your Father in heaven" (Matt 5:16).

— Evangelism Is . . . —

1. Shaking salt and shining light.
2. Doing what Jesus did—being friends with sinners.
3. A matter of involvement, not isolation.

— Key Verse —

"Let your light so shine before men, that they may see your good works and glorify your Father in heaven." (Matt 5:16)

— Good Quotes —

What is God's plan to deal with this darkened, decaying world? His plan is us! It's us. There is no one else. It isn't going to be given to anyone else. It doesn't belong to famous evangelists. They'll never touch the people you touch. It doesn't belong to great preachers, or people on the radio or television, or people who write books. It belongs to all of us. This is God's divine plan.

—John MacArthur[1]

Instead of being salt and light too many Christians have chosen to act like saltshakers and lightbulbs.

—A country preacher whose name I do not recall

Notes

1. J. MacArthur, sermon, "You Are the Light of the World: Matthew 5:14–16," http://www.gty.org/Resources/Sermons/2208, accessed June 11, 2009.

Part 2

Meaning

7

Evangelism Is . . .

Telling Good News

Dave Earley

M any years ago, 900 years before the time of Christ, war was raging. The
Samarians were besieged by their enemy and were experiencing a severe
famine (2 Kgs 6:24). Food was in such scarce supply that inside the gates of
the besieged city people were literally going crazy from hunger. They would
pay absolutely any price for food. They were so starved and crazed by hunger
they'd eat anything they could get their hands on, even to the point of eating
their own children (2 Kgs 6:25,28–29). Death was inevitable and imminent.

Four men with leprosy were outside the gates of the city. Leprosy is a scaly
skin and nerve disease that can cause severe tissue damage, loss of sensation, and
disfigurement. Because leprosy is transmitted following close personal contact,
people suffering from leprosy were shunned by the community. They lived as
outcasts and beggars in little packs, scavenging for food like wild dogs.

With the entire city starving, there was no chance of anyone giving the lepers food. So they decided their only hope was to surrender to the enemy rather
than starve to death. So they headed out to the enemy camp (2 Kgs 7:3–4).

They were astounded by what they found.

When they got there, they found no one to surrender to because the enemy
camp was entirely abandoned. God had sent thunder that sounded like the
chariots and horses of a great army. The invaders were so scared they fled back
home with only the clothes on their backs (2 Kgs 7:5–7).

The four lepers had won the lottery, hit the jackpot, and found the pot
of gold at the end of the rainbow all at once. They found plenty of food, fine

clothes, and riches left for the taking. They ate their fill like madmen and took things to hide and to hoard.

Yet something was not right.

A little voice inside them got their attention. They looked at their unexpected good favor and decided they could not keep the good news to themselves. Then they said to one another, "We're not doing right. This is a day of good news and we are keeping it to ourselves. . . . Let's go at once and report this to the royal palace" (2 Kgs 7:9 NIV).

They realized they had a moral obligation to share the good news. So they did.

Of course, the people of Samaria were skeptical at first. They thought it had to be a trick. This news of free food and riches just lying there for the taking was too good to be true. Yet after checking out the story, they found the lepers had told them the truth and saved their lives. Deliverance and plenty awaited every person in the city. Tens of thousands of people would have died if the lepers hadn't shared the good news.

We Are like the Lepers

As I read this story, I find myself identifying with the lepers on several levels. Prior to our acceptance of the Lord Jesus as our Savior, we are all in many ways like those lepers.

1. We had spiritual leprosy. Sin clung to us, ate at us, and made us dangerously contagious and completely unclean.

2. We lived in a world of people starving for the truth and love that only God could supply. These spiritually starving people will pay any price to get even a taste of any cheap substitute for the genuine soul nourishment of the love of God.

3. We existed under the sentence of impending death.

4. We decided anything was better than this wasting away.

5. One day we left the comfort of what we had known to surrender to something unknown.

6. As we lifted our hands in surrender, we found that God had already gone ahead of us and run off the enemy.

7. We were not only spared from death, but God had a feast awaiting us. We could feed our starving bellies with the bread of life and drink deeply from the stream of salvation. At God's table we found the best food we'd ever eaten; a new robe of righteousness and great riches were ours for the taking. It was so

good to be full. It was exciting to be rich. We were no longer starving beggars but were now rich and free.

8. Our first impulse might have been to hide some of the goodies and keep them for ourselves. Yet there was/is more than we could ever enjoy. There was/is plenty for everybody "back in the city." All those starving people can be fed. The poor can be made rich. Their lives can be spared.

9. Like the lepers we must realize that hiding and hoarding life-giving goodies is wrong. Like the lepers we must say, "We're not doing right. This is a day of good news and we are keeping it to ourselves. . . . Let's go at once and report this." The message of Jesus is good news. We cannot keep it to ourselves. We must go and tell somebody. We can at least tell them where the food is. If they refuse to eat it, that is their responsibility, but we at least have to tell them. They may be skeptical at first, but we still must tell them.

We were former spiritual lepers starving and unclean until we surrendered to God. There is good news in Jesus, and we must go tell somebody about it.

Evangelism Is Sharing Good News

The story of the Samaritan lepers has everything to do with evangelism. It is a story about the moral obligation to share good news. As the lepers said when they found the riches, "We're not doing right. This is a day of *good news,* and we are keeping it to ourselves." A literal translation of the word "gospel" (*euangelos*) is "good message" or "good news."

In some spheres the word *evangelism* has obtained a negative connotation, but nothing could be further from the truth. The word *evangelism* literally means "to communicate good news."

Jesus' death on the cross to pay for our sins and open the way for us to get to God is good news. In fact, it's the best news. But having such information does others no good unless, or until, we share it. We have to proclaim the good news.

"Evangelism Is One Beggar Telling Another Beggar Where to Find Bread"[1]

This quote by D. T. Niles is my favorite description of evangelism. Evangelism is a positive opportunity to help someone else. It is not talking down to someone as if you were better; you aren't better. It's not looking down a self-righteous nose and saying, "Sinner repent!" It's realizing that spiritually we are all beggars in need of living bread. We have found that Jesus is the living bread. Evangelism is telling someone how to meet the living bread, the Lord Jesus Christ. "This is the bread which comes down from heaven, that one may eat of it and not die. I am the living bread which came down from heaven. If anyone eats of this bread, he will live forever" (John 6:50–51).

The Bible and Sharing Good News

The Bible is full of references to sharing the good news. The words *gospel* or *good news* are used 130 times in the Bible, 109 times in the NT. So many references make clear that sharing the good news is something every follower of Jesus must take seriously.

1. The Old Testament prophesied that the ministry of the Messiah would be to proclaim the good news. Jesus fulfilled this prophecy.

> He went to Nazareth, where he had been brought up, and on the Sabbath day he went into the synagogue, as was his custom. And he stood up to read. The scroll of the prophet Isaiah was handed to him. Unrolling it, he found the place where it is written: "The Spirit of the Lord is on me, because he has anointed me to preach *good news* to the poor. He has sent me to proclaim freedom for the prisoners and recovery of sight for the blind, to release the oppressed, to proclaim the year of the Lord's favo.r" (Luke 4:16–19 NIV, italics added; see Isa 61:1–3)

2. Jesus equated people's commitment to the gospel to their commitment to Him.

> For whoever wants to save his life will lose it, but whoever loses his life for me and for the *gospel* will save it (Mark 8:35 NIV, italics added)

> "I tell you the truth," Jesus replied, "no one who has left home or brothers or sisters or mother or father or children or fields for me and the *gospel* will fail to receive a hundred times as much in this present age (homes, brothers, sisters, mothers, children and fields—and with them, persecutions) and in the age to come, eternal life." (Mark 10:29–30 NIV, italics added)

3. The Great Commission is the command for us to proclaim the good news. "He said to them, 'Go into all the world and preach the *good news* to all creation.'" (Mark 16:15 NIV, italics added)

4. The gospel is the power of God unto salvation. "That is why I am so eager to preach the *gospel* also to you who are at Rome. I am not ashamed of the *gospel*, because it is the power of God for the salvation of everyone who believes: first for the Jew, then for the Gentile" (Rom 1:15–16 NIV, italics added).

5. The good news must be proclaimed so people can hear, believe, and call upon the name of the Lord for salvation.

> For, "Everyone who calls on the name of the Lord will be saved." How, then, can they call on the one they have not believed in? And how can they believe in the one of whom they have not heard? And how can they hear without someone preaching to them? And how can they preach unless they are sent? As it is written, "How beautiful are the feet of those who bring *good news!*" (Rom 10:13–15 NIV, italics added)

6. Paul viewed proclaiming the good news as his priestly duty, his great ambition, and his driving compulsion.

> I have written you quite boldly on some points, as if to remind you of them again, because of the grace God gave me to be a minister of Christ Jesus to the Gentiles with the priestly duty of proclaiming the *gospel* of God, so that the Gentiles might become an offering acceptable to God, sanctified by the Holy Spirit. (Rom 15:15–16 NIV, italics added)

> It has always been my ambition to preach the *gospel* where Christ was not known, so that I would not be building on someone else's foundation. (Rom 15:20 NIV, italics added)

> Yet when I preach the *gospel*, I cannot boast, for I am compelled to preach. Woe to me if I do not preach the *gospel!* (1 Cor 9:16 NIV, italics added)

7. Paul was flexible with his methods but never changed the message of the gospel.

> Though I am free and belong to no man, I make myself a slave to everyone, to win as many as possible. To the Jews I became like a Jew, to win the Jews. To those under the law I became like one under the law (though I myself am not under the law), so as to win those under the law. To those not having the law I became like one not having the law (though I am not free from God's law but am under Christ's law), so as to win those not having the law. To the weak I became weak, to win the weak. I have become all things to all men so that by all possible means I might

save some. I do all this for the sake of the *gospel*, that I may share in its blessing. (1 Cor 9:19–23 NIV, italics added)

8. Paul defined "the gospel" as the good news of the death, burial, and resurrection of Jesus for our sins.

Now, brothers, I want to remind you of the gospel I preached to you, which you received and on which you have taken your stand. By this *gospel* you are saved, if you hold firmly to the word I preached to you. Otherwise, you have believed in vain.

For what I received I passed on to you as of first importance: that Christ died for our sins according to the Scriptures, that he was buried, that he was raised on the third day according to the Scriptures. (1 Cor 15:1–4 NIV, italics added)

9. Satan attempts to blind the minds of unbelievers from seeing the glory of the gospel. "And even if our *gospel* is veiled, it is veiled to those who are perishing. The god of this age has blinded the minds of unbelievers, so that they cannot see the light of the *gospel* of the glory of Christ, who is the image of God" (2 Cor 4:3–4 NIV, italics added).

10. Our conduct needs to match our message, the gospel. "Whatever happens, conduct yourselves in a manner worthy of the *gospel* of Christ" (Phil 1:27 NIV, italics added).

We Must Share the Good News

The Bible is clear. We must be aware of the spiritual hunger of the unbelievers. We should care that they will spiritually starve to death without the living bread, Jesus. We need to share the good news of the death, burial, and resurrection of Jesus Christ for our sins. We cannot keep it to ourselves. We are obligated to share the good news so spiritual beggars can find living bread.

⁓ Evangelism Is . . . ⁓

1. One beggar telling another beggar where to get bread.
2. Actively believing that the gospel is the power of God unto salvation.
3. Sharing the gospel or good news.
4. Telling the good news of the death, burial, and resurrection of Jesus for our sins.

⚊ Good Quotes ⚊

To evangelize is to tell a good message. In the New Testament
the term implies a good message, as in a victory.
While some people might attempt to make us feel as
though evangelism imposes on the privacy of others,
let us never forget we are telling the Good News—Jesus has
conquered sin, death, and the grave!

—ALVIN REID[2]

The simple definition of evangelism: Those who know,
telling those who don't.

—LEITH ANDERSON[3]

Notes

1. D. T. Niles, *That They May Have Life* (New York: Harper and Brothers, 1951), 96.

2. A. Reid, *Introduction to Evangelism* (Nashville, TN: B&H, 1998), 9.

3. L. Anderson from sermon "Making More Disciples," http://www.Sermon-Central.com, accessed July 21, 2009.

8
Helping People Become Good Enough

Dave Earley

I was talking with a young man named Rob not long ago. As the conversation turned to spiritual things, I asked him, "What would happen to your soul if you died today? Let's say a meteorite fell out of the sky and crushed you. Do you think you would go to heaven?"

"Yes," he said. "I think I might."

"What if God were to ask you, 'Why should I let you into heaven?'" I asked. "What would you say to God?"

"I guess I would answer, 'Because I am a pretty good person and have lived a good life,'" he responded.

"But," I asked, "how do you know if it is good enough?"

The Goal of Evangelism

The apostle Paul was an expert evangelist. It was his consuming passion. He was especially burdened about his people, the Hebrews. Of them he wrote, "Brethren, my heart's desire and prayer to God for Israel is that they may be saved" (Rom 10:1 NKJV).

"That they may be saved." What is the goal of a missionary? It is to help people be saved. What is the goal of evangelism? It is that people would be saved.

The word *saved* means "being delivered from the penalty and punishment of death that results from sin and delivered to an abundant life on earth and eternal life in heaven." It is the result of having your sin paid for. So the goal of evangelism is helping another person experience salvation from sin and death and deliverance to life with God.

Lost People Need a Relationship with God

"For I bear them witness that they have a zeal for God, but not according to knowledge." (Rom 10:2).

Note the word "knowledge." The word Paul chose for knowledge (*epi-ginosko*) refers to "knowledge gained only through personal experience and personal relationship." By using it here, Paul tells us that the Jews knew about God but did not personally know God. They knew of God in their heads but had yet to experience Him in their hearts. They had a religion dealing with God but not a personal relationship with God. Real Christianity is not about religion, ritual, or rules. It is about a relationship with God.

Lost People Lack Righteousness Before God

Being saved or not being saved is a matter of having the right type of righteousness, the type that makes you good enough for God. God is holy. He is sinless, righteous, and perfect. In order to relate to Him, we need a perfect level of holiness, sinlessness, and moral perfection as well. In other words, we need a pure righteousness.

The answer God is looking for when it comes to getting into heaven is an answer involving righteousness. The issue is, Do you have the righteousness necessary to get into heaven? Is the type of righteousness you have good enough?

The Issue Is Righteousness

In Rom 10:3–4, Paul mentions righteousness four times and discusses two types of righteousness. One is inadequate for entrance into heaven, and the other is required for entrance into heaven. "For they being ignorant of God's righteousness, and seeking to establish their own righteousness, have not submitted to the righteousness of God. For Christ is the end of the law for righteousness to everyone who believes" (Rom 10:3–4).

A person may ask, "Well how do I know which righteousness I have?"

Go back to the question I asked Rob: "What would you say to God if He were to ask you, 'Why should I let you into heaven?'" The way a person answers that question reveals the type of righteousness they have.

Often a person's answer will include some of the following basis for righteousness:

- I attend church regularly.
- I pay my taxes.
- I do not lie, cheat, or steal.
- I am sexually pure.
- I have never murdered anyone.
- I give my money in the offering at my church.
- I was baptized, sprinkled, or confirmed.

If someone's answer is based on any of those actions, he is indicating that he, like the Jews, is seeking to establish his own righteousness. When I tell people this, I have had people say to me, "What's wrong with my righteousness? It's pretty good, isn't it? It's better than most!"

I answer, "That may be true, but the issue is not, Is your righteousness better than most? The issue is, Is your righteousness good enough to please God?" The issue also isn't, "Do *you* think it is good enough?" or "Do *I* think it is good enough?" or "Does *your mom* think it is good enough?" The issue is, "Does *God* think it is good enough?"

The Bible has much to say about righteousness. According to the earlier verses from Romans, it all boils down to the fact that we all have one of two types of righteousness (Rom 10:3–4).

Their Own Righteousness

The big problem with my own righteousness is that it is not good enough. The OT tells us that compared to the perfect righteousness God expects, our righteousness is like an unclean, filthy rag (Isa 64:6). That's not very impressive. When he wrote those words, Isaiah was speaking to a group of religious Jews, but the assessment applies to all of us. Compared to what God expects, our righteousness is at its best ugly, dirty, and stained.

In the book of Romans, Paul is saying the same thing Isaiah said. In sizing up the righteousness of humanity, Paul concluded, "There is none righteous, no, not one" (Rom 3:10).

I was in an evangelizing discussion with a man one day, and I asked him the two questions: "If you died tonight, would you know for sure you would be with God in heaven?" And, "If yes, how can you be sure?"

He puffed out his chest and said, "Yes, because I keep the Ten Commandments."

I smiled and said, "That's great, could you name them for me please?"

He blushed deeply, stammered, and was able to name only two of the 10. I said, "Let's be honest. If you don't even remember them, how do you know you have kept them?"[1]

No one is perfect when it comes to God's standard of righteous. The apostle John wrote, "If we say that we have no sin, we deceive ourselves" (1 John 1:8).

Missing the Mark

The standard of righteousness needed in order to earn eternal life is perfection. When Paul wrote, "All have sinned, and come short of the glory of God" (Rom 3:23 KJV), the word he used for *sin* means "to miss the mark." It came from archery contests where the archers tried to hit the bull's-eye. The first ring next to the bull's-eye was called "Sin 1"; the second ring was called "Sin 2," etc. Paul says that when it comes to the moral, spiritual, perfect righteousness of God we have all missed the bull's-eye. Maybe you have come close, and you are at Sin 1, or maybe you have totally blown it and are at Sin 101. The point is that we have all missed the bull's-eye—all of us except Jesus.

Our righteousness is not good enough. It falls short of the necessary perfection. We have all missed the mark. We have all sinned.

How Good Is Good Enough?

Often when I talk with someone about the fact that their own righteousness is not good enough, they ask me, "So how good is good enough?" I tell them that Jesus answered that question. He made a stunning statement that reveals the inadeuacy of our self-righteousness: "For I say to you, that unless your righteousness exceeds the righteousness of the scribes and Pharisees, you will by no means enter the kingdom of heaven" (Matt 5:20).

Scribes and Pharisees loved rules. They thought the 600 rules of the OT were inadequate so they added hundreds more! Pharisees were externally righteous people. They gave at least 10 percent of every single thing they had to the temple. They fasted from food for two full days a week. They attended synagogue several times a week, plus all holidays, even when they were on vacation.

They followed all of their rules with the goal of being good enough in the eyes of God. They wanted to accrue as much self-righteousness as humanly possible. Yet Jesus said that the righteousness of the Pharisees was still not good enough!

Our righteousness is not enough to get us into heaven. Neither is it good enough to overcome the stain of sin and make us saved. It is not enough to get us to God.

God's Righteousness

> My little children, these things I write to you, so that you may not sin. And if anyone sins, we have an Advocate with the Father, Jesus Christ the righteous (1 John 2:1).

Notice the last four words above: "Jesus Christ the righteous." The bad news is that we don't have good enough righteousness. The good news is that Jesus does. He is not only the Son of God but also God the Son. His mother was a virgin. Why? So He could have the humanness of man without the stain of sin. "For we do not have a High Priest who cannot sympathize with our weaknesses, but was in all points tempted as we are, yet without sin" (Heb 4:15).

Notice those last two words: "without sin." Jesus was no ordinary man. He was the sinless Son of God. Why am I a Christian and not a Mormon, a Buddhist, or a Muslim? The answer is because Jesus was different from Joseph Smith, Siddharthe the Buddha, or Mohammed. Jesus never sinned. Jesus attained the required righteousness. He hit the bull's-eye.

God's Accounting Book

When I was talking with Rob about righteousness, I drew something I have done dozens of times to help people understand the simplicity of the gospel. I took a clean napkin at the table where we were eating lunch. On it I drew the following chart as we talked, read several Scriptures, and talked about the fact that all have sinned and our self-righteousness is inadequate.

But we are all like an unclean thing, and all our righteousnesses are like filthy rags. (Isa 64:6)

As it is written: "There is none righteous, no, not one." (Rom 3:10)

All have sinned, and come short of the glory of God. (Rom 3:23 KJV)

My Righteousness	Christ's Righteousness
US	
+SIN Isa 64:6; Rom 3:10; 3:23	

Then we read Rom 6:23: "For the wages of sin is death, but the gift of God is eternal life in Christ Jesus our Lord." We talked about the fact that sin has a price tag—death. Physical death is separation of a soul from a body. Spiritual death is separation of a soul from God. Because we have all sinned, we all deserve death and separation from God. So I added to the chart the result of sin, which is death, as you can see below.

My Righteousness	Christ's Righteousness
US	
+SIN Isa 64:6; Rom 3:10; 3:23	
DEATH Rom 6:23a	

After that, I drew the other page "Christ's Righteousness" and got to the good news. We read several verses about the fact that Jesus did not sin.

My little children, these things I write to you, so that you may not sin. And if anyone sins, we have an Advocate with the Father, Jesus Christ the righteous. (1 John 2:1)

For we do not have a High Priest who cannot sympathize with our weaknesses, but was in all points tempted as we are, yet without sin. (Heb 4:15)

My Righteousness	Christ's Righteousness
US	JESUS
+SIN Isa 64:6; Romans 3:10; 3:23	–SIN 1 John 2:1; Heb 4:15
DEATH Rom 6:23a	

We talked about the fact that because Jesus did not sin, He did not deserve death. Instead, He deserved life and union with God forever in heaven. We read Rom 6:23 again, focusing on the last part: "For the wages of sin is death, *but the gift of God is eternal life in Christ Jesus our Lord.*"

My Righteousness	Christ's Righteousness
US	JESUS
+SIN Isa 64:6; Rom 3:10; 3:23	–SIN 1 John 2:1; Heb 4:15
DEATH Rom 6:23a	LIFE Rom 6:23b

But we did not stop there. I said to Rob, "You and I have sinned, and we deserve death. Correct?

"Correct," he said.

I continued, "Jesus never sinned so He deserves life and union with God. Correct?"

"Correct," he said.

"So what was the big thing Jesus did for us?" I asked. "In order to remember it, a lot of people wear it around their necks."

"He died for us on a cross," Rob answered.

"Correct," I said, as I drew an arrow from the word *Jesus* to the word *death.*

My Righteousness	Christ's Righteousness 2 Cor 5:21; 1 Pet 3:18
US	JESUS
+SIN Isa 64:6; Rom 3:10; 3:23	–SIN 1 John 2:1; Heb 4:15
DEATH Rom 6:23a	LIFE Rom 6:23b

"Yes, Jesus died for us," I said. "But *why* did Jesus die for us?"

Rob grew quiet. Then he said. "Because we have all have sinned and deserve death."

Then I drew an arrow from the word *us* to the word *life*.

We read Rom 6:23 again, underlining some key words: "For the wages of sin is death, but the gift of God is *eternal life in Christ Jesus* our Lord."

"Oh, now I understand," Rob said. "Jesus died for us in order to give us life."

"This is right," I said. "The one who did not deserve to die, Jesus, died so the ones who do deserve to die, us, can have eternal life."

Then we read this verse: "For Christ also suffered once for sins, the just [Jesus the righteous] for the unjust [us, the not so righteous], that He might bring us to God" (1 Pet 3:18).

"According to this verse, why did Jesus die?" I asked.

"To bring us to God," Rob answered.

"Correct," I said.

We read this verse: "For He made Him who knew no sin to be sin for us, that we might become the righteousness of God in Him" (2 Cor 5:21).

"According to this verse, why did Jesus die?" I continued.

"To provide us with the type of righteousness that would give us a relationship with God," Rob answered.

"Absolutely correct," I said.

"We need to look at one more thing," I said. "Let's see how to receive this gift of eternal life." We read Eph 2:8–9: "For by grace you have been saved through faith, and that not of yourselves; it is the gift of God, not of works, lest anyone should boast" (Eph 2:8–9).

"So it takes faith," Rob said. "That's the only way we can be good enough for God."

"That's right," I said. "In order to receive God's gift, you have to have faith, committed belief, all-out trust, complete reliance in Jesus. That is the only way to get the righteousness needed to be saved."

After that Rob got down on his knees and gave his life to God by faith in Jesus Christ.

⚊ Evangelism Is . . . ⚊

1. Helping people realize they are not good enough for God without Jesus.
2. Helping people become good enough for God through faith in Jesus.

⚊ Key Verse ⚊

For He made Him who knew no sin to be sin for us, that we might become the righteousness of God in Him. (2 Cor 5:21)

⚊ Good Quote ⚊

If I had one hour with a man, I would spend the first 55 minutes explaining to him that he is lost. Then I would spend the last 5 minutes telling him how to be saved.

—UNKNOWN

Notes

1. At this point you may want to turn to the Ten Commandments, beginning with the ones about lying and stealing.

9

Leading People to True Conversion

Dave Earley

If I were not totally committed to Christ, Doug might have been my hero. He was a couple of years older than me, had his own apartment, and drove a fast new car. He was extremely handsome, very bright, and had a great personality. He also had a killer smile, was well built and athletic. On top of that, he was a truly nice guy. He worked hard and was rapidly advancing up the corporate ladder. The girls absolutely adored him.

Doug worked as an assistant manager for the company I worked for one summer. Being two of the few young single guys, we naturally hung out together. On our days off we lifted weights and ran together. I soon realized that while Doug had it all together outwardly he was empty on the inside. He had been successfully seduced by the world into loving and living for the big three: money, sex, and power. The Bible clearly states that they don't satisfy and will not last.

> Do not love the world or anything in the world. If anyone loves the world, the love of the Father is not in him. For everything in the world—the cravings of sinful man, the lust of his eyes and the boasting of what he has and does—comes not from the Father but from the world. The world and its desires pass away, but the man who does the will of God lives forever. (1 John 2:15–17 NIV)

As I spent time with Doug, he shared with me more and more of his past, his struggles, and his dreams of the future. As he came to trust me, I shared with him about how Jesus was changing my life. When it came to Jesus, Doug was curious but not convinced.

Near the end of the summer, I finally got him to attend church with me on my last Sunday before leaving for college. Doug had rarely attended church. It was odd to see him in a setting where he was uncomfortable and even awkward at times. But the people were friendly, and he paid careful attention. The pastor did a good job of presenting the gospel in his message that day.

After church Doug and I went to lunch. We had a good talk about church and more importantly about Jesus. I could tell that he had taken some steps toward God as a result of attending the church service. He had gone from being curious about Jesus to being convicted of his need for Jesus, but he still was not convinced.

This is where I made a well-meaning mistake. I really cared about Doug and desperately wanted him to know Christ. I knew that in a few days our paths would separate because I would be leaving for school, and he was being transferred to the main office before getting his own store to run. So I presented the gospel again to Doug. I could tell that he understood the main points. He was separated from God through sin. Jesus died to pay for his sin. He needed to call upon Jesus to save him from his sin. Then he could experience eternal life.

Doug said that he believed all of those things. I could see a level of conviction in his face. So instead of being grateful for the progress made, I jumped ahead of God. I disregarded the check in my spirit and pressed on in my own strength and wisdom. I verbally twisted his arm to pray with me and ask Jesus into his life. Doug was reluctant.

"This is all new to me, Dave," he said.

"Yes but it has been true all of your life," I countered.

"I guess you are right," he said. "But I really like my life just as it is. I don't want to change."

"Jesus can make it even better," I said. "What will it hurt if you get saved right now?"

"Nothing I guess," he shrugged.

I could tell he was uncomfortable. But now it was no longer the holy discontent of the conviction of the Holy Spirit. It was the discomfort of being pressed to do something he didn't want to do. Yet I pressed on. I wanted him to be saved so badly.

"Doug, repeat this prayer after me," I said. "Dear God, I admit that I have sinned."

Politely Doug repeated the words after me. We went through the prayer, and I said, "Amen." He repeated it after me, sounding relieved.

I looked up with a proud smile. Then I asked Doug, "So what will be different about your life from now on?"

I expected him to tell me he was going to quit getting drunk, stop chasing/using young women, and no longer live for money. I thought he was going to say that he was going to start reading his Bible and begin regularly going to Bible studies and church. But that's not what he said.

"Nothing," he said. "Nothing is going to change. I told you, I really like my life just as it is, and I am not ready for Jesus to mess it up. I want to go to heaven, but I am not ready to live for Jesus."

I felt like an idiot. Even though I had been doing many things right, I had tried to get ahead of God. Impatiently, I had rushed the plowing, planting, and watering process and pressed my friend to make a commitment he was not ready to make. I had misread the situation. He had gone from curious about Jesus to convicted by the Holy Spirit, but he was not yet convinced of the awfulness of his sin and of the supremacy of a life lived for God. He was unwilling to turn from his old life and turn to God. So even though Doug had repeated a prayer after me, he clearly was unconverted.

Four Steps to True Salvation

1. CURIOUS: Curious about who Jesus is and what Jesus did and can do for you.
2. CONVICTED: Convicted by the Holy Spirit of your sin and the resulting judgment.
3. CONVINCED: Convinced that Jesus is the sinless Son of God and that salvation comes only through Him.
4. CONVERTED: Converted or turned around through active faith that leads you to turn from sin and to God for salvation.

When I prematurely tried to lead my friend Doug to Christ, he was somewhere between convicted and convinced. Because I rushed the process, he was not truly converted at that time and gave no evidence of a changed life.

Jesus Sorted Out the Merely Curious

In the sixth chapter of the Gospel of John, we find that Jesus had been busy healing the sick. To top that off, He had performed the amazing miracle of feeding 5,000 men with a boy's lunch of five small barley loaves and two small fish

(John 6:1–15). The crowds were curious about the identity of this miracle man so they followed Him in droves wondering what He would do next and hoping He would meet more of their needs (John 6:26–28).

As the chapter unfolds, Jesus discerned the shallowness of their dedication. By bringing them to a point of decision about His identity, He called them to the level of commitment to Him that would make them true followers (John 6:29–65). Sadly, at this point some turned back, but not all.

> From this time many of his disciples turned back and no longer followed him.
>
> "You do not want to leave too, do you?" Jesus asked the Twelve.
>
> Simon Peter answered him, "Lord, to whom shall we go? You have the words of eternal life. We believe and know that you are the Holy One of God." (John 6:66–69 NIV)

While salvation often begins with *curiosity*, it takes more than curiosity in Jesus to experience true conversion. It takes experiencing the *conviction* of the Holy Spirit as He convinces us of our sin, our lack of true righteousness, and the resulting judgment (John 16:8). It takes being *convinced* that Jesus is indeed the Christ, the sinless Son of God, by believing the Word of God (John 16:30–31). It takes confident faith that He truly has the words of life and a resulting *commitment* to follow Jesus (John 6:68–69). Truly following Jesus will result in our turning from our old lifestyles of sin and turning to God in complete trust in Jesus and in determined obedience to His Word. Such a turning results in a truly changed life.

Two Sides of True Conversion

Both the Hebrew and the Greek words for conversion mean "to turn." True conversion is a turning *from* something (sin) and turning *to* Someone (God). It has two sides, one positive and one negative.

The positive side of conversion is turning *to* God (Acts 9:35; 11:21; 15:19; 2 Pet 2:25). Some refer to the positive side as faith. The negative side of conversion is turning *from* sin, which is often called repentance. Combined, they result in true conversion.

Paul proclaimed both sides of conversion. He said, "I have declared to both Jews and Greeks that they must turn to God in repentance and have faith in our Lord Jesus" (Acts 20:21 NIV). Later he described both sides when he summed up his ministry by saying that he "declared first to those in Damascus and in Jerusalem, and throughout all the region of Judea, and then to the

Gentiles, that they should repent, turn to God, and do works befitting repentance" (Acts 26:20).

Three Aspects of True Conversion

True conversion not only has two sides, but it also impacts a person on three levels—intellect, emotion, and will. In order to experience true conversion, a person must *know* something, *feel* something, and *do* something.

1. Know. In order to be converted, a person must know of his lost condition (Rom 3:20; Ps 51:3–4; Ezek 36:31) and know that Jesus is the divine remedy for sin (Rom 10:13,17; Ps 109:10; Phil 3:8). True conversion is a result of knowing and believing the basic facts of the gospel—the death, burial, and resurrection of Jesus for our sins.

2. Feel. In order to be converted, a person must have a broken and contrite heart over his sin (Jer 31:19; Ps 51:17; 2 Cor 7:10f) and feel drawn to Christ (John 6:44,65; 1 Thess 2:13). True conversion is a result of feeling the guilt and shame for one's sin.

3. Act. In order to be converted, a person must also turn *from* his sin (Acts 26:18; Ezek 14:6; 2 Cor 7:11) and turn *to* Christ in reliance on Him alone for salvation (Acts 15:11; 16:31; Phil 3:9). This faith is expressed by calling on the Lord to save you (Rom 10:9,13). This repentance in changing the way you live.

Many of the people who respond to an invitation, pray a prayer, and fill out a card have never experienced true conversion. The gospel has penetrated their intellect and even their emotions but not their will. Faith does not become *saving* faith until it impacts all three.

James wrote that even demons have a faith that impacts their intellect (they know there is one God) and emotions (they shudder), but it does not save them because it does not result in a change in their behavior.

> What does it profit, my brethren, if someone says he has faith but does not have works? Can faith save him? If a brother or sister is naked and destitute of daily food, and one of you says to them, "Depart in peace, be warmed and filled," but you do not give them the things which are needed for the body, what does it profit? Thus also faith by itself, if it does not have works, is dead.
>
> But someone will say, "You have faith, and I have works." Show me your faith without your works, and I will show you my faith by my works. You believe that there is one God. You do well. Even the demons believe—and tremble! (Jas 2:14–19)

Simple, Not Easy

Being converted is simple yet not necessarily easy. It is not easy to admit our sinfulness. We are not comfortable admitting our utter inability to save ourselves. It is not always easy to leave behind a lifestyle of self-centered sin. It is difficult to turn our lives over to a new master.

Jesus described the simple difficulty of true conversion as the difference between going through a wide gate and a narrow one. True conversion is like going through a small gate and following a narrow path. Jesus is the gate, and the Christian life is the path. "Enter through the narrow gate. For wide is the gate and broad is the road that leads to destruction, and many enter through it. But small is the gate and narrow the road that leads to life, and only a few find it" (Matt 7:13–14 NIV).

Not That Complicated

While not easy, true conversion is relatively simple to understand. Even a child can be converted. While true conversion is a miraculous act of God, on the human side, it can be as simple as A, B, C. Each of those letters stands for one of the three aspects of true conversion.

Admit. To be saved or truly converted, a person must *acknowledge* his lost condition and *admit* that Jesus is the divine remedy for sin. There are some truths they must know. They must use their intellect.

Believe. To be saved or truly converted, a person must *believe* that Jesus died for his sins and that He rose from the dead.

Call. To be saved a person must *confess* that Jesus is Lord and *call* upon the name of the Lord (Rom 10:9,13). This shows a willingness to *do* what God desires.

Not Converted Because of a Boat

Steve and Debbie were in a Bible study group Cathy and I had in our home. The group was made up of young adults who were interested in Christianity. One by one members of the group were getting saved. Debbie had already gotten saved, but Steve was not ready. He was an engineer who had no church background. It was all new to him.

Week after week God worked on his heart. We had watched him move from being curious about Jesus to convicted by the Holy Spirit about his need for Christ. We saw Steve become convinced that Jesus is Lord and that he needed Jesus to save him. But something was holding him back.

One night Cathy and I went to visit Steve and Debbie at their home. We hoped to get the opportunity to lead Steve to Christ. While Cathy and Debbie were talking in the kitchen, Steve took me out into his huge garage. He showed me his "toys," as he called them—a sports car, a classic motorcycle, and a brand-new boat.

I oohed and aahed over his toys. Then I turned the conversation to spiritual things and asked Steve point-blank what was keeping him from giving his life to Christ.

"That boat," he said, pointing at the shiny new boat. "I just bought it this summer. I am afraid that if I get saved, Jesus may want me to give it up."

"Thanks for being honest," I said. I really wanted to try to talk him into praying to be saved anyway, but the Lord was prompting me to be quiet.

"I guess that is not a very good reason," he said. "But I saved my money for three years to buy it."

He looked really guilty. I bit my lip and determined not to be the one who talked him into praying a prayer he did not really mean.

"But then it is just a boat," he said, shaking his head as we walked out of the garage.

The Rest of the Story

In our house five nights later, as we were wrapping up Bible study, it was Steve's turn to share what God was saying to him through the Word that night. "Well," he began, with a guilty look on his face, "the last few weeks you guys have been getting saved and talking about how good you now feel inside. I have been thinking that it was all well and good for you, but I am doing just fine without being saved." He continued, "But the last few days I have been feeling miserable inside. I guess I have been running from God. So," he paused, ". . . anyway, I know I need to get saved."

"Do you believe Jesus died for your sins and rose from the dead?" I asked.

"Yes," he said.

"Are you willing to turn from your sin?"

"Yes," he said.

"Will you call Jesus Lord and do *whatever* He says?" I emphasized *whatever*. Steve and I both knew why.

"Yes," he said.

"Then let's get on our knees and you tell Him all about it."

And he did!

By the way, I think he sold the boat after a while because he was not using it much anyway.

⚊ Evangelism Is . . . ⚊

1. Helping people experience true conversion.
2. Leading people to turn to God by faith and from sin in repentance.
3. Knowing when to be quiet and let the Holy Spirit do His work.

⚊ Key Verse ⚊

*"Assuredly, I say to you, unless you are converted
and become as little children, you will by no means enter
the kingdom of heaven." (Matt 18:3)*

⚊ Good Quotes ⚊

*Before you or I can have any well-grounded, scriptural hope,
of being happy in a future state, there must be some great,
some notable, and amazing change pass upon our souls.*
— George Whitefield [1]

*Conversion is about a change of heart that results in a change
of living. Conversion to Jesus Christ involves the whole
person, that is, not only the way we think, but also the way
we behave and the way we engage and construct our self,
community and society.*
— Kim Thoday [2]

Notes
1. G. Whitefield, in his sermon "Mark of True Conversion," quoted on Peacemakers.net, accessed March 17, 2009.
2. K. Thoday, "Conversion (Luke 19:1–10)," posted by John Mark Ministries, http://jmm.aaa.net.au/articles/4544.htm.

10

A Process Leading to an Event

Dave Earley

Both Dr. David Wheeler and I teach large classes composed of hundreds of first-year college students. Every semester I ask for volunteers and bring four single young ladies up in front of the class. I ask them to give their honest response to a series of scenarios.

Scenario 1. What if a reasonably attractive young man came to class as I was beginning to lecture? Let's say that he sat next to you but did not speak to you. Immediately after class he got down on one knee, pulled out a diamond ring, and asked, "Will you marry me?"

Then I ask each of the girls, "Would you marry him?"

After giggling a bit, they always give the same answer: "No!"

Then I ask, "Why?"

You can guess their responses. "I don't even know him."

Then I ask, "What would you think of him?"

"I would think he was crazy," is their most common response.

Scenario 2. What if a reasonably attractive young man came to class as I was beginning to lecture? Let's say that he sat next to you but did not speak to you. Immediately after class he invited you to join him for coffee at Starbucks. You went and talked for about half an hour and had a decent time. The next thing you know, he got down on one knee, pulled out a diamond ring, and asked, "Will you marry me?"

Then I ask each of the girls, "Would you marry him?"

After some laughing, they still give pretty much the same answer: "No!"
Then I ask, "Why?"

You can guess their responses. "I still don't really know him."

Then I ask, "What would you think of him?"

"I would still think he was nuts," is their most common response.

Scenario 3. Let's say that a reasonably attractive young man came to class as
I was beginning to lecture. Let's say that he sat next to you but did not speak to
you. Immediately after class he invited you to join him for coffee at Starbucks.
You went and had a decent time. Then he sat by you in class the next day, and
immediately after class he got down on one knee, pulled out a diamond ring,
and asked, "Will you marry me?"

Then I ask each of the girls, "Would you marry him?"

After looking at me like I am crazy, 95 percent of the girls still say, "No!"
Four percent usually ask how cute he was, and 1 percent ask how big the diamond was.

Then I ask, "Why wouldn't you marry him?"

You can guess their responses. "I still would barely know him. Marriage
is a big commitment. I need to know a guy pretty well before I agree to marry
him."

At this point I ask the entire class to respond to this scenario.

Scenario 4. Let's say that you have never been to church in your life and
have never read the Bible. You had heard the name *Jesus* but usually as a curse
word or as a part of a joke. You had heard of "born-again Christians" but do
not personally know any. One day a born-again Christian stops you on the
street and asks you if you would like to trust Jesus as your personal Savior.
What would you say?

A Big Commitment

Marriage is a serious commitment. It is supposed to last a lifetime. No reasonably sane, secure American girl chooses to marry someone she does not know
fairly well. Therefore people will spend months or even years getting to know
all they can about a person and finding out if that person can be trusted.

In a similar way, trusting Jesus as your Lord and Savior is a significant
commitment, which the Bible likens to marriage. Jesus is called the Bridegroom
(Eph 5:25–27; Rev 19:7–9). It will last throughout eternity.

No reasonably sane, secure person would ever agree to commit his life to
Jesus as Lord and Savior if he did not know Him fairly well. He will usually

take time to get to know more about Jesus before committing his life to Him.

Ideally a marriage is a process (getting to know and trust each other) leading to the event (the wedding ceremony) resulting in a lifetime spent together. Evangelism is similar. There is usually a process whereby the unbeliever gets to know about Jesus and the gospel, leading to an event, the act of faith and repentance, resulting in eternity spent growing in relationship with Jesus.

Effective evangelism introduces unbelievers to a relationship with Jesus. It respects the process and does not rush it. It leads people step-by-step to an eternal marriage with the heavenly Bridegroom Jesus Christ.

Stair-Stepping People to Salvation

One of my mentors is Dr. Elmer Towns. In his book *Winning the Winnable*, he discussed the process whereby most people come to salvation. In chapter 2, he told the story of the process by which he was saved.

> I did not become a Christian the first time I heard the gospel. Even though I grew up in church and knew religious terminology, I was not seeking God nor was I concerned with my eternal destiny. I went to a youth rally when I saw Christian young people who had something I did not have. I wanted to be like them.
>
> Next I went to hear Jack Wyrtzen, a youth evangelist preach the gospel. For the first time I sensed I was lost and going to hell. I did not go forward to get saved, but I was no longer satisfied in my sin.
>
> Then I went to a revival meeting where I heard the gospel. I was told to invite Jesus Christ into my heart to be saved. I did it on July 25, 1950. It took several stair-steps for me to realize my need and to be saved. When we witness to our unsaved friends we must recognize the steps they need to take to be saved.[1]

Later in the book Towns mentioned that according to his research in the 1980s, people generally needed to hear the gospel 3.4 times before they accepted Christ.[2] My guess is that in today's world the number of times someone needs to hear the gospel before accepting Christ would be much higher. Obviously, someone can be saved the first time he or she hears the gospel. But most people need to be stair-stepped toward a lasting commitment to Christ. Salvation is a process leading to an event. Effective evangelism leads people step-by-step to the event of trusting Christ as their Savior.

Salvation Is like a Birth

One metaphor often used by the New Testament for the salvation experience
is that of the new birth. Jesus referred to salvation as being born again (John
3:3,5). Peter also used the analogy of birth in reference to salvation (1 Pet 1:23).
In his first letter John the apostle stated that salvation is a birth that comes as a
result of faith in Christ (1 John 5:1).

A birth is a process that culminates in an event. The event is recorded on a
birth certificate with a distinct date and time measured to the exact minute. Yet
the event of the birth is the product of a nine-month process we call *gestation*
for the baby and *pregnancy* for the mother. Salvation is similar to a birth in that
there is usually a process often involving months or even years, leading to the
moment the person gives his or her life to Christ.

A healthy baby is usually one that has gone full-term. The process was not
cut short. Spiritually when people have been given the necessary time to digest
the meaning of the gospel and respond to it, the odds of their continuing to live
for Christ after their decision are much higher.

Evangelism Is like Harvesting a Crop

Although most of us aren't farmers, we do understand that there is a process
involved in harvesting a crop. For example, if a farmer wants to harvest a crop
of corn, he does not merely hop on his tractor, ride out into the fields, and
start collecting corn. A lengthy process must be followed. First he has to plow
the ground. Then he must plant the seed. The young plant must be fertilized,
watered, and weeded. It also must be given time to grow. This entire process
must be followed before the event of the harvest can occur.

The apostle Paul likened the process of the evangelization of the Corinthians to farming. He said that their conversion was the result of spiritual planting
and watering prior to the reaping.

> I planted the seed, Apollos watered it, but God made it grow. So neither
> he who plants nor he who waters is anything, but only God, who makes
> things grow. The man who plants and the man who waters have one
> purpose, and each will be rewarded according to his own labor. For we
> are God's fellow workers; you are God's field. (1 Cor 3:6–9 NIV)

In one sense everyone you meet is a spiritual field. Our responsibility is to
work together to plow the soil, plant the seed, water the seed, and wait for God

to bring the harvest. Salvation is a process leading to an event. Effective evangelism understands that before there can be a harvest, the soil of the unbeliever's
heart must be plowed, planted, and watered first.

Evangelism Is a Process Leading to an Event

A missionary named James Engel wanted to depict a typical journey a person
takes to conversion and after. He put each step a person, or even a group of
persons, may take toward Christ on a scale. The point is that not everyone is
on the same point on the scale. Some are closer to soul-saving repentance and
faith than others. If we understand roughly where a person (or a whole target
group of people) stands spiritually on this scale, we can adjust the way we present the gospel to them accordingly.[3] Engel's scale was later modified to include
God's role and the role of the gospel communicator, along with that of the
unbeliever's response. Study this chart carefully.

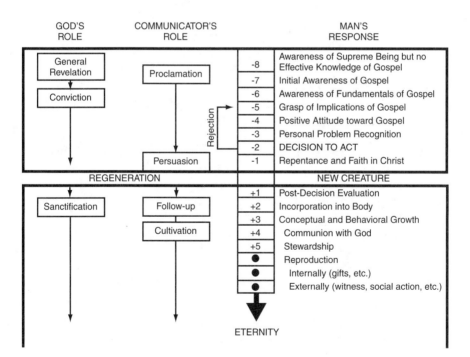

As we study Engel's scale, it is helpful to keep in mind that not every-one comes to Christ in exactly these steps or always in this order. The process of salvation is somewhat mysterious (see John 3:8) and is not always linear, but there is definitely a process (John 3:3). Engel's scale is generally true of most people. When this is understood, the benefit of this scale is immense.

- It explains why some decisions for Christ bear no fruit. The person was led to make a decision before he was really ready.
- It helps us understand why some people are more receptive to the gospel than others.
- It enhances our appreciation for the need to stair-step people to Christ.
- It also aids our ability to value repeated efforts to help people take incremental steps to Christ as opposed to turning people off by treating evangelism as an isolated, high-pressured sales job.

Adjust Your Methods

In the last few years Thom Rainer's team of researchers has conducted interviews with unchurched and formerly unchurched persons. In his book *The Unchurched Next Door,* he quotes a formerly unchurched, 40-something, African-American man referred to as "Franklin R."

> Ten years ago I claimed to be an agnostic. But just a year ago I was ready to accept Christ; I was just waiting for someone to tell me about Jesus. The best way to reach me ten years ago would have been much different from the way to reach me a year ago. Last year someone invited me to go to his church. I gladly accepted the invitation, heard the gospel, and accepted Christ, all within six weeks.[4]

People who are farther from God may need a different type of evangelistic approach than someone on the verge of trusting Christ. Those who are a –7 or –8 on Engel's scale probably need *prayer* evangelism (praying for God to open their heart) and *presence* evangelism (getting to know them and looking for ways to show them the love of Jesus) more than *proclamation* evangelism (telling them the facts and implications of the gospel).

Redefine Success

In the past, evangelism success was viewed solely as helping someone across the finish line of faith and repentance. This was not the view of the apostle Paul who stated that the one who plants the seed and the one who waters it are equally a part of the process as God who grants the harvest. Engel's scale shows us that if we understand something of the journey a person must take in order to discover God, then we know that helping someone take one more step toward God is successful evangelism.

Patiently Build Trust

When Cathy and I moved into our first home, we were a bit surprised to discover that our next-door neighbors were from North Vietnam. Tony had escaped when the Communists from North Vietnam captured Saigon. Now Tony worked as an engineer, and Twat stayed home with their two young sons, David and Jonathan. Their goal was to live the American dream.

I had always been taught to equate evangelism with the event of reaping a harvest. Someone else plowed the soil, planted the seed, and watered it. Then the act of evangelism was getting people to ask the Lord to save them. But with our new neighbors, and especially their sons, we faced an open field. I could not merely show up, give the gospel, and expect a harvest. There was nothing to harvest because no seed had been sown. They were Buddhists. Only Tony had any exposure to Christianity, and that was limited.

We found it easiest to establish a relationship with David and Jonathan. They loved to come to our house, play with our sons, and call Cathy and me their American mom and dad. We also made a point of treating Tony and Twat with great respect. They were nice people and easy to get along with. They appreciated the fact that we obviously loved their children. Tony and I often engaged in long talks over the fence. Often he would help me fix my lawn mower or give me needed advice on home maintenance.

One Saturday afternoon Tony and I were having one of our usual over-the-fence conversations when he made a statement that floored me. "We have decided that you may make David and Jonathan Christians." After four years of building trusting friendships and patiently plowing, planting, and watering the seed of the gospel, this was the first indication of response.

That next Sunday morning we took David and Jonathan with us to church. They loved church and learning more about Jesus. After a few months, during the last day of Vacation Bible School, as I presented the gospel and gave an invitation to respond, they gave their lives to Christ. They grew in Christ and stayed involved in our church until they moved away a couple of years later. Trying to minister to our neighbors was a great lesson to me in the often slow process of helping people far from God journey to Jesus.

— Evangelism Is . . . —

1. A process leading to an event.
2. Leading people step-by-step to the event of trusting Christ as their Savior.
3. Helping someone take one more step toward God.

— Good Quote —

When we bring someone to a decision to trust Christ in the course of a conversation or two, we can be sure of one thing: considerable preparation and laboring has already occurred in that life before we arrived on the scene.

—JIM PETERSEN[5]

Notes

1. E. Towns, *Winning the Winnable* (Lynchburg, VA: Church Leadership Institute, 1986), 13.

2. Ibid., 15.

3. J. F. Engel and W. Norton, *What's Gone Wrong with the Harvest?* (Grand Rapids, MI: Zondervan, 1975).

4. F. R. quoted in T. Rainer, *The Unchurched Next Door* (Grand Rapids, MI: Zondervan, 2003), 20.

5. J. Petersen, *Evangelism as a Lifestyle* (Colorado Springs, CO: NavPress, 1980), 24.

11

Evangelism Is . . .

Spiritual Farming

David Wheeler

The church was born into an agricultural society. Most of the people lived in the country and farmed. Even village dwellers had a garden and raised a few animals. If you were not a fisherman or a carpenter, you likely would have been a farmer. The idea of plowing, planting, and harvesting would have been easily understood. Therefore, when the apostle Paul was trying to help the Corinthian Christians understand the nature of evangelism, he used the analogy of the harvest. "I planted, Apollos watered, but God gave the increase. So then neither he who plants is anything, nor he who waters, but God who gives the increase. Now he who plants and he who waters are one, and each one will receive his own reward according to his own labor. For we are God's fellow workers; you are God's field" (1 Cor 3:6–9).

In Paul's harvest analogy the gospel is the seed. Paul and Apollos were harvest workers along with God. The hearts of the Corinthians were the field of soil. The "increase" or harvest is the result of the gospel's producing new life in the heart of a lost person.

We need to understand several key truths about the principles of the spiritual harvest.

1. The harvest is a process, not an event. As we mentioned in a previous chapter, effective evangelism respects the processional nature of evangelism.

2. More than one element is involved in the harvest. In order to ensure a harvest, someone must plant seed. The seed must be watered. God has to make it come to life, grow, and bear fruit.

3. Different people can play different roles in the harvest. Some can plant; others can water.
4. Every aspect is equally important. If no one plants the seed, there can never be a harvest. If no one waters the seed, it will never grow and produce fruit.

Effective evangelism never violates the principles of the harvest. The best way to recapture success in evangelism is to return to these principles. The harvest principles are taught throughout the Scriptures.

Plow the Fields Through Prayer

"Those who sow in tears shall reap in joy. He who continually goes forth weeping, bearing seed for sowing, shall doubtless come again with rejoicing, bringing his sheaves with him" (Ps 126:5–6).

We can renew our effectiveness in evangelism if we will plow the fields of lost people's hearts with our prayers. We focus too much of our prayers on the physical needs of the saved instead of the spiritual needs of the lost. Minette Drumwright, the former director of the International Prayer Strategy for the International Mission Board of the Southern Baptist Convention, once observed, "In our churches we spend more time praying to keep sick saints out of heaven than we do praying lost people into heaven."

Why not keep a list of unsaved people and pray for each person by name daily? Maybe your church could have a master list of unsaved people, and every time a family, a small group, a Sunday school class, or the church comes together to worship, the people on the list are prayed for by name.

I also suggest that you engage in prayer walking. It is a powerful way to plow the soil and impact your neighborhood. Simply encourage participants to walk through their communities praying for unsaved neighbors by name, asking God to open doors to serve and to share a verbal witness of the gospel. There is no greater preevangelism activity for a congregation than mapping out a geographic vicinity and encouraging Christians to saturate the area with aggressive prayer that is specifically aimed at attacking spiritual darkness.

Plow the Field with Humble, Loving, Need-Meeting Service

Hard hearts crumble under the power of Christlike, servant-minded evangelism. In the following chapters we will discuss in detail the power of seeing and meeting needs, practicing empathy, and actively sharing Christ.

Plant the Seed of the Gospel

Once the soil has been plowed, the seed needs to be sown. In order to have a large harvest, many seeds must be planted. The more seeds we sow, the larger the harvest we expect to receive.

In the analogy of spiritual farming, the idea of planting simply means sharing the gospel. It is verbally telling the lost person of the death, burial, and resurrection of Jesus Christ.

In order to see many people come to Christ, we need to tell many people about Christ. The more we tell, the more will be saved. Consider the parable of the Sower as recorded in Matt 13:3–9:

> Then He spoke many things to them in parables, saying: "Behold, a
> sower went out to sow. And as he sowed, some seed fell by the wayside;
> and the birds came and devoured them. Some fell on stony places, where
> they did not have much earth; and they immediately sprang up because
> they had no depth of earth. But when the sun was up they were scorched,
> and because they had no root they withered away. And some fell among
> thorns, and the thorns sprang up and choked them. But others fell on
> good ground and yielded a crop: some a hundredfold, some sixty, some
> thirty. He who has ears to hear, let him hear!"

The modern farmer would call this sloppy sowing! Why would someone throw seeds in an area near rocks and thorns? But in biblical times farmers were less strategic about the scientific approaches used today. All they knew was that the seed had to be spread. In many cases farmers would go out into an open field that was grown over and would begin to throw seed as liberally as possible. So naturally some of the seed fell among rocks, thorns, and such. The next step was to use rocks or sharp implements to scratch the ground where the seed was spread in hopes of somehow embedding the seed further into the soil.

While this approach to farming seems wasteful, it exemplifies the importance of the harvesting process. In order to ensure a bountiful harvest, the ground has to be broken (plowed), and the seed has to be spread (planted).

God Gives the Increase

> Therefore hear the parable of the sower: When anyone hears the word
> of the kingdom, and does not understand it, then the wicked one comes
> and snatches away what was sown in his heart. This is he who received
> seed by the wayside. But he who received the seed on stony places, this

is he who hears the word and immediately receives it with joy; yet he has
no root in himself, but endures only for a while. For when tribulation or
persecution arises because of the word, immediately he stumbles. Now
he who received seed among the thorns is he who hears the word, and the
cares of this world and the deceitfulness of riches choke the word, and
he becomes unfruitful. But he who received seed on the good ground is
he who hears the word and understands it, who indeed bears fruit and
produces: some a hundredfold, some sixty, some thirty. (Matt 13:18–23)

Notice the last sentence: "But he who received seed on the good ground
is he who hears the word and understands it, who indeed bears fruit and produces: some a hundredfold, some sixty, some thirty." Be encouraged never to
stop plowing and planting. Even though some of the seed will be destroyed
by the enemy and others will turn away for lack of commitment or because of
persecution, the biblical principles of the harvest are always the same. According to Christ, the blessing comes when the seed falls on good ground where a
person both "hears the word and understands it." The eternal payoff comes
when the new Christian "bears fruit and produces: some a hundredfold, some
sixty, some thirty." As Paul said, if we plow, plant, and water, God will give an
increase (1 Cor 3:6).

The Fields Are Ready to Harvest

One day Jesus had a fascinating dialogue with a Samaritan woman, as we shall
examine in detail in chapter 15. His disciples had been getting food while He
spoke with a woman by a well. When His disciples returned, they were surprised to find that Jesus, the Jewish rabbi, was speaking to a woman, let alone
a Samaritan woman with a bad reputation. Jesus used the opportunity to teach
them about the harvest.

Do you not say, "There are still four months and then comes the
harvest"? Behold, I say to you, lift up your eyes and look at the fields,
for they are already white for harvest! And he who reaps receives wages,
and gathers fruit for eternal life, that both he who sows and he who
reaps may rejoice together. For in this the saying is true: "One sows and
another reaps" (John 4:35–37).

Jesus wanted them to realize that as long as we are willing to go to all types
of people, we will always find souls ready for the gospel. He also wanted them
to understand that the harvesting process is a team sport. Some sow and some
reap, but both can rejoice together.

Justin's Life Is Changed

Justin was not a Christian, and everyone at school knew it! But a young lady from a small congregation in rural Georgia invited him to attend church with her. Surprisingly, he did. At church he was given a warm welcome from the youth group. They even sat with him during the worship services. It was not long before Justin became involved in a small-group Bible study.

After several months of visiting church, members of the youth group invited Justin to go with them to SuperWow, a student conference sponsored by the Georgia Baptist Convention. A Christian contemporary rock group, Big Daddy Weave, led worship. The Skit Guys dramatized the good news. The SuperWow speaker, Thomas Young, preached the gospel. As a result, Justin committed his life to Christ.

Justin followed up SuperWow by professing his new Christian faith before the entire church body. His next step was to identify with Christ through public baptism. However, before being baptized, Justin asked permission to speak to the congregation.

In his brief testimony he shared about a friend from school who had been witnessing to him about Christ on a regular basis. One day Justin was at his friend's house. Finding his friend's journal, he began to read his friend's deepest thoughts and desires. Justin wept as he told the congregation about reading the following journal entry: "Lord, please do something special for Justin today and accomplish something magnificent in his life."

Justin was deeply touched by his friend's request of God. As a result of this and many other prayers, Justin eventually surrendered his life to Christ.

Spiritual Farming in Action

Spiritual seed-sowing recognizes that most unbelievers need multiple encounters with the gospel before eventually coming to faith. For instance, in Justin's life a number of Christians provided a consistent stream of touches with the gospel. They were unknowingly working together under the organization of the Holy Spirit to bring Justin to the Savior.

Think about it. A friend invited Justin to church. The gospel was preached to him. A friendly church welcomed him. A youth group accepted him. A Bible study teacher taught him. The SuperWow speaker, Thomas Young, related the truths of Scripture to him. A Christian contemporary rock group, Big Daddy Weave, led him to worship. The Skit Guys dramatized the good news before him. The youth pastor addressed his curiosity and answered his questions. All of this occurred while his friend (and others) prayed for him. His friend even kept his name before God in a prayer journal. As we know, the end result was Justin's salvation!

Alisha Is Saved

Eighteen-year-old Alisha was our waitress one Sunday evening at an Atlanta restaurant. As she approached the table to take our order, we asked her if there was anything we could pray for in reference to her life. She began to relate the story of how her grandmother and others had been planting seeds by sharing Christ with her. To our elation she eventually responded with an amazing request, "Please, pray for someone who can tell me how to be saved!"

Of course we were more than happy to be the answer to her prayer request. After a few minutes of sharing the gospel with her, she bowed her head and asked Christ to invade her life! WOW!

Again, much like Justin, the harvest came only after numerous seeds of the gospel had been planted in her life through her grandmother and others. This did not occur because of clever or persuasive words. On the contrary, we were just fortunate enough to be there when the seed of the gospel was ready to be harvested in her life. With this in mind, I could not help but recall the words of Christ in John 4:38, "Others have labored, and you have entered into their labors."

Keys to Effective Spiritual Farming

Be prayerful. Seed-sowing is a spiritual voyage. Prayer is necessary as you set sail with a sense of adventure and abandon. Perhaps we could pray a version of the prayer Justin's friend prayed, "Lord, please do something special in my life today, and accomplish something magnificent for others through me."

Be positive. You should share Jesus in a positive manner. Never use His name to win an argument or to put down another person.

Be accepting. Accepting people is not the same as condoning their sinful behavior. Jesus loved people as they were, always leading them to become what He knew they could be through Him.

Be consistent. Pray every day that God will help you touch people with the good news of Christ. In other words, *live every day with the intention to do something eternal.* Seek to establish habits that will yield a life that bears spiritual fruit.

Be intentional. I often say, *that which we intentionally ignore will unintentionally not get done!* While true evangelism always depends on the Holy Spirit, sharing your faith does not happen by accident. It must be an intentional and conscious commitment of every Christian.

Be creative. Be creative (but not strange) in looking for ways to light your world with spiritual touches that exemplify the love and message of Christ in practical ways.

Be active. The law of the harvest is simple. The more you spread the gospel seed, the greater the likelihood that people will respond. Psalm 126 is true, "Sow in tears . . . reap in joy" (v. 5).

Spiritual Farming Is . . .

1. Spiritual farming is an investment in a process. It is a mistake to define evangelism narrowly in terms of merely sharing the information of the gospel. While that is obviously an essential and vital part of our responsibility, as spiritual farmers we are called to surrender ourselves to the total process of plowing, planting, and harvesting.

2. Spiritual farming is time-consuming. Farming is not a brief process. It is a year-round commitment to working the soil and preparing the fields for the harvest. The same is true with spiritual farming. Praying for unsaved friends (plowing), investing in their lives through serving and sharing (planting), and being patient as the Holy Spirit draws people to Himself is usually time-consuming.

3. Spiritual farming is hard work. Farming requires a lot of sweat and commitment. There are no shortcuts, and it is never easy. It is a daily affair with the soil and the potential harvest. Spiritual farming requires the same work ethic. Regardless of frustrations, rejection, or spiritual warfare, we must continue to work the fields.

4. Spiritual farming is worth the wait. In Luke 15, Jesus tells the parable of the Lost Sheep. After explaining the importance of a shepherd who leaves 99 sheep to locate the one that is lost, He concludes, "I tell you that in the same way there will be more rejoicing in heaven over one sinner who repents than over ninety-nine righteous persons who do not need to repent" (Luke 15:7 NIV). The harvest is worth the investment!

— Evangelism Is . . . —

1. Spiritual farming.
2. Plowing in prayer, planting through sharing the gospel, and being patient as the Holy Spirit draws people to Himself.
3. Being willing when the harvest is ready.

— Key Verse —

"Do you not say, 'There are still four months and then comes the harvest'? Behold, I say to you, lift up your eyes and look at the fields, for they are already white for harvest!" (John 4:35)

— Good Quotes —

The law of the harvest is simple. The more you spread the gospel seed, the greater chance that people will respond.

—TOBY FROST[1]

We cannot harvest where no seed has been planted.

—WILL MCRANEY[2]

Our job is to be seed flingers, not seed protectors watching over God's business as though He had a limited supply.

—STEVE SJOGREN[3]

Notes

1. Shared in a phone conversation by Dr. T. Frost, former team leader for the Event Evangelism Unit of the North American Mission Board of the Southern Baptist Convention, March 2007.
2. W. McRaney Jr., *The Art of Personal Evangelism* (Nashville, TN: B&H, 2003), 46.
3. S. Sjogren, *Conspiracy of Kindness* (Ventura, CA: Regal Books, 2003), 97.

12

Helping People
Lose Their Religion

Dave Earley

If all you have is religion you will never even see heaven.

—JESUS CHRIST[1]

Religion is dung.

—PAUL THE APOSTLE[2]

"Lose Your Religion!"

A few years ago my church mailed out 10,000 postcards emblazoned with the words, "Lose Your Religion!" On the back of the card, I paraphrased the words of Jesus, "If all you have is religion, you will never see the kingdom of heaven" (John 3:3). I also paraphrased the words of the apostle Paul, who said that "religion is dung" (Phil 3:3–10).

As I had expected, we received some interesting e-mails that week. People wanted to know how I, as the pastor of a well-known church, could be so dead set against religion.

My point was simple: Religion by itself is not enough. Religion will not get anyone to heaven. Real Christianity is a *relationship* into which you must be spiritually born. You must be born again.

Nic at Night

Nicodemus hoped his clandestine meeting would go unnoticed in the clamor of the Passover celebration. Power, position, prestige—he potentially had much to lose. Meeting with Jesus, the unsanctioned teacher, could cost Nicodemus dearly.

Nicodemus was not merely a Pharisee. He was a member of the Sanhedrin, the elite group of 70 men who ruled Israel in all matters regarding religion. Religion—that's what had raised his curiosity about Jesus. The miracles Jesus had performed had piqued Nicodemus's interest to see if this man really was who some said He was, the Messiah.

So Nicodemus came at night and sat down across from Jesus. Peter, James, and John probably sat in the background, joined by a few of Nicodemus's assistants. They may have been surprised by the unthreatening manner with which Nicodemus approached Jesus. But Nicodemus was soul thirsty. Jesus wisely whetted his appetite then drew from his lips a question.

> There was a man of the Pharisees named Nicodemus, a ruler of the Jews. This man came to Jesus by night and said to Him, "Rabbi, we know that You are a teacher come from God; for no one can do these signs that You do unless God is with him."
>
> Jesus answered and said to him, "Most assuredly, I say to you, unless one is born again, he cannot see the kingdom of God."
>
> Nicodemus said to Him, "How can a man be born when he is old? Can he enter a second time into his mother's womb and be born?" (John 3:1–4)

"How Can a Man Be Born When He Is Old?"

Jesus said that no one could even *see* heaven without being born again. But Nicodemus wasn't sure what it meant to be "born again." He knew that a second physical birth made no sense. So Jesus explained.

> Jesus answered, "Most assuredly, I say to you, unless one is born of water and the Spirit, he cannot enter the kingdom of God. That which is born of the flesh is flesh, and that which is born of the Spirit is spirit. Do not marvel that I said to you, 'You must be born again.' The wind blows where it wishes, and you hear the sound of it, but cannot tell where it comes from and where it goes. So is everyone who is born of the Spirit" (John 3:5–8).

Religion Is Not Good Enough

Sometimes it's easier to understand what a person is saying by first determining what he or she is *not* saying. Clearly, in telling Nicodemus that he had to be born again, Jesus was *not* saying that people needed to be religious to enter the kingdom of heaven. Nicodemus did not need to become religious because he already was religious. As we read in John 3:1, he was a member of the Jewish ruling council.

In order to be on that select council of 70, a man had to be a Pharisee. Pharisees were the most religious of the Jews. Their whole life was religion. The word *Pharisee* is from a word meaning "separate." The Pharisees were noted as those who kept away from anyone or anything they considered to be religiously unclean. They fasted two days every week and never missed attending services at synagogue. The Pharisees felt the OT had too *few* religious rules in it so they added hundreds of their own.

But Nicodemus was more than a Pharisee; he was a leader of the Pharisees! He was a part of the ruling council known as the Sanhedrin. These 70 men were the most religious of the Pharisees.

If anyone was religious, it was Nicodemus. Yet his religion was not good enough. Jesus looked Nicodemus in the eye and told him that he had to be born again. That must have been a little unnerving for Nicodemus. If his religion wasn't good enough, whose would be? Would yours?

Recently I asked a man this question: "If you died today, are you certain you would be welcomed into heaven?"

He said, "I guess so."

I asked him, "On what basis would God let you in?"

He replied, "Well, I go to church."

I asked, "If I sat in a garage a few hours every week, would it make me a car?"

He laughed and said, "Of course not."

I replied, "Sitting in a garage will no more make you a car than attending a church will make you a Christian. Jesus said that you need to be born again."

Being Good Is Not Good Enough

When Jesus said that to enter heaven a person must be born again, He was also not saying that being born again equals doing good works and acquiring self-righteousness. As we discussed in chapter 8, the Bible teaches that only one person in history was "good enough." Only one person hit the bull's-eye of the righteousness required by God. That person is Jesus Christ. He is the only one who earned a relationship with a perfect God by living a sinless life. Yet He died in our place on the cross and rose again from the dead. Our relationship with God is not the result of the religion we have or good works we do. It is the result of believing in what Jesus has done. It is not something we earn. It's a gift we receive.

You see, if we could get to heaven by being really religious or really good, why did Jesus have to die for our sin? No matter how good we are, we are not perfect. No matter how much good we do, we can't erase the stain of our past sins.

The First Birth Is Not Good Enough

I recently saw a bumper sticker that said, "Born once. It was good enough." I thought, *Not according to Jesus.* Jesus taught that the first birth is insufficient. Our first birth is corrupted by our sin nature, called "the flesh." "The Spirit gives life; the flesh counts for nothing" (John 6:63 NIV). "I know that nothing good lives in me, that is, in my sinful nature. For I have the desire to do what is good, but I cannot carry it out" (Rom 7:18 NIV).

"What Is Wrong with These Boys?"

I have three active sons. One week when they were all under the age of six, God used them to teach me the truth of the sinfulness of the flesh nature. It was Dad's night home to watch the boys; Cathy was at a ladies' meeting at church. I brought home what I considered to be an educational movie on Huck Finn. In this entire two-hour movie there is only one questionable moment. In a scene lasting less than a minute, Huck's father came home drunk and made a fool out of himself.

After the movie I popped them in the bathtub when the phone rang. So I left the older two boys on their own in the bathroom for about five minutes. Then Cathy came home. I proudly told her what a great job I had done with the boys that night.

The next thing we heard was wild whooping and yelling. I stormed into the bathroom, and it was covered with water. They had cups full of bathwater and were swirling it around and laughing wildly.

I put my hands on my hips, did my best tough dad imitation, and said, "What is going on here?" I demanded.

"We're drunk," they said. "Drunker than skunks." Then they laughed delightedly.

"Where on earth did you get the idea of being drunk?" I asked.

"From Huck Finn's dad," they replied innocently.

"He was a drunk," said Daniel, the oldest.

"Drunker than a skunk," added his younger brother, Andrew.

I could not believe it. We had watched a 120-minute educational movie, and what did they learn? How to be drunks!

Later that week we sat down to a wonderful meal my wife, Cathy, had prepared. We bowed our heads to pray, and I immediately heard a whooshing sound. It was followed by muffled laughing and more "whooshes." I opened my eyes and saw our family premeal prayer time break into a full-blown food fight.

Exasperated, Cathy looked at me and said, "Dave, what is wrong with these boys?"

All of a sudden I understood something profound about our sin nature and said, "Well, theologically speaking, they are sinners."

"How Many Murders?"

After church one Sunday, a lady became upset with me because I had mentioned that apart from Jesus we are all sinners.

"Sinner?" she said. "That is such a strong term. I resent being called a sinner."

I asked her, "How many murders does it take to be a murderer?"

"One," she replied. "It only takes one."

"So," I continued, "how many sins does it take to be a sinner?"

"Oh," she said pausing.

"Now I see what you mean." Later she asked, "So how do I get born again?"

We have seen that being born again is not a matter of religion or good works. Now let's look at what it *does* mean to be born again.

A Second Birth

Jesus told Nicodemus that he had to be born *again*. In other words, He was telling Nicodemus that he needed a *second* birth. His first birth was insufficient. Being born again is not something you *do*. It's something you *experience.* Jesus was crystal clear: You will not experience the kingdom of God unless you experience a second birth.

I asked a gentleman if he was born again. He told me, "Sure, I've been a Christian all my life." That's not what Jesus was saying. He said we need a *second* birth. We need to be born *again*.

A Spiritual Birth

Nicodemus was thinking in physical terms when he asked, "How can a man be born when he is old? Can he enter a second time into his mother's womb and be born?" (John 3:4).

Jesus responded that being "born again" is not only experiencing a second birth but also experincing a *spiritual* birth. "Jesus answered, 'Most assuredly, I say to you, unless one is born of water and the Spirit, he cannot enter the kingdom of God. That which is born of the flesh is flesh, and that which is born of the Spirit is spirit'" (John 3:5–6).

By describing births of both water *and* the Spirit, Jesus contrasted physical birth with spiritual birth. He said we need both.

Jesus described the physical birth in verse 5 when He said "born of water." When a woman is pregnant, a sack of water protects the baby inside her. She knows the baby is ready to come when the water breaks. When the baby is born, it's all wet. The physical birth involves being "born of water."

By saying, "That which is born of the flesh is flesh," Jesus was further referring to physical birth. When we are born physically, we mark the event with a certificate that gives the date, time, and place of our arrival. Note carefully that Jesus said the physical birth alone will not get us into the kingdom of God. We need a spiritual birth. We need to be "born of water *and* the Spirit" (John 3:5). Jesus added, "The wind blows where it wishes, and you hear the sound of it, but cannot tell where it comes from and where it goes. So is everyone who is born of the Spirit" (John 3:8).

How to Be Born Again

Later in this chapter Jesus answered this question with the statement that has become the most quoted verse in the Bible. Note that being born again is a result of believing in Jesus. "For God so loved the world that he gave his one and only Son, that whoever believes in him shall not perish but have eternal life" (John 3:16 NIV).

John's Gospel reaffirms this statement and adds clarity to it. We are born again when by faith we receive Jesus Christ as our Savior. "Yet to all who received him [Jesus], to those who believed in his name, he gave the right to become children of God [i.e., be born again]" (John 1:12 NIV).

— Evangelism Is . . . —

1. Helping people lose their religion and discover a relationship with Jesus.
2. Helping people experience a spiritual new birth into a real relationship with God through Jesus Christ.

— Three Important Questions —

Let me ask several vitally important questions:

1. Do you know the date, time, and place of your spiritual birth?
2. Do you know for sure that you have been born again?
3. If you are not absolutely certain that you have been born again, will you respond to God and be born again today, on this date, at this time, at this place? This is a chance to make sure.

Below is a simple prayer hundreds have prayed when they were serious about turning their lives over to Jesus Christ. It incorporates the gospel and the elements of true conversion. Read through it. If you mean it, you can say it to God.

Dear God,

I admit that I have sinned. I admit that my religion alone is not going to give me a relationship with You. I admit that my goodness is not good enough. I admit that I need to be born again.

I believe that Jesus is God's Son. I believe that Jesus never sinned. I believe that Jesus died to pay for my sins. I believe that Jesus rose from the dead to give me eternal life.

Right now I call upon the name of the Lord Jesus to save me. I ask the Holy Spirit to come into my heart and make me a new person. I ask that I may be born again as a child of God. I surrender the throne of my heart to You. I ask to experience Your love and power.

I am willing to do anything You tell me to do. I am willing to stop doing anything that displeases You. I ask for the power to follow You all the days of my life.

In Jesus' name, amen.

If you said that prayer to God and meant it, you might want to fill out the spiritual birth certificate below. Also, please send me an e-mail (dearley@ liberty.edu) so I can rejoice with you and pray for you.

My Spiritual Birth Certificate

On _____ ____, 20___,

I, _____ _____,

was born again by responding to God's Word and called upon the name of the Lord to save me. I am now born again as I have admitted my sin, believed in Jesus Christ to pay for my sin, and committed my life to Him.

Notes

1. See John 3:1–7.
2. See Phil 3:7–10.

13

Being a Missionary, Not a Mission Field

Dave Earley

Are You a Missionary or a Mission Field?

In its nontechnical sense the term *missionary* is simply "a person with a mission." A Christian missionary is a person with the mission of positively impacting others with the life-changing message of Jesus Christ. A "mission field" is "someone needing the ministry of a missionary." A mission field is a person or persons yet to be impacted by the life-giving message of Jesus.

So that returns us to the question: Are you a missionary or a mission field?

You are either one or the other. There is no middle ground.

If you have been wonderfully impacted by the message of Jesus Christ, you are obligated to live as a missionary sharing the truth of Jesus with others. If you are still sorting Christianity out, you can't really be expected to act as a missionary because in a sense you are still a mission field.

First-Century Missionary

The apostle Paul was one of the first cross-cultural missionaries of the church. He was also one of the most effective. His passion was planting churches. He started successful churches in Philippi, Ephesus, Galatia, Corinth, and

Thessalonica. Born a Jew and trained as a rabbi, he had a deep devotion to his people, the Jews. This devotion did not lessen when he met Jesus Christ but rather intensified and purified. In his letter to the Romans, we see this when he declares, "I tell the truth in Christ, I am not lying, my conscience also bearing me witness in the Holy Spirit, that I have great sorrow and continual grief in my heart. For I could wish that I myself were accursed from Christ for my brethren, my countrymen according to the flesh" (Rom 9:1–3).

The Goal of Missions

Brethren, my heart's desire and prayer to God for Israel is that they may be saved. (Rom 10:1).

Note those last five words: "That they may be saved." What is the goal of a missionary? It is to help people be saved. Yes, they may serve them, feed them, clothe them, doctor them, and/or teach them; but it all is with the greater purpose of helping them be saved.

As we said earlier, the word "saved" in its fullest sense means "delivered *from* the penalty and punishment of death that results from sin and delivered *to* an abundant life on earth and eternal life in heaven that comes from having your sin paid for." So the goal is salvation from sin and death *and* deliverance to life and God.

In Rom 10:2–8 Paul discusses the necessity of lost persons to obtain the required righteousness of God so they can be saved. We discussed this process in detail in chapter 8, "Helping People Become Good Enough."

The Process of Salvation

In Rom 10:9–17 Paul outlines the process in which unbelievers trade their inadequate righteousness for the righteousness that is only available through faith in Jesus Christ. This passage describes six steps by which they trade their self-righteousness for the required righteousness of Christ. They are given from the last step to the first.

6. The lost person *confesses* that Jesus is Lord (10:9–10) . . . but only after . . .
5. They *call* upon the name of the Lord to save them (10:12–13) . . . but only after . . .
4. They *believe* in Jesus (10:14) . . . but only after . . .

3. They *hear* about Jesus (10:14) . . . but only after . . .
2. Someone *preaches or proclaims* to them the truth about Jesus (10:14) . . . but only after . . .
1. That someone was *sent* to the lost person (10:15–17).

Confess

> That if you confess with your mouth the Lord Jesus and believe in your heart that God has raised Him from the dead, you will be saved. For with the heart one believes unto righteousness, and with the mouth confession is made unto salvation. (Rom 10:9–10)

Confession is a public, verbal expression of the inward, personal commitment. This alone doesn't give someone God's righteousness but rather states that they now have it as a result of having heard, believed, and called upon the name of Jesus to save them. Historically this confession of Jesus as Lord occurs when people are publicly baptized. At baptism a confession is made through their testimony and their baptism. I genuinely doubt the reality of anyone's salvation who is not willing to confess Jesus is Lord by following His command to be baptized.

Call

> For there is no distinction between Jew and Greek, for the same Lord over all is rich to all who call upon Him. For "whoever calls on the name of the LORD shall be saved." (Rom 10:12–13)

True belief always results in action. According to Rom 10:12–13, the action needed for salvation is "calling on the Lord." This is a prayer that usually includes several keys elements. I call them the ABCs.

Admitting sin—admitting the need for forgiveness and salvation because of your sin; acknowledging your inadequacy to save yourself.
Believing in Jesus as Savior—believing that He alone is the sinless Son of God, that He died on the cross to pay for your sin, and that He rose from the dead to give you new life.
Calling on Jesus—calling out to Jesus verbally in prayer to save you from your sins; calling on Jesus to be your Lord.

Most lost people are not used to praying at all, let alone aloud. Often when new believers are at this point, I offer to lead them in a simple prayer. I say to them, "If you would like, I can say a sample prayer. If it resonates in your heart, you can repeat it after me to God. He is listening. If you mean it, He will answer your prayer and save your soul."

> Dear God,
>   I admit that I have sinned. I know I cannot get to heaven on my own righteousness.
>   I believe that Jesus never sinned. I believe that He died to pay for my sin and that He literally rose from the dead to give me new life.
>   Right now, I want to call upon You to save me. I want His righteousness credited to my account. I want to live to obey You the rest of my life.
>   In Jesus' name, amen.

Believe

> That if you confess with your mouth the Lord Jesus and *believe* in your heart that God has raised Him from the dead, you will be saved. For with the heart one *believes* unto righteousness, and with the mouth confession is made unto salvation. For the Scripture says, "Whoever believes on Him will not be put to shame." . . . How then shall they call on Him in whom they have not *believed*? And how shall they believe in Him of whom they have not heard? . . . So then *faith* comes by hearing, and hearing by the word of God. (Rom 10:9–11,14,17, italics added)

Belief is the key. Notice how many times the words "believe," "believed," and "faith" are mentioned in the above verses. Salvation is the result of believing certain truths. These truths include:

- There is a God.
- I am responsible to God.
- I have erred in my responsibility; I have sinned.
- Sin has some negative consequences: death/separation from God.
- Jesus never sinned.
- Jesus died to pay for my sin.
- I believe His righteousness is good enough.
- I can have His gift of eternal life by receiving it.

It is possible to hear the gospel and never be saved. A person must believe it, trust it, rely on it, and act upon it. The word *believe* as it is used in the Bible is always expressed by commitment and action.

Note that Rom 10:9 says, "That if you confess with your mouth the Lord Jesus and believe *in* your heart that God has raised Him from the dead, you will be saved." People are saved when they believe *in* Jesus.

Romans 10:14 asks, "How then shall they call on Him in whom they have not believed? And how shall they believe *in* Him of whom they have not heard?" People are saved when they believe *in* Jesus.

John 3:16 states, "For God so loved the world that He gave His only begotten Son, that whoever believes *in* Him should not perish but have everlasting life." Eternal life is given to those who believe *in* Jesus.

Believe In

One summer while on vacation, our family visited Niagara Falls. The falls span a length of 1,060 feet and stand at a height of 176 feet; 150,000 gallons of water pour over the falls every second. They are so large you can hear the water pounding over them several miles away.

Across one of the main streets is a statue of a man on a tightrope. His name is Jean Francois Gravelet, the great Blondin. He was the first tightrope walker to appear at Niagara Falls. He was a professional artist and showman trained in the great tradition of the European circus. At age 31, he came to America and made the announcement that he would cross the gorge of the Niagara River on a tightrope.

On June 30, 1859, Blondin became the first man to walk across Niagara Falls on a tightrope. But he did more than that. In his life he crossed the falls several times in a variety of ways including blindfolded, on a bicycle, with his hands and feet manacled, and even with his manager on his back.

Yet none of these stunts compare with Blondin's greatest feat. As a boy, I heard an old pastor tell how one day Blondin put a wheelbarrow on his tightrope and asked the crowd if they believed he could wheel it across. They yelled, "We believe!"

Then he wheeled it across and back. Then he called out, "Who believes I can put a man in my wheelbarrow and wheel him across?"

The excited crowd yelled, "We believe."

So he looked into the faces of that crowd and said, "Who will be first?"

The point is that Blondin was not asking the crowd what they believed *about* him and his wheelbarrow. He was asking if they believed *in* him. In the same way eternal life is not a matter of standing on the side having nice beliefs *about* Jesus. It is a matter of believing *in Him*. Unbelievers will never cross over into eternal life until they get *in* the wheelbarrow by believing *in* Jesus.

If you were in the crowd that day, you could not get across the Niagara by being pretty good or joining a church but only by having the faith to get *in* the wheelbarrow. In the same way, you do not receive eternal life merely by being pretty good or joining a church but only by having the faith to get in Jesus' wheelbarrow. You must have the faith to trust in Him to be the complete and total payment for your sins.

Hear

How then shall they call on Him in whom they have not believed? And how shall they believe in Him of whom they have not *heard*? And how shall they *hear* without a preacher? And how shall they preach unless they are sent? As it is written: "How beautiful are the feet of those who preach the gospel of peace, who bring glad tidings of good things!" . . . So then faith comes by *hearing*, and *hearing* by the word of God. (Rom 10:14–15,17, italics added)

Hearing is a huge part of salvation. This word *hearing* refers to more than comprehending sound in the eardrum. *Hearing*, as Paul uses it here, involves active listening—taking it in, thinking it over, and determining to act.

I've been sharing the gospel for about 30 years. I have found that there are times when people really hear. You can tell because they are listening intently. They may nod their head, or they may look puzzled or look down. But the easiest way to tell if they have *heard* is that they respond. They realize the voice they are hearing is more than my voice; in a sense it is the voice of God. He is knocking at the door of their heart. He is pointing out their sin, their need, and His awesome love. He is drawing them to Himself.

My parents took me to church every Sunday of my life. I am sure that I physically heard the story of the death, burial, and resurrection of Jesus for my sins many times. But I did not *hear* it spiritually until I was older. The first time I spiritually *heard* it, the ramifications scared me so much I jumped up in the middle of a pastor's sermon and ran out of the back of the church.

Thankfully, God gave me another chance. Even though I continued to go to church, it wasn't until a year and a half later that I spiritually *heard* the gospel again. This time, instead of running out the back of the church, I jumped up and ran to the front of the church. There I believed in Jesus as my Lord and Savior. I called upon Him to save me. A few weeks later I confessed Jesus as Lord when I was baptized.

Preach or Proclaim

> And how shall they hear without a *preacher*? And how shall they *preach* unless they are *sent*? As it is written: "How beautiful are the feet of those who *preach* the gospel of peace, who bring glad tidings of good things!" (Rom 10:14–15, italics added)

The word *preach* literally means "to tell good news." The word *preach* sounds formal, like some man in a suit and tie in a church on a Sunday standing behind a pulpit pointing his bony finger in your face. That is one way to preach but certainly not the only way. Anytime we tell the good news of the death, burial, and resurrection for our sins to another person, we are preaching the gospel. It could be over coffee at Starbucks, across the fence with a neighbor, during bedtime prayers with your kids, over the phone with a loved one in another state, over the Internet, or in a Sunday school class with a group of bright-eyed kids. The issue is not *how* we preach but *that* we preach.

Sent

> And how shall they preach unless they are *sent*? As it is written: "How beautiful are the feet of those who preach the gospel of peace, who bring glad tidings of good things!" (Rom 10:15, italics added)

The word Paul uses for "sent" is the word *apostello* from which we get our words *apostle* and *missionary*. Being sent is the first step of the evangelism process: someone is sent on a mission with the message—the missionary. People who get saved most often do so because someone made the effort to tell them about Jesus. You do not always have to go across the ocean to be a missionary. Sometimes you just have to go across the street.

People who are saved are then sent to tell others the good news about Jesus. So the process is an ongoing cycle: We are saved. Then we are sent to tell others how to be saved. In other words, if we are saved, we are missionaries. We must go and tell others. If you have been saved, you have been sent to tell others the good news.

The ardent young God follower Isaiah experienced the sending/going process.

> Also I heard the voice of the Lord, saying:
> "Whom shall I *send*,
> And who will *go* for Us?"
> Then I said, "Here am I! *Send* me."
> And He said, "*Go*, and *tell* this people . . ." (Isa 6:8–9, italics added).

Jesus was continually reminding His followers of the sending/going process. He wanted them to live, as we are to live, as missionaries, not mission fields.

> "*Go* home to your friends, and *tell* them what great things the Lord has done for you, and how He has had compassion on you." (Mark 5:19, italics added)

> "*Go* therefore and make disciples of all the nations, baptizing them in the name of the Father and of the Son and of the Holy Spirit." (Matt 28:19, italics added)

> And He said to them, "*Go* into all the world and preach the gospel to every creature." (Mark 16:15, italics added)

> "As You *sent* Me into the world, I also have *sent* them into the world." (John 17:18)

> So Jesus said to them again, "Peace to you! As the Father has sent Me, *I also send you.*" (John 20:21)

Missionary or Mission Field?

There are only two types of people reading this chapter right now: missionaries and mission fields. Which are you?

‒ Evangelism Is . . . ‒

1. Going and telling the good news of Jesus Christ.
2. Living as a missionary, not a mission field.

‒ Key Verse ‒

And how shall they hear without a preacher? And how shall they preach unless they are sent? As it is written: "How beautiful are the feet of those who preach the gospel of peace, who bring glad tidings of good things!" (Rom 10:14–15)

~ Good Quotes ~

Every Christian is either a missionary or an imposter.

— CHARLES HADDON SPURGEON

*God is a missionary God, so the church
is to be a missionary church.*

— CRAIG VAN GELDER[1]

The US is the fifth largest mission field on earth.

— GEORGE HUNTER[2]

Notes

1. C. Van Gelder, *The Essence of the Church* (Grand Rapids, MI: Baker, 2000), 98.
2. G. Hunter, "The Rationale for a Culturally Relevant Worship Service," *The Journal of the Society for Church Growth, Worship and Growth* 7 (1996): 131.

14

Releasing a Virus

David Wheeler

When you hear the word *virus*, what type of thoughts come to mind?

- The deadly Ebola virus?
- Swine flu?
- A pesky cold?
- A corrupting influence or poisonous person?
- A segment of self-replicating code planted illegally in a computer program that is designed to damage or shut down a computer system or network?

We have negative impressions for good reason. Viruses strike quickly and relentlessly. They can replicate efficiently and change constantly. As fast-moving targets with infinite, clever disguises, they continually foil modern medicine and technology.

But can viruses ever be positive? What if we could apply the contagious nature of the virus to spreading the gospel of Jesus Christ? Imagine if sharing the good news was as easy as shaking hands with someone or sneezing in a crowded room.

Further imagine the newly infected people turning around and transferring the message to someone else and so on as the virus of the gospel spreads like wildfire. Is that so unimaginable?

Greg Stier, in his book *Outbreak*, asks us to consider such a favorable application of the virus. He argues that the birth and early growth of the church was viral in nature. Christianity spread throughout the entire province of Asia in less than two years, through all of the Roman Empire within 30 years, and became the dominant religion of Europe within 300 years.[1]

When a virus inhabits an organism, its job is not merely to compromise or disrupt its host but to take complete control. Once that happens, the virus replicates itself and goes on to repeat the process in other cells.

As Christians, we can learn much from a virus. When Jesus invades our lives, "He wants every aspect of every Christian life to be completely under His control, and He won't stop until that happens."[2] The infecting process begins at salvation and continues until Christ reigns supreme. Unfortunately for some Christians this final phase never occurs because they never fully surrender to Jesus. As a result their testimony is compromised, and they may never be able to spread the gospel to others effectively.

The Gospel Is a Positive Virus

In may ways the gospel is viral in nature. It can radically and wonderfully impact the people it infects. It not only transforms their life on earth, but it also gives them eternal life in heaven. It can be highly contagious and sweep through families and tribes. Therefore, it has incredible power. "For I am not ashamed of the gospel of Christ, for it is the power of God to salvation for everyone who believes, for the Jew first and also for the Greek" (Rom 1:16).

Paul, the Viral Evangelist

The apostle Paul is a good example of someone who was thoroughly infected by the gospel virus. After his initial encounter with Christ, he became a walking epidemic, evangelizing a wide swath of Asia.

In his previous life Paul was a hard-core Pharisee and a stickler for the law of Moses who literally hunted Christians. So to the first-century observer Paul's conversion from Christian killer to Christianizer was a stunning testimony and an unmistakable act of God.

Stier suggests three essentials for the gospel to spread effectively: it must have a courageous carrier, be an infectious message, that is also highly contagious in character. Paul's ministry had all these elements.[3]

Paul Was a Courageous Carrier

Paul was an incredible, church-planting missionary. As a viral evangelist, he traveled from town to town preaching the good news, enduring arrest, imprisonment, and beatings, and was even stoned. Yet, by the grace of God, Paul persevered, and the gospel prevailed. Churches sprang up on several continents through Paul's efforts. Many who heard him were transformed and became carriers themselves.[4]

The Gospel Was Powerfully Infectious

When Paul was imprisoned in Rome, he used his circumstances as a way to spread the gospel. Paul states that he eventually shared the gospel with all of the guards in the prison. How did he do it? "Because of my chains, most of the brothers in the Lord have been encouraged to speak the word of God more courageously and fearlessly" (Phil 1:14 NIV).

Someone said that Paul launched a gospel chain reaction. You see, every few hours a new guard would be chained to Paul. Therefore, Paul had a captive audience, and he would evangelize the guard. Then when that guard went off duty, he would carry the gospel with him. Every new guard chained to Paul became infected with the gospel and a carrier of the good news.

The gospel Paul shared powerfully infected others with the desire to share it. Wherever the gospel was spoken—Asia, Athens, Rome—people were changed and also emboldened to propagate the message. Just as a sneeze is involuntary, forceful, and infectious, so was their uttering of the gospel.

The gospel is powerfully infectious. When someone has truly been saved, they cannot keep the good news to themselves. They have to tell somebody.

Much like a plague that naturally infects living things in a geographical area, the religious leaders of the first century found genuine Christianity can sweep seemingly out of control and be impossible to harness. Once the infection called the good news has room to spread through evangelism, if left unhindered, it will naturally create an epidemic of spiritual multiplication.[5]

The Gospel Was Highly Contagious

> Some indeed preach Christ even from envy and strife, and some also from goodwill: The former preach Christ from selfish ambition, not sincerely, supposing to add affliction to my chains; but the latter out of love, knowing that I am appointed for the defense of the gospel. What then? Only that in every way, whether in pretense or in truth, Christ is preached; and in this I rejoice, yes, and will rejoice. (Phil 1:15–18)

Paul states that some were preaching the gospel in the hopes that it will anger more people and thereby hasten his death. But his perspective was, "So what, as long as Christ is preached." Of course he hoped that people would adopt his teachings and live holy and authentic lives. That was important. But what mattered even more was that people were being exposed to Christ's message of salvation.[6]

Unstoppable

When a virus is airborne, it is on the loose and virtually unstoppable.[7] This is what happened when Peter preached the gospel in Jerusalem on the day of Pentecost (Acts 2). Jerusalem became the virtual epicenter of a shock wave that rippled through Asia, the Mediterranean world, the Roman Empire, and into Europe. The gospel has an innate power that is unstoppable.

What Has Changed?

What has changed since the gospel spread through the world in the first century? We have. We have lost the passion of the first followers of Jesus. Nearly every day teenagers across the world are strapping bombs to their backs and driving into marketplaces and restaurants with the aim of killing themselves and harming others for the sake of Allah. At the same time, American Christian teenagers are swapping churches in order to take advantage of bigger shows and more technical gadgets. How about strapping the cross to our backs as Jesus commands in Mark 8:34 when He states, "Take up your cross and follow Me."

What has changed? A lot. Our high-tech, media-immersed culture suffers from a short attention span and growing boredom so anything short of extreme is seen as dull.

Students Make Great Carriers

"To start an outbreak of biblical proportions today, we need carriers who are courageous. It will take a supernatural confidence for us to push past the barriers of embarrassment and rejection so the message can go out."[8]

Because they thrive on adrenaline, students are ideal gospel carriers. Evangelism can be scary, and that's just the point; the fear and trembling Paul endured are "prerequisites for the ultimate extreme sport—sharing your faith."[9]

Paul Borthwick observed how many of our culture's unchurched kids "pursue risk-taking lifestyles with religious fervor. . . . Meanwhile, our youth group kids stay locked in the safety zone. . . . Today's young people need to be called to a life of danger for the sake of following Christ. Many of them are just waiting for the church to give them something big, something significant, something risky to do."[10]

What's the Solution?

First, start with Jesus. Jesus is extreme! For example, during His nighttime rendezvous with Nicodemus (John 3), Jesus puzzled the upstanding Pharisee by telling him that he must be born again (3:3), a physical impossibility. This is not what Nicodemus wanted to hear. In his book *Real Life Jesus*, Mike Cain notes that Jesus was giving us an incredibly difficult assignment; He was telling us that our only hope of entering the kingdom of God is to do something we cannot possibly do. It requires a miracle! "He [Jesus] is saying one of the things that our culture doesn't want to hear"—the fact that we cannot change our own hearts. We need someone to intervene. And that is exactly what Jesus says he has come to do."[11] When we accept His Son, Jesus Christ, God does an extreme miracle in us. If we can convey this to people, it certainly will get their attention.

Second, don't be distracted. First-century cultures had their share of distractions as well. The Greeks were polytheists preoccupied with philosophy and their brand of religion. Acts 17:21 says that the "Athenians and the foreigners who lived there spent their time doing nothing but talking about and listening to the latest ideas" (NIV). Speaking in Athens, Paul observed that the Greeks were "very religious" (17:22). Although it was a religion different from that which Paul would explain, he used it as a bridge to reach them.

The Romans were polytheists, as well. Even the monotheistic Jews suffered infighting between their various factions: "the liberal Sadducees, the conservative Pharisees, the radical Zealots, the communal Essenes, and others."[12] Amid all this confusion the Christian church was born, grew, and thrived. Was it because it had better marketing or slicker salesmen? No, it simply had a credible, compelling message, communicated in a way that was relevant to the culture of the day. Today the message is just as compelling and just as relevant.

Third, be confident. Never forget that you are empowered through the same Holy Spirit and the same God to impact the world for Christ! It is easy to read the Bible and come away with the impression that the biblical characters were superheroes who lived on a spiritual plain way above contemporary Christians. Nothing could be farther from the truth! Before Peter stood up and preached the gospel boldly at Pentecost and thousands responded in Acts 2, he denied his Savior three times (Matt 26:69–74). In addition, before Moses led the children of Israel out of Egyptian slavery toward the promised land, he had become angry and killed an Egyptian guard (Exod 2:11–12).

God is as active today as He was in biblical days. His desire is still to have a viral explosion of the gospel to every nation. As always, His means of accomplishing this goal is the obedience of His children to the call of the Great Commission. God has never required superhuman attributes to be effective in ministry. He requires only faithful and surrendered hearts. He will do the rest!

Viral Evangelism Is Organic

True evangelism does not require cumbersome programs. On the contrary, evangelism should be a natural (organic) expression of every believer. Genuine Christians should be infected by the evangelism virus. It does not start at the church building; rather it organically initiates from the heart and soul of dedicated believers who are on mission with God to impact the unsaved world with the message of Christ. It is not something you try to do as an expression of your duty to Christ. It is who you are in Him. Just as Christ lives in us as Christians, He should also freely minister through us as His disciples.

Viral Evangelism Is Multiplication in Action

The gospel was never meant to be a private or individual affair reserved only for the solitude and silence of a believer's soul. It was meant to be lived out in community among Christians and unbelievers. Just as the human body was designed naturally to multiply cells in order to maintain health and to fulfill its purpose, the same is true with Christians and how they should live out their existence in this world. Multiplication of the gospel through evangelism should be an involuntary desire of every Christian. Just like the analogy of the virus, the gospel should naturally multiply.

⌐ Evangelism Is . . . ⌐

1. Viral in nature. It is both contagious and infectious.
2. Organic, not requiring programs.
3. Involuntary, just like breathing. One should not have to be continually reminded in order to participate.

⌐ Key Verse ⌐

For I am not ashamed of the gospel of Christ, for it is the power of God to salvation for everyone who believes, for the Jew first and also for the Greek. (Rom 1:16)

⌐ Good Quotes ⌐

I can't think of better candidates to be courageous carriers [of the gospel] than teenagers. We live in a student culture obsessed with adrenaline. What better rush than evangelism? Fear and trembling are prerequisites for the ultimate extreme sport—sharing your faith.

—GREG STIER[13]

The magnitude of our mission surpasses the ordinary mind. All the world is our parish. There is no limit. All must hear and heed the Master's call. The Bible says that every single individual must accept or reject the person of the Lord Jesus Christ. . . . Our ministry is to preach the Word "in season" or "out of season."

—CLIFT BRANNON[14]

He [Jesus] lost no opportunity to impress on His followers the deep compulsion of His own soul aflame with the love of God for a lost world. Everything He did and said was motivated by this consuming passion. His life was simply the revelation in time of God's eternal purpose to save for Himself a people. Supremely, this is what the disciples needed to learn, not in theory, but in practice.

—ROBERT COLEMAN[15]

➤ Application ➤

Over the next month, read the Gospel of John and highlight anytime that Jesus goes viral and impacts someone else as it relates to spreading the gospel. At the same time, pay special attention to the attitudes of the disciples and how they responded to Jesus' viral message. For example, in John 4 in the story of the woman at the well, how did the disciples respond to Jesus' interest in the woman and the souls of the Samaritans?

Then read the book of Acts and look for ways the gospel spread throughout the world. How did the early believers participate in the viral spread of the gospel? How does this impact the overall mission of the church? How should this impact your behavior as a Christian in the twenty-first century?

Notes

1. G. Stier, *Outbreak* (Chicago, IL: Moody, 2002), 24.

2. Ibid., 25.

3. Ibid., 26.

4. Ibid.

5. Ibid., 28–30.

6. Ibid., 31.

7. Ibid., 37.

8. Ibid., 27.

9. Ibid.

10. Ibid.

11. M. Cain, *Real Life Jesus: Meaning, Freedom, Purpose* (Nottingham, England: InterVarsity Press, 2008), 68–69.

12. Stier, *Outbreak*, 39.

13. Ibid., 27.

14. C. Brannon, *Successful Soul Winning* (Philadelphia, PA: National Publishing Co., 1981), 133.

15. R. E. Coleman, *The Master Plan of Evangelism* (Grand Rapids, MI: Revell, 1996), 62.

Part 3

Manner

15

Following the Example of Jesus

Dave Earley and David Wheeler

On one occasion Jesus needed to pass from Jerusalem, the hub of religious life in Judea, north to his homeland in Galilee. The shortest distance was to pass through a small section of territory known as Samaria. Traditionally Jews looked down on Samaritans as biological and religious half-breeds. The prejudice was so intense that Jews would not pass through Samaria but bypassed setting foot in their territory, even though it was the most direct route from Judea to Galilee. Yet on this occasion Jesus led His disciples directly into Samaria.

Once there His disciples left Jesus sitting by a well while they went to get supplies. There Jesus encountered an unsaved woman. His dealings with her form a template for how we can evangelize others. As you read through this chapter, we will point out key aspects of the Jesus model for evangelism.

1. Jesus Stepped Out of His Comfort Zone and Took the Initiative to Start the Conversation

Jesus spoke with her. Even though He was weary, He did not turn down the opportunity to start the conversation. "So He came to a city of Samaria which is called Sychar, near the plot of ground that Jacob gave to his son Joseph. Now Jacob's well was there. Jesus therefore, being wearied from His journey, sat thus by the well. It was about the sixth hour. A woman of Samaria came to draw water. Jesus said to her, 'Give Me a drink'" (John 4:5–7).

Launching conversations with lost people is not always comfortable or convenient, but we must do it anyway. We need to realize that if some lost people are ever going to hear the gospel we will have to tell them.

2. Jesus Crossed Barriers to Bring Her the Gospel

In those days Jews would not speak to Samaritans, but Jesus broke the ethnic barrier to speak with her. In those days religious men would not speak with women, but Jesus crossed the gender barrier to share with her. In those days, godly men did not speak with sinful women—and as we shall see, this woman had quite a reputation—but Jesus spoke to her. This obviously made a deep impression on this woman that Jesus would break down the wall of prejudice to speak to her. "Then the woman of Samaria said to Him, 'How is it that You, being a Jew, ask a drink from me, a Samaritan woman?' For Jews have no dealings with Samaritans" (John 4:9).

In a broader sense we need to realize that Jesus was the premier cross-cultural missionary. He left the culture of heaven to come to earth. He left the glories of the Godhead to become a man. He left the freedom of being a man by becoming a poor Jewish baby, born in a barn.

Effective evangelists are ready, willing, and able to cross any barrier with the good news of Jesus Christ. Issues of prejudice have little importance compared with the larger issue of taking the good news to lost people. When necessary we should be cross-cultural missionaries willing to cross any barrier to take the gospel to the lost person who needs to hear it.

This may mean taking the gospel across the street to our immigrant neighbors. It may also mean traveling overseas to obey the mandate of making disciples of all nations, even to the ends of the earth (Matt 28:19–20; Acts 1:8).

3. Jesus Turned the Conversation to Spiritual Matters

In one sentence Jesus turned the conversation from being about His asking her for a drink to the possibility of her having living water. He moved from His physical need for water to *her* need of living water. "Jesus answered and said to her, 'If you knew the gift of God, and who it is who says to you, "Give Me a drink," you would have asked Him, and He would have given you living water'" (John 4:10). As He had done with Nicodemus earlier, Jesus used a commonly understood physical reality (in Nicodemus's case, birth; in her case, thirst) to build a bridge to spiritual issues.

Often as we engage people in everyday conversations, they will say something that can become the springboard into a spiritual conversation. Wise evangelists will prayerfully listen for an opportunity to turn an ordinary dialogue into an eternally significant conversation.

4. Jesus Listened to Her

When Jesus mentioned "living water," the woman immediately launched into a commentary about Jesus' lack of material resources to meet His need. "The woman said to Him, 'Sir, You have nothing to draw with, and the well is deep. Where then do You get that living water? Are You greater than our father Jacob, who gave us the well, and drank from it himself, as well as his sons and his livestock?'" (John 4:11–12).

Jesus carefully listened to her words and planned His response. Listening is an essential, powerful tool and an aid for building any relationship. If we want lost people to listen to us when we share the gospel, we must first listen to them as they share with us. Never underestimate the role of listening in building an evangelistic relationship.

As a professor, I (David Wheeler) always spend the last class period of the semester discussing what the students gained most from the class. I recall one young lady who used this opportunity to share how her brother was won to Christ by listening. The young lady told how she had gotten saved and was the only Christian in her family. Initially she tried to strong-arm her family with the gospel. All of her lengthy discourses and endless apologetic presentations did nothing more than turn her family off to her and to Christ.

She told the class how her perspective changed when we discussed the power of listening in our class. She was convicted that she needed to go back home and love and accept her family regardless of their spiritual condition. She also made the commitment to become a better listener. It was not long before her family relationships began to blossom.

Soon after, she received a late-night phone call from her brother. He was in trouble and landed in jail. This was not the first time her brother had gotten in serious trouble, but it was the first time he had called her. He had always felt uncomfortable in the past reaching out to her because the last thing he wanted was another sermon from her. He felt that she always preached at him and condemned him.

On this night, however, because she had spent several months repairing the relationship through listening, he reached out to her for help. She got to share the gospel with him. Her prayers were answered as he surrendered his life to Christ.

5. Jesus Refused to Be Sidetracked but Stayed Focused on God's Provision for Her Spiritual Need

When the woman mentioned Jacob, she was referring to the Hebrew patriarch claimed by both Samaritans and Jews. Rather than getting caught up in the age-old Jewish-Samaritan issue of the spiritual heritage of Jacob's descendents, Jesus stayed focused on the primary issue: her need for eternal life as portrayed by living water.

> Jesus answered and said to her, "Whoever drinks of this water will thirst again, but whoever drinks of the water that I shall give him will never thirst. But the water that I shall give him will become in him a fountain of water springing up into everlasting life." The woman said to Him, "Sir, give me this water, that I may not thirst, nor come here to draw." (John 4:13–15)

Because talking about spiritual matters might make unsaved people feel guilty or uncomfortable, they will often bring up an issue or a question to get the conversation off their need for God. Don't get sidetracked.

6. Jesus Did Not Pick the Fruit Too Quickly

When the woman said, "Give me a drink," could it mean that she was ready to respond to Christ? Or could it mean that she was just being sarcastic and still doubted? In either case, unlike most of us, Jesus was careful not to pick the spiritual fruit too early. Regardless of the woman's motivation, Jesus was intentional in His actions yet patient enough carefully to engage the woman in a dialogue that ultimately leads to the truth.

7. Jesus Pointed Out Her Sin

> The woman said to Him, "Sir, give me this water, that I may not thirst, nor come here to draw."
> Jesus said to her, "Go, call your husband, and come here."
> The woman answered and said, "I have no husband."

Jesus said to her, "You have well said, 'I have no husband,' for you have had five husbands, and the one whom you now have is not your husband; in that you spoke truly." (John 4:15–18)

The woman had asked Jesus about giving her the living water. In response to her request, Jesus first confronted her regarding her sin. We soon find out that this woman's primary sin was immorality. She had gone through several husbands and was now cohabiting with a man who was not her husband. Pointedly but politely, Jesus moved the conversation to her sin when He mentioned her husband. When she tried to deflect it, He spoke directly about her obvious need.

We all know that immorality is breaking the Seventh Commandment: "You shall not commit adultery" (Exod 20:14). Still Jesus did not yell at her or whack her on the head with a Bible. He simply raised the issue of her husband(s) and reminded her of her present sinful situation.

Often in our eagerness to help lost people get into heaven, we fail to point out sin in their lives. The reason people are lost is because of sin. The reason people will not get to heaven is because of sin. The reason they are empty, lonely, and frustrated is because of sin. If we want people to be truly saved, we must address the issue of their sin. No one senses their need to be saved until they understand that they are lost. The noted English pastor and Bible scholar Martyn Lloyd-Jones notes: "A gospel which merely says, 'Come to Jesus' and offers him as a Friend, and offers a marvelous new life without convincing of sin, is not New Testament evangelism. . . . True evangelism must always start by preaching the Law."[1]

Kirk Cameron and Ray Comfort make the case that most evangelistic methods fail adequately to address the issue of sin in general and breaking God's law in specific. In their gospel presentation, they advocate reading through the Ten Commandments.[2]

Please note that unlike many approaches to evangelism, Jesus had already established rapport with the woman before attacking the issue of her sin. Dealing with sin is always imperative and essential; the issue is how one accomplishes the task. In a contemporary/relational culture, this should be done in a sensitive manner. Most people will not receive the truth until they first see the truth demonstrated in other believers. Like Jesus, His followers must be genuine and real.

8. Jesus Refused to Let Her off the Hook

The woman said to Him, "Sir, I perceive that You are a prophet. Our fathers worshiped on this mountain, and you Jews say that in Jerusalem is the place where one ought to worship."
Jesus said to her, "Woman, believe Me, the hour is coming when you will neither on this mountain, nor in Jerusalem, worship the Father. You worship what you do not know; we know what we worship, for salvation is of the Jews. But the hour is coming, and now is, when the true worshipers will worship the Father in spirit and truth; for the Father is seeking such to worship Him. God is Spirit, and those who worship Him must worship in spirit and truth." (John 4:19–24)

When Jesus pointed out this woman's sin, she jumped a step in understanding and observed, "Sir, I perceive that You are a prophet." But then she immediately got offtrack again going back to the age-old Jewish-Samaritan issue of *where* to worship, Mount Gerazim or Jerusalem. He carefully corrected her focus, moving it from *where* to worship to the more important issue, *whom* to worship.

Lost people often miss the key issues. Our job as effective evangelists is patiently to pull them back on track, back to the core issues of the gospel.

9. Jesus Called for the Woman to Submit Her Life and "Worship the Father in Spirit and Truth"

A proper understanding of worship always involves the issue of total submission and surrender to the lordship of the Father. Note that Jesus said that the "Father is seeking such to worship Him." Consider the implications: Jesus shared with a Samaritan woman, and He affirmed that God is "seeking" worshippers, even Samaritans! Wow! Regardless of religious traditions and personal preferences, always be careful not to limit God's grace and mercy to a certain segment of society or culture.

10. Jesus Introduced Himself to Her

"The woman said to Him, 'I know that Messiah is coming' (who is called Christ). 'When He comes, He will tell us all things.' Jesus said to her, 'I who speak to you am He'" (John 4:25–26). In response to the woman's statement, "I know the Messiah is coming," Jesus affirmed His deity with the words, "I who speak to you am He." A point comes in spiritual conversations when we need to get to the issue of Jesus Christ. He is the most important issue in the matter of salvation.

> Jesus said to him, "I am the way, the truth, and the life. No one comes to the Father except through Me." (John 14:6)

> Nor is there salvation in any other, for there is no other name under heaven given among men by which we must be saved. (Acts 4:12)

The Woman Leaves Her Water Pot

> The woman then left her waterpot, went her way into the city, and said to the men, "Come, see a Man who told me all things that I ever did. Could this be the Christ?" Then they went out of the city and came to Him. (John 4:28–30)

As a result of her conversation with Jesus, the woman was spiritually ignited. She immediately "left her waterpot" and ran into the city. There she summoned the town to come and hear Jesus.

Often the best evangelists are not the professors with PhDs in theology but instead are those who most recently have met Jesus. They have the best contacts with lost people and the most enthusiasm for telling others about Jesus. We all must be willing to leave our water pots immediately for the sake of inviting the world to meet Christ.

— Evangelism Is ... —

1. Following Jesus' format.
2. Crossing cultural barriers to share the gospel.
3. Boldly and wisely addressing the issue of sin.
4. Not being sidetracked by noneternal issues.

— Good Quotes —

Most men and women are not looking for religion, nor do they often have the time or inclination to ask themselves questions about the meaning of life. . . . But most men and women are looking for love.

—ARTHUR McPHEE[3]

> *The Christian life is not just a private affair of your own.*
>
> —JOHN R. W. STOTT[4]

Notes

1. M. Lloyd-Jones quoted in Kirk Cameron and Ray Comfort, *The Way of the Master* (Wheaton, IL: Tyndale, 2002), 4.

2. Cameron and Comfort, *The Way of the Master*, 129.

3. A. G. McPhee, *Friendship Evangelism* (Grand Rapids, MI: Choice Books, Zondervan, 1978), 56.

4. J. R. W. Stott, *Basic Christianity* (Grand Rapids, MI: Eerdman's, 1999), 139.

16 Not Following the Example of the Disciples

Dave Earley and David Wheeler

I (David Wheeler) was interviewed several years ago by a Baptist church in Texas about the possibility of becoming their senior pastor. During the brief time of courtship, it became evident that we were headed in two different ministerial directions. When they informed me of their decision to move on to other candidates, while I was not shocked, out of curiosity I asked them to explain their reasoning.

I was amazed by their blunt honesty. They replied, "We want our pastor to be much more concerned with the affairs of the church and the present membership, . . . to be in the office every day from 9:00 a.m. until 5:00 p.m. in case we call or drop by. . . . Frankly, you are way too evangelistic for us. . . . We (the pulpit committee) agree that the whole concept of evangelism makes us uncomfortable!"

This pulpit committee was not the first group of Christians to place a low value on evangelism. Unfortunately many Christians today have the same perspective. Two thousand years ago another group of Christ followers also had misplaced priorities.

The Disciples Failed to Prioritize Evangelism

In the previous chapter we looked at how Jesus went about sharing the good news with a Samaritan woman. But Jesus and the Samaritan woman were not the only characters in this story. Also at the well that day were Jesus' disciples.

In John 4 we read that after Jesus led her to understand that He was the Messiah, she left her water pot and invited the entire town to meet Jesus. In a sense she was the catalyst for a citywide crusade. At this time Jesus' disciples returned to the scene. From the disciples we learn several negative lessons about how not to do effective evangelism.

1. The Disciples Overlooked the Woman and Didn't Affirm Her or Acknowledge Her Spiritual Need

When they returned from getting food, the disciples saw Jesus wrapping up His dialogue with the Samaritan woman. "And at this point His disciples came, and they marveled that He talked with a woman; yet no one said, 'What do you seek?' or, 'Why are You talking with her?'" (John 4:27). The disciples were, no doubt, uncomfortable being in Samaria much less coming back to find that Jesus had been publicly speaking with a Samaritan woman of questionable morals. Nevertheless, they were silent. They not only said nothing to Jesus, but they also said nothing to the woman.

This may not sound like much, but their silence speaks volumes. It is almost as if they did not want to say anything that might prolong their stay. They obviously ignored the woman as if she did not matter. Either they just didn't pay attention, or, worse, they were too proud to speak to her.

Unlike Jesus, the disciples did not affirm the woman's humanity or the eternal value of her soul. Their hearts were hardened by years of religious traditions and cultural perceptions. As a result, the disciples' reaction communicated that they did not care about her!

Most of us miss countless opportunities to make a difference because we either don't notice people or don't care enough about them to get involved in their lives. We will never see anyone come to Christ if we don't actively acknowledge, affirm, and care about them.

2. The Disciples Ignored Jesus and What He Was Doing

Not only did the cultural and religious prejudice blind the disciples from the need and potential of the woman, but it also blinded them to Jesus Himself. "In the meantime His disciples urged Him, saying, 'Rabbi, eat'" (John 4:31). Through the disciple's obsession to make sure Jesus eats as quickly as possible, they actually appear to be rude and ignore Him. After all, the quicker Jesus eats, the quicker their nightmare is over, and they are able to leave Samaria.

When we refuse to open our eyes to the needs of the world around us, we do ourselves a double disservice and lose on two levels. Not only do we lose the joy of being used by God to make a difference, but we also lose out on noticing what God is doing.

God is always working around us. Those who are sensitive to His ways will rejoice with Him and join Him in His work. In doing so, He opens our eyes to the needs around us, then empowers us to meet the needs.

3. The Disciples Missed the Obvious Spiritual Opportunity Right in Front of Their Faces

Here was a lost woman who was ripe for salvation, and they missed it. Here was Jesus showing them an eternal opportunity in the midst of a daily routine, and they did not notice. All they thought about was the food. They failed to realize that real soul-nourishing "food" is doing God's work, not feeding your face.

"But He said to them, 'I have food to eat of which you do not know.' Therefore the disciples said to one another, 'Has anyone brought Him anything to eat?' Jesus said to them, 'My food is to do the will of Him who sent Me, and to finish His work" (John 4:32–34).

Sadly, unlike the woman and Jesus, the disciples were so distracted by the physical dimension of food and eating, they missed the spiritual point entirely. The woman was willing to drop her water pot to pursue a Savior. Yet the disciples were not willing to drop their religious prejudice and cultural dislike for the Samaritans in order to see the spiritual harvest.

4. The Disciples Failed to See the Spiritual Harvest Ripe Before Them

"Do you not say, 'There are still four months and then comes the harvest'? Behold, I say to you, lift up your eyes and look at the fields, for they are already white for harvest!" (John 4:35)

Jesus told His disciples to wake up and look around. Not only was a woman open to salvation, but a whole town was also ready for harvest. To them evangelism of Samaritans was not an option. Even as the people were coming to Jesus, the disciples were too blinded by their location and the cultural hatred for the Samaritans to rejoice over what God was doing. Although it was directly in front of them, the disciples refused to see the harvest!

Often opportunity is in the eye of the beholder. For example, a hundred years ago two new salesmen were sent to sell shoes to a recently civilized South American tribal people. One man cabled back regarding their sales territory, "Bad field. No one wears shoes here. Send me somewhere else." The other man, seeing the opportunity, cabled back, "Great field! No one has shoes here. Send me more shoes."

When the disciples saw the Samaritans, they saw a large group of people who weren't worth their time because they weren't Jewish. When Jesus saw the Samaritans, He saw a whole group of people who were ripe for salvation. So while they mumbled about sandwiches, Jesus evangelized a woman and started a spiritual revival.

Jesus' excitement is in obvious contrast to the disciples' unconcern over the lost state of the Samaritans. To Him the harvest was at hand. If we would only look at people through Jesus' eyes, we could see the deep thirst in their souls.

5. The Disciples Failed to Understand the Role They Could Play in the Harvest

"And he who reaps receives wages, and gathers fruit for eternal life, that both he who sows and he who reaps may rejoice together. For in this the saying is true: 'One sows and another reaps.' I sent you to reap that for which you have not labored; others have labored, and you have entered into their labors." (John 4:36–38)

Jesus, the Master Teacher and Mentor, used this incident as an opportunity to teach His followers some key truths about spiritual farming. (We discussed "spiritual farming" in chap. 11.) Jesus was able to begin reaping a harvest among the Samaritans because they were a prepared field. They already had an understanding of God and an appreciation for His Word. They simply needed someone to connect them with the Savior.

In order for a spiritual harvest ever to be reaped, someone must first plow (primarily through prayer) and plant (the gospel seed). A paraphrase of John 4:36–38 could be, "Some of you will harvest where you have not plowed or planted; others will plow and plant without directly experiencing the harvest. In either case, someone has to plow and plant for the harvest to come!"

In short, spiritual farming is the responsibility of all of us. Every believer is called to be a good farmer who faithfully seeks to plow through prayer and to plant the gospel seed. Then God will honor the efforts and grant a harvest. The only way to kill the harvest is to forsake the plowing and planting!

6. The Disciples Did Not See How Big the Harvest Could Be

And many of the Samaritans of that city believed in Him because of the word of the woman who testified, "He told me all that I ever did." So when the Samaritans had come to Him, they urged Him to stay with them; and He stayed there two days. And many more believed because of His own word. Then they said to the woman, "Now we believe, not because of what you said, for we ourselves have heard Him and we know that this is indeed the Christ, the Savior of the world." (John 4:39–42)

We especially love two words in these verses: "many" and "many more." Jesus shared with one woman, yet "many of the Samaritans . . . believed." After staying with them for two more days, "many more believed." They grasped salvation and eventually claimed it as their own. This is the principle of natural multiplication. One convert led to a citywide revival.

This should always be the natural progression of salvation. It begins by way of the Holy Spirit in the hearts of men and women who are redeemed. However, it must never stop multiplying. In fact, consider that many biblical scholars believe that the Samaritan revival initiated through Philip in Acts 8 was simply a natural progression that began with the occurrence in John 4.

Never Underestimate the Power of One

One Samaritan woman testified to her town, and many believed in Jesus.

One man, Noah, built a boat that saved the human race.

One man, Moses, stood up to Pharaoh and delivered the Hebrews from Egypt.

One woman, Deborah, delivered Israel from the Canaanite oppression.

One man, David, defeated the Philistines when he killed their champion, Goliath.

One woman, Esther, had the courage to approach the king and see her nation spared from extermination.

One man, Peter, preached a sermon that led 3,000 to be saved.

One salesman and Sunday school teacher, Edward Kimball, led a young man named Dwight to Christ. Dwight Moody became a blazing evangelist who it is said, led one million souls to Christ in his short lifetime.[1] Wilbur Chapman received the assurance of his salvation after talking with Moody and went on to become a noted evangelist himself. The drunken baseball player Billy Sunday was an assistant to Chapman before becoming the most famous evangelist of his day. One of the fruits of Sunday's ministry was the forming of a group of Christian businessmen in Charlotte, North Carolina. This group brought the evangelist Mordecai Ham to Charlotte in 1934. A tall awkward youth named Billy Graham was converted during those meetings.[2] According to his staff, as of 1993, more than 2.5 million people had "stepped forward at his crusades to accept Jesus Christ as their personal Savior."[3] Millions of souls trace their spiritual lineage back to the influence of one man, a simple Sunday school teacher, Edward Kimball.

Someone said, "To the world you may just be one person, but to one person you may be the world." To this we might add, to you they may seem like just one lost soul, but to God that may be a soul who can shake the whole world.

Never Underestimate the Power of One Multiplied

What the disciples did not understand and Jesus did was the exponential power of multiplication. Jesus understood that often the fastest way to reach the many is through the slow process of multiplication. Walter Henrichsen has written:

> Some time ago there was a display at the Museum of Science and Industry in Chicago. It featured a checkerboard with 1 grain of wheat on the first, 2 on the second, 4 on the third, then 8, 16, 32, 64, 128, etc. Somewhere down the board, there were so many grains of wheat on the square that some were spilling over into neighboring squares—so here the demonstration stopped. Above the checkerboard display was a question, "At this rate of doubling every square, how much grain would be on the checkerboards by the 64th square?"
>
> To find the answer to this riddle, you punched a button on the console in front of you, and the answer flashed on a little screen above the board: "Enough to cover the entire subcontinent of India 50 feet deep."
>
> Multiplication may be costly, and in the initial stages, much slower than addition, but in the long run, it is the most effective way of accomplishing Christ's Great Commission . . . and the only way.[4]

When we lead people to Christ, we must stay with them to help them get established in their faith. Then they can also be carriers of the good news, and the message of the gospel will multiply through their consistent witness.

The Disciples Eventually Changed

After seeing the resurrected Christ, the disciples radically changed. It was as if their spiritual eyes were suddenly opened and now they understood. Everything they had heard Jesus say and had seen Jesus do came alive to them. Instead of treating people and the harvest as they did with the Samaritan woman, they began to follow Jesus' example. They noticed people and their needs, and they acted to meet those needs. As a result vast numbers of souls came to Christ.

For example, when Peter and John went to the temple to pray, they noticed a lame man begging by the side of the road. Rather than silently passing by, they stopped and ministered to him in the power of the name of Jesus (Acts 3:1–10). Later they all ministered to scores of sick and demonized people (Acts 5:12–16).

On top of that, when Samaria began to turn in vast numbers to Christ through the ministry of Philip, the apostles actively responded. Instead of ignoring the Samaritans, as they had before, they sent Peter and John to minister to them (Acts 8:17–25).

You Can Make a Difference

Like the disciples, all of us need to be enlightened to the power of biblical multiplication through investing our lives on a daily basis. We should read this chapter several times, being honest about our spiritual attitudes. Are we like Jesus who reached out to a helpless and hopeless woman with no fear of political or religious retribution? Or are we like the disciples, who at the time refused to open their eyes and accept that God could be working outside of their limited understanding?

The truth is, just as the disciples changed when they were confronted by the coming of the Holy Spirit, we need to remain in His presence as well. Since the Holy Spirit is the discerner of all truth, if we are willing, He will mold us into the image of Christ. God can erase our deepest fears and prejudiced attitudes and replace them with courage (Acts 4:18–20) and boldness (Acts 4:31) to proclaim the gospel at any cost!

We never know if our obedience for a *moment* could start a *movement* of God that might impact our communities, schools, workplaces, or maybe the world! Yes, just like the woman in John 4, you *can* make a difference!

— Evangelism Is . . . —

1. Seeing people and acknowledging their needs.
2. Seizing opportunities to share Jesus.

— Key Verse —

"Do you not say, 'There are still four months and then comes the harvest'? Behold, I say to you, lift up your eyes and look at the fields, for they are already white for harvest!" (John 4:35)

— Good Quotes —

I believe that God holds you responsible for everyone He brings into your sphere of influence. . . . When we have ruptured relationships horizontally with people, we also have a ruptured relationship vertically with God. It is not that we do not know the Lord. It is just that He is really not Lord of our lives. We are not willing to let Him be Lord of everything and accept, love, and forgive people on His conditions.

—Oscar Thompson[5]

Here finally is where we must all evaluate the contribution that our life and witness is making to the supreme purpose of Him who is the Savior of the world. Are those who have followed us to Christ now leading others to Him and teaching them to make disciples like ourselves? . . . What really counts in the ultimate perpetuation of our work is the faithfulness with which our converts go out and make leaders out of their converts, not simply more followers.

—Robert Coleman[6]

Notes

1. W. R. Moody, *The Life of Dwight L. Moody, by His Son* (New York: Fleming H. Revell, 1900), taken from the back cover.
2. http://www.wheaton.edu/bgc/archives/faq/13.htm.

3. "God's Billy Pulpit," *Time*, November 15, 1993, http://205.188.238.109/time/magazine/article/0,9171,979573,00.html.

4. W. Henrichsen, *Disciples Are Made Not Born* (Carol Stream, IL: Victor Books, 1979) 143.

5. W. O. Thompson, *Concentric Circles of Concern* (Nashville, TN: B&H, 1999), 20.

6. R. E. Coleman, *The Master Plan of Evangelism* (Grand Rapids, MI: Revell, 1993), 102–3.

17

Cooperating with the Holy Spirit

Dave Earley

I'm convinced more than ever that the absolute highest value in personal evangelism is staying attuned to and cooperative with the Holy Spirit.

—BILL HYBELS AND MARK MITTELBERG[1]

Anytime a person gives his or her life to Jesus Christ, it is never a solo operation. There are always at least three persons involved: (1) the nonbeliever hears the gospel and receives Jesus by faith and repentance, (2) the person who shares the gospel with the nonbeliever, and (3) the Holy Spirit who applies the gospel to the understanding of the nonbeliever.

The key to being effective in evangelism is simply learning to cooperate with what the Holy Spirit is already doing and saying to the person we are trying to reach. I am convinced that the times I have been least effective in evangelism have been those times when I either tried to go it alone, without being sensitive to the Holy Spirit, or worse, tried to be the Holy Spirit in the life of the lost person.

Meet the Most Important Person in Your Spiritual Life, the Holy Spirit

Some churches talk a great deal about the Holy Spirit. Others rarely do. While the Bible does speak more often about God the Son and God the Father, it also has much to say about God the Holy Spirit. Let me give you a quick overview:

The Holy Spirit Is God

The Bible teaches the tri-unity of God. Historically, Christians have believed in one God who expresses Himself in three persons. These three persons are God the Father, God the Son, and God the Holy Spirit. All three are equally God.

When the Bible refers to the Holy Spirit, He is described as having attributes that are only found in God. The Holy Spirit is everywhere present (Ps 139:7). He is all-knowing (1 Cor 2:10–11). He is all-powerful (Gen 1:2; Luke 1:35). He is eternal (Heb 9:14). He is holy (Luke 11:13). Beyond that the Holy Spirit is frequently referred to as God (Acts 5:3–4; 2 Cor 3:18; Gen 1:1–2; Luke 4:18). He is equated with the Father and the Son (Matt 28:19–20).

The Holy Spirit Is a Person

Some have mistakenly referred to the Holy Spirit as an "it." This could not be more inaccurate. The Holy Spirit is every bit as much a person as is God the Father or God the Son. He has intellect (1 Cor 2:10–11; Eph 1:17; Rom 8:27), emotion (Eph 4:30), and will (1 Cor 12:11). He has creativity (Gen 1:2). He has love (Rom 15:30). Beyond that He is referred to with a personal pronoun (John 15:26; 16:13–14).

The Holy Spirit is *not* a ghost who will scare the nonbeliever. He is *not* an impersonal force that will zap the nonbeliever. He *is* a person who will lovingly pursue the nonbeliever and speak to his or her heart.

The Holy Spirit Is Primary in God's Work on Earth Today

The gospel is all Jesus—His death, burial, and resurrection for our sins. Yet the application of the gospel to the heart of the unbeliever is the work of the Holy Spirit. He is the person of the Godhead who is primary in God's work today on planet Earth.

Old Testament Times	Gospel Times	Current Times
1400 BC–4 BC	4 BC– AD 30	AD 30–Tribulation
God the Father	God the Son	God the Holy Spirit

Billy Graham has noted, "Man has two great spiritual needs. One is forgiveness. The other is for goodness. . . . We need this two-sided gift God has offered us: first, the work of God the Son for us; second, the work of God the Spirit in us."[2]

Since the day of Pentecost in about AD 30, the Holy Spirit has been primary in God's work on planet Earth. The Bible tells us that Jesus sat down because His primary work was finished: "who being the brightness of His glory and the express image of His person, and upholding all things by the word of His power, when He had by Himself purged our sins, sat down at the right hand of the Majesty on high" (Heb 1:3).

Just because Jesus' work on Earth was finished, that did not mean God's work was complete. In describing His departure, Jesus explained the turning over of responsibility to the Holy Spirit:

> I go to prepare a place for you. . . .
>   And I will pray the Father, and He will give you another Helper, that He may abide with you forever—the Spirit of truth, whom the world cannot receive, because it neither sees Him nor knows Him; but you know Him, for He dwells with you and will be in you. I will not leave you orphans; I will come to you (John 14:2,16–18).

The Holy Spirit Is the Primary Player in Bringing a Lost Person to Salvation

I own almost 40 books that deal directly with the subject of evangelism. I am shocked that only a handful of them mention the role of the Holy Spirit in effective evangelism. A quick survey of the Bible reveals the essential role of the Holy Spirit in bringing people to Christ.

Convincing of the Need. "And when He has come, He will convict the world of sin, and of righteousness, and of judgment: of sin, because they do not believe in Me; of righteousness, because I go to My Father and you see Me no more; of judgment, because the ruler of this world is judged" (John 16:8–11).

Everyone who is saved has become so as the result of the convincing work of the Holy Spirit. As we share the gospel, the Holy Spirit speaks to the heart of the nonbeliever convincing and convicting them, pursuing and persuading them. Jesus said that the Holy Spirit convicts them of sin, righteousness, and judgment.

Until nonbelievers are convinced that they are lost, they have no motivation or desire to be saved. As we share the gospel, the Holy Spirit uses the Word of God to convince the nonbeliever of his sin. Because of the work of the Holy Spirit, the nonbeliever will be persuaded regarding the reality, the weight, and the guilt of his sin. Yet the Holy Spirit does not stop there.

He also convinces the nonbeliever of righteousness. Only the Holy Spirit can open the eyes of the nonbeliever to see both his own lack of real righteousness and the perfect, sinless righteousness of the Savior, Jesus Christ.

Beyond that the Holy Spirit also convinces the nonbeliever of judgment. As the Holy Spirit works in the heart of the nonbeliever, he will grasp the severity of his sin and recognize how much the sin deserves to be punished.

Not enough can be said about the supreme importance of the Holy Spirit in convincing and convicting the lost person of sin, righteousness, and judgment. Unless this work occurs, a nonbeliever does not, cannot experience salvation. Yet the work of the Holy Spirit in bringing a lost soul to salvation does not end there.

Giving New Life. Earlier we discussed the familiar story of Jesus' sharing with a seeker named Nicodemus. That dialogue (John 3:1–8) describes salvation as a new birth. When someone is saved, he is born again spiritually; a new life is given. Jesus further states that while a physical birth is immediately visible, a spiritual birth is less obvious yet no less real. The work of the Holy Spirit is compared with the work of the wind. Although we cannot see wind, we can see its results. So it is with the Holy Spirit: we cannot physically see the Holy Spirit birth a new spiritual baby, but we will no doubt see the results in the life of the new believer. "The wind blows where it wishes, and you hear the sound of it, but cannot tell where it comes from and where it goes. So is everyone who is born of the Spirit" (John 3:8).

Entering a Life. Often those who share the gospel encourage nonbelievers to ask Jesus into their hearts. While this is not exactly wrong, it is also not exactly accurate. When people call upon the name of the Lord to save them, Jesus does not enter their hearts. The Spirit of the Lord or the Holy Spirit comes *into* their lives.

"And I will pray the Father, and He will give you another Helper, that He may abide with you forever—the Spirit of truth . . . dwells with you and will be *in you*" (John 14:16–17, italics added). "But you are not in the flesh but in the Spirit, if indeed the Spirit of God dwells *in you*. Now if anyone does not have the Spirit of Christ, he is not His" (Rom 8:9, italics added).

The Holy Spirit takes up residence in their lives. In doing so, He makes the new Christian's body His temple, a place where God is to be worshipped: "Or do you not know that *your body is the temple of the Holy Spirit* who is *in you*" (1 Cor 6:19, italics added).

The Holy Spirit Is Essential in Helping a Saved Person Grow and Serve

The work of the Holy Spirit does not end when a person gets saved. The Holy Spirit becomes our primary Comforter (John 14:16–17) and Teacher (John 14:26; 1 Cor 2:12; 2 Pet 1:21). As His life flows unhindered through us, He becomes our Life Changer (Gal 5:22–23). He is our Spiritual Gift Giver (1 Cor 12:4–11). The Holy Spirit is the most important person in your spiritual life.

Beyond that He is described as our Guide (Rom 8:14; 1 Thess 5:19), and Power Giver (Eph 3:16; Luke 24:49; Acts 1:8). In order to lead other people to Christ, we need the spiritual guidance and spiritual power given by the Holy Spirit. The Holy Spirit is the most important person in your ministry life.

The Holy Spirit Partners with a Believer in Effectively Sharing the Gospel

I often ask witnessing Christians this question: "How many of you have ever shared the gospel with a lost person and found yourself saying things that were clearer and more intelligent than you imagined you could?" They always nod their heads and answer, "Yes." Why? The Holy Spirit actively partners with us when we share the gospel. Effective evangelism is simply cooperating with Him.

Read carefully the Great Commission promise of Jesus: "'Go therefore and make disciples of all the nations, baptizing them in the name of the Father and of the Son and of the Holy Spirit, teaching them to observe all things that I have commanded you; and lo, *I am with you always*, even to the end of the age.' Amen." (Matt 28:19–20, italics added).

Think about what Jesus is promising. He says that when we set our lives on making disciples of all types of people, He is *with* us in the process. The Bible tells us that Jesus is seated at the right hand of the Father in heaven (Eph 1:20; Heb 8:1). So how can He be with us when we fulfill the Great Commission?

Jesus is with us in the person of the Holy Spirit. If you want to experience the presence of the Spirit, make disciples.

Cooperate with the Holy Spirit

The Holy Spirit wants people saved more than we do. He has supernatural power we do not have to convict lost people of sin, righteousness, and judgment. The Holy Spirit is omniscient. He knows exactly what is going on in lost people's lives and thoughts as we are talking with them. Only the Holy Spirit has the power to regenerate a lost person into a new creation in Jesus Christ. Therefore, it only makes sense that if we hope to evangelize anyone effectively, we should rely on Him.

Effective evangelism is actively cooperating with the Holy Spirit as He works to open the eyes of lost people and bring them to God. When you share the gospel, the Holy Spirit gives you wisdom you did not know you had. He also gives you sensitivity you could not possibly have on your own.

"I Was on My Way to a Drinking Problem"

Prior to giving my life completely to Jesus, I had a problem with drinking alcohol. When I was in middle school, my family was going through some tough times. In order to escape, I began to make wine. I also thought having access to alcohol as a middle school student would increase my popularity. I used the wine to get myself and my friends drunk on weekends. Before long I had a thriving little business going. Speeding down the wrong road headed in the wrong direction, I was miserable.

Because of a nonjudgmental Christian friend and a spiritually passionate youth pastor, I was compelled to not discount the Lord. I could see that they had what I needed. When I gave my life full out to Jesus a few years later, I was filled with genuine joy and immediately stopped drinking alcohol and have not tasted it since that time.

I rarely share this story when I am evangelizing another person, but one day as I was sharing Christ with a businessman, I felt especially prompted by the Holy Spirit to mention how Jesus had freed me from alcohol. I had no way of knowing at the time that the man's wife had just threatened to leave him because of his drinking. When I said, "I was on my way to a real drinking problem," it caught his attention and gave me the key to his heart. The Holy

Spirit used my story of freedom from alcohol to touch this man deeply and bring him to Jesus.

Let us encourage you as you share your faith: don't rely solely on yourself. You can't convict or convince anyone, but the Holy Spirit can. You can't know everything that is going on in the other person's life or mind, but the Holy Spirit does. You can't save anyone, but the Holy Spirit can. Since the Holy Spirit plays such a key role in bringing a person to salvation, it behooves us to rely on His help.

Jesus Promised the Enabling Empowerment of the Holy Spirit

The last words a person says are often considered important. The last words of the most important person who ever lived, Jesus, are certainly considered to be some of the most significant words ever uttered. Interestingly they involve the promise of the Holy Spirit and evangelism. "But you shall receive power when the Holy Spirit has come upon you; and you shall be witnesses to Me in Jerusalem, and in all Judea and Samaria, and to the end of the earth" (Acts 1:8).

The First Evangelists Relied on the Power of the Holy Spirit

When Jesus promised to give His followers the power of the Holy Spirit as we share the gospel, He did more than say some nice-sounding words. He gave a promise that His followers relied upon and employed effectively.

For example, the first message ever given in the first church in history was the detailed proclamation of the gospel by the apostle Peter. As Peter and the others were controlled by the Holy Spirit, they boldly proclaimed the death, burial, and resurrection of Jesus for our sins. The Holy Spirit so empowered Peter's words that 3,000 were saved and baptized that day (Acts 2:1–41).

Later Peter and John were arrested for preaching Jesus. Instead of being intimidated into silence, they relied on the power of the Holy Spirit to aid them as they fearlessly proclaimed Christ (Acts 4:1–12). Their boldness stunned the authorities (Acts 4:13). Not sure what to do with them, the authorities threatened Peter and John, then let them go. The response of the apostles wasn't to back off sharing their faith. No way. They did just the opposite. They cried out to God for more boldness to speak God's Word. God's answer came in the form of the Holy Spirit.

> "Now, Lord, look on their threats, and grant to Your servants that with all boldness they may speak Your word, by stretching out Your hand to

heal, and that signs and wonders may be done through the name of Your holy Servant Jesus."

And when they had prayed, the place where they were assembled together was shaken; and they were all filled with the Holy Spirit, and they spoke the word of God with boldness (Acts 4:29–31).

— Evangelism Is . . . —

1. Recognizing that anytime a person gives his or her life to Jesus Christ it is never a solo operation. At least three persons are always involved: (1) the nonbeliever who hears the gospel and receives Jesus, (2) the person who shares the gospel with the nonbeliever, and (3) the Holy Spirit who applies the gospel to the understanding of the nonbeliever.
2. Valuing the Holy Spirit as the person of the Godhead who is primary in God's work today on Earth.
3. Cooperating with what the Holy Spirit is already doing and saying to the person you are trying to reach.
4. Relying on the Holy Spirit to give you wisdom and guidance you could never have on your own.

— Key Verses —

*"But you shall receive power when the Holy Spirit
has come upon you; and you shall be witnesses to Me in
Jerusalem, and in all Judea and Samaria, and to the
end of the earth." (Acts 1:8)*

*And when they had prayed, the place where they were
assembled together was shaken; and they were all filled with
the Holy Spirit, and they spoke the word of God
with boldness. (Acts 4:31)*

⁓ Good Quote ⁓

The Holy Spirit accompanies the gospel. It is our privilege to turn on the drawing power by proclaiming the gospel. . . . His drawing follows our giving out of the gospel.

—DANNY LOVETT[3]

Notes

1. B. Hybels and M. Mittelberg, *Becoming a Contagious Christian* (Grand Rapids, MI: Zondervan, 1994), 59.

2. B. Graham, *The Holy Spirit: Activating God's Power in Your Life* (Nashville, TN: Thomas Nelson, 2000), xi.

3. D. Lovett, *Jesus Is Awesome* (Springfield, MO: 21st Century Press, 2003), 240.

18

Washing Feet

David Wheeler

In his book *Safely Home*, Randy Alcorn tells the fictional story of a fervent Christian named Quan. He was unjustly thrown into jail for publicly proclaiming his faith in China. Alcorn paints a portrait of the nature of evangelism through Quan's humble servant evangelism. Alcorn shares:

> The guard peered into Quan's cell through the little, barred window, which was two handbreadths across. . . . Quan could see the contempt in his eyes.
>
> "Stop smiling!" he yelled.
>
> "I am not smiling," Quan said.
>
> "Yes, you are!" shouted the guard.
>
> . . . Suddenly, Quan stood and pressed his face against the bars. "Guard!" Quan called. When he didn't come, he called louder. "Su Gan!"
>
> The guard came back and rattled the door violently. "Who told you my name? Be silent or I will come in and make you silent!"
>
> "Su Gan, sir, please, I have a request for you."
>
> "Unless you can pay me, I care nothing for your requests."
>
> "Can I do some labor for you?"
>
> Quan saw in the jailer's eyes surprise mixed with contempt.
>
> "This prison is so filthy," Quan said. "There is waste everywhere. The rats and roaches feed on it. . . . Quan can help you. Let me go into the cells one by one and clean up this filthy place. Give me water and a brush and soap, and I will show you what I can do!"[1]

From this point, Alcorn picks up the story after several weeks in which Quan chooses to serve the jailer and the other prisoners by the disposing of human waste from the filthy jail cells. Again, you will notice how God uses his Christlike attitude. The story picks up with Quan addressing a Christian visitor to the jail named Ben. Alcorn continues:

> Ben stood in the chilly winter air. As usual, he waited nervously, trying to keep warm and to will Quan out of the black hole. Someone was being led out of the building now, a frail, older man with a pronounced limp and yellow skin, as if he had jaundice or hepatitis.
> . . . He felt his heart freeze. "Quan?" He tried to disguise his horror. They touched right index fingers through the fence. "You smell like . . . soap."
> "Yes." Quan beamed, his face and voice surprisingly animated. "This is better than I smelled last time, yes? I have wonderful news! You must tell my family and house church. God has answered prayer. He has given me a ministry!"
> "What?"
> "I go from cell to cell, bringing Yesu's message."
> "But I thought you were in an isolated cell."
> "God opened the door. I go to the other men. Most have never had anyone else come into their cell except to beat them. I help and serve them as I clean their cells. I bring them the love of Yesu. Twelve men I have visited. When I left their cells, six I did not leave alone."
> "What do you mean?"
> "When I left, Yesu was with them. Three were already believers, one of them a pastor. . . . Three more bowed their knees to Yesu, who promises never to leave or forsake them. . . . I will teach as I wash."
> "The guards let you do this?"
> "The smell that used to cling to the guards is now almost gone. Their shoes are not ruined. The prisoners are excited . . . to realize that even if they die here, they will have eternal life."
> "Sounds more like a revival meeting than a prison."[2]

The Towel and Basin

Even though it is fictional, the story of Quan is an amazing representation of servant evangelism. Next to the Holy Spirit, the Bible, and the gospel message, there is nothing more powerful or useful in the call of evangelism than "the towel and the basin."

Jesus, the Servant

In the time of Christ, the streets were unpaved, and men either wore sandals or went barefoot. Meals were eaten reclining around low tables. Obviously, it was entirely possible that the man eating next to you or across from you would have his dirty feet near your face, making for an unappetizing meal. Therefore, a servant usually greeted guests at the door and washed their feet.

On the night of the last supper, Jesus gathered with His disciples in a rented room to celebrate the Passover. There was no host and no servant to wash feet. Jesus, realizing the situation, used it as a chance to show love in action. How did He do it? He did it with a basin and a towel.

> Now before the Feast of the Passover, when Jesus knew that His hour had come that He should depart from this world to the Father, having loved His own who were in the world, He loved them to the end. And supper being ended, . . . Jesus, knowing that the Father had given all things into His hands, and that He had come from God and was going to God, rose from supper and laid aside His garments, took a towel and girded Himself. After that, He poured water into a basin and began to wash the disciples' feet, and to wipe them with the towel with which He was girded. (John 13:1–5)

His actions were motivated by love: "having loved His own who were in the world, He loved them to the end" (13:1). Servant evangelism is not a program. It is service motivated by love. Notice that this picture of humble service involved action. Look at all the verbs: "Jesus *rose* from supper and *laid aside* His garments, *took* a towel and *girded* Himself. After that, He *poured* water into a basin and *began to wash* the disciples' feet." Servant evangelism is more than good intentions and warm feelings. It is love in action.

Jesus did not do His act of service merely to show His love for His disciples. He had another objective. He wanted to leave us a vivid portrait of the way He desires us to live. We should also be willing to "wash feet."

> So when He had washed their feet, taken His garments, and sat down again, He said to them, "Do you know what I have done to you? You call Me Teacher and Lord, and you say well, for so I am. If I then, your Lord and Teacher, have washed your feet, you also ought to wash one another's feet. For I have given you an example, that you should do as I have done to you." (John 13:12–15)

Our natural inclination is to be served, not to serve others. Even Jesus' disciples wrestled with an entitlement mentality. James and John's desire to sit in authority prompted Jesus' clear call for us to be servants as well.

But Jesus called them to Himself and said to them, "You know that those who are considered rulers over the Gentiles lord it over them, and their great ones exercise authority over them. Yet it shall not be so among you; but whoever desires to become great among you shall be your servant. And whoever of you desires to be first shall be slave of all. For even the Son of Man did not come to be served, but to serve, and to give His life a ransom for many." (Mark 10:42–45)

Every Christ follower should heed Jesus' instruction to become a "servant" and "slave of all." Just as Jesus washed the disciples' feet, Christians are to do the same for a hurting world that is dying to see authentic examples of a loving Savior! In the end Christians must understand that unbelievers will not accept what we say about Christ until they first see the truth manifested in our lives. We are implored by the biblical example to wrap our faith in the flesh of daily living.

A Humble Pastor

I have had many influential leaders and mentors in my life, but few had the lasting impression of a humble pastor named Milton Worthington. It is impossible to overestimate his impact on a young boy considering the call of ministry.

Such was the case at a weekend youth retreat when I was 13 years old. After finishing the morning Bible study and observing the Lord's Supper, I was horrified when the leaders pulled out several towels and water basins. Having never observed foot washing before, I recall looking around hoping to use a bathroom break as an escape. Pastor Worthington walked over and kindly asked, "David, have you ever participated in washing feet?" I am sure he could tell that I was frightened when I responded, "No sir." He then asked if he could teach me.

He gently removed my shoes and socks. Then he tenderly splashed water on my feet and washed them. After that he rinsed my feet and dried them with a towel.

As this humble pastor washed my feet, it was as if Christ sat in front of me, showing me what I must become in order to follow Him. In this pastor I saw no pride or self-absorbed desires, just compassion and surrender. The impact of the experience has never escaped me!

An Agnostic

While I was in college, a young man named Steve began attending a weekly prayer group in our dorm. When asked about his faith, he quickly responded that he was an agnostic in search of the truth.

After several weeks spent building a relationship, Steve was invited to stay after one of the meetings to discuss his questions related to Christianity. He seemed intrigued and even stated that he wanted to "believe," but he "just couldn't *see* it." At that point one of the coworkers in the prayer group stood up and quickly left the room, only to return a few minutes later with towels and a basin of water. After setting the basin at my feet, he turned to Steve and said, "If you can't see what faith in Christ is all about, we will show you." He proceeded to wash my feet, allowing me to return the privilege. Afterward, we prayed and sang a few worship songs. It was evident that the Holy Spirit was present.

Steve later explained that when he returned to his dorm room that evening, he was confused about what he believed and vowed never to return to the prayer group. However, this radically changed early the next morning. After lying in bed from midnight until about 3:30 a.m., desperately trying to forget what he had "seen and heard" (see Acts 4:18–20), all he could think about was Christ and especially the humble demonstration of washing feet. After hours of feeling God's conviction for sin and being unable to rest, he slipped to his knees and told Christ, "If You are there and if You are as real as I saw and experienced tonight, I need You, Lord Jesus, to save me. I surrender everything. . . . Please come into my life!"

Steve was saved. His life was radically changed through the power of genuine faith as demonstrated through washing feet. We call this biblical approach "servant evangelism."

The Power of Servant Evangelism

Servant evangelism is a combination of simple acts of kindness *and* intentional sharing of the gospel. Servant evangelism involves intentionally sharing Christ by putting love in action.

1. Servant Evangelism Opens the Door to Share the Gospel

Practicing simple acts of kindness with an *intentional* aim of sharing Christ wonderfully opens the door for the greatest act of kindness a Christian can give: sharing the gospel. Servant evangelism is intentionally evangelistic. However, it never coerces in a manipulative or negative sense.

When doing an act of kindness for a nonbeliever, the Christian witness can say, "I am doing this to show the love of Jesus in a practical way." Often people ask, "Why are you doing this?" Then, as the Holy Spirit opens the door, the Christian can briefly share a testimony and possibly the facts of the gospel. If the other person is not open for discussion, the witness goes no further except possibly to offer Christian literature or prayer.

I have found that servant evangelism leads to a full presentation of Christ much more often than if the concept of service is ignored. When simple acts of kindness are coupled with an intentional and prayerful attempt to share the gospel, it powerfully enables the Holy Spirit to convict and to draw people to Himself.

2. Servant Evangelism Is Low-Risk Evangelism

It provides an entry-level way to involve everyone in the ministry of outreach. One does not need unusual communication skills, an extroverted personality, a slick sales pitch, or multiple hours of training to participate in servant evangelism. This approach redirects one's focus away from selfish inhibition and fear onto those being served.

While some people are terrified to witness verbally, they can wash cars, hand out lightbulbs, give away balloons or popsicles, mow yards, or rake leaves. In doing so, shy people can learn to be more bold and intentional with their faith.

3. Servant Evangelism Is Effective at Reaching People in Today's Culture

Servant evangelism is easily adaptable. In a post-Christian culture, it offers a demonstration of the gospel coupled with an explanation of salvation. Too many people have rejected Jesus but not because they do not know *of* Him. They have rejected a caricature of Jesus. For some, their concept of Christianity needs to be changed. Calvin Miller, retired homiletics professor at Beeson Divinity School, Birmingham, Alabama, has argued for the need of a "sensory apologetic,"[3] a living, breathing argument for truth about God. Servant evangelism addresses this need to a skeptical world.

4. Servant Evangelism Provides the Opportunity for Personal Evangelism in a Natural Mode of Fellowship and Community

You are not alone! In many cases the church has become way too individualistic. While evangelizing on an individual basis is biblical and appropriate, the strength of the church as believers serve together is an example of authentic community and fellowship. These opportunities are ripe for mentoring and teaching.

One of the most unique qualities of servant evangelism is the numerous opportunities for a large group of church members in such service projects as car washes, offering sodas at a park, raking leaves, shoveling snow, and so on.

The body of Christ can be on mission "learning" together as they serve the community.

Timid or inexperienced witnesses can learn to share their faith by watching more experienced witnesses. As the old saying goes, "Evangelism is more caught than taught."

5. Servant Evangelism Is Fun!

Nothing is more rewarding and fun than serving others. This is especially true when Christians choose to fellowship and serve as they seek opportunities to point people to Christ. There is no need to feel guilty; it is OK to have fun and serve Christ at the same time!

6. Servant Evangelism Creates a Lifestyle That Permeates Every Aspect of a Christian's Life

Once you have learned the mind-set of service, you will find that you can share Christ anywhere, anytime, 24-7. You can do it at work, school, in your neighborhood, or at a sporting event. The key is to be intentional.

7. Servant Evangelism Exemplifies the Ministry Model and Passion of Christ

Effective servant evangelists have adopted what is called the "Philippians 2 Attitude."[4] In Philippians 2, we are told to take on the humble servant attitude of Jesus.

> Let this mind be in you which was also in Christ Jesus, who, being in the form of God, did not consider it robbery to be equal with God, but made Himself of no reputation, taking the form of a bondservant, and coming in the likeness of men. And being found in appearance as a man, He humbled Himself and became obedient to the point of death, even the death of the cross. (Phil 2:5–8)

— Evangelism Is . . . —

1. Washing feet.
2. Love in action.
3. Humbly serving and intentionally sharing.
4. Communicating the nature and message of Christ.
5. As much being as it is doing. It is both!

— Key Verse —

*"For even the Son of Man did not come to be served,
but to serve, and to give His life as a ransom for many."
(Mark 10:45)*

— Good Quotes —

*Kind words can be short and easy to speak
but their echoes are truly endless.*

—Mother Teresa[5]

*The basic idea behind servant evangelism projects is
very simple. It is not difficult to begin loving people in
practical ways. We need to avoid the human tendency
to make things overly complicated.*

—Steve Sjogren[6]

*If believing the way they duz makes them
the way they iz . . . it bards looking into.*

—From *Loves Enduring Promise* on the
Hallmark Channel

Where Do You Go from Here?

For more helpful information including hundreds of servant evangelism ideas, numerous examples of outreach cards, and lots of good online links, refer to www.ServantEvangelism.com. The site is updated and monitored frequently by Steve Sjogren. As a struggling church planter in the 1980s, he coined the phrase "servant evangelism."

Notes

1. Taken from *Safely Home* by Randy Alcorn. Copyright © 2001 by Tyndale House. Used by permission of Tyndale House Publishers, Inc. All rights reserved, 273–74.

2. Ibid., 276–77.

3. A. Reid and D. Wheeler, *Servanthood Evangelism* (Alpharetta, GA: North American Mission Board, 1999), 14.

4. S. Sjogren, Evangelism Conference, May 16, 1995, Vineyard Community Church, Cincinnati, OH.

5. S. Sjogren, *Conspiracy of Kindness* (Ventura, CA: Regal Books, 2003), 15.

6. Ibid., 129.

19

Spiritual Warfare

Dave Earley

I understood that evangelism involves spiritual war, but I am not sure how deeply I believed it. One day that all changed.

When Cathy and I and a team of young adults moved to Columbus, Ohio, to plant a new church, we started with 12 people and saw it grow in just a few years to several hundred who met with us each Sunday to worship. Best of all, we were reaching lost people with the gospel of Jesus Christ. All was going so well. Then it happened.

I woke up on a Tuesday morning in intense pain—sharp, stinging pain. I got out of bed and looked down at my arm. Every painful area was marked with an angry red welt. My legs and back were worse with burning red welts everywhere.

I went to my doctor who was stunned.

"Twenty-two!" the doctor exclaimed shaking his head. "Twenty-two boils."

"I have only had one boil in my life," I said. "How could I get 22 at the same time?"

He proceeded to quiz me on everywhere I had been recently, everything I had done, and everything I had eaten. He sighed, shaking his head. (I don't like it when doctors shake their heads.)

"I have never seen anything like it . . . so many boils coming so fast," he muttered. "I have never read anything like it . . . except in the book of Job." The light of insight flashed in his eyes. "This is a long shot, but it is worth asking. What are you preaching on Sunday?" (My doctor is a believer.)

"Spiritual warfare," I said. "I am preaching on the devil and demons."

"Bingo!" he said. "This can only be spiritual warfare."

Then he said words I did not want to hear. "If the boils are not gone by Friday, I will have to use a razor blade and lance each one."

The coming of the boils and the visit to the doctor had happened on a Tuesday. I went home from the doctor and told Cathy what he had said. She called some of our prayer warriors and asked them to pray for a miracle.

Friday morning I was back at the doctor's. "Gone," he muttered shaking his head. "All gone. Never seen anything like it. Boils don't come and go that quickly. Your people must have done some strong praying on your behalf."

In the early years of starting our church, I was ignorant of the enemy's schemes, and the enemy took advantage of that. Every Saturday evening was miserable at my house, especially if we expected a big crowd of lost people on Sunday morning. The kids would be healthy all week but wake up vomiting on Saturday night. Or they would be well behaved all week but act rotten on Saturday night. Or Cathy and I would get along great all week but get in an argument over some trivial little thing on Saturday night. Plus almost every Saturday night at about 12:30 a.m., right after we had fallen asleep, the phone would ring. It would either be a wrong number or a drunk.

After a few years of this, I began to see a pattern. (I am a little slow.) So after the boils incident I swallowed my pride, and that Sunday night in church I explained to our people what was going on. Then I asked them to pray for me especially on Saturday nights.

The next Saturday night was heaven in my home. The kids were happy and healthy. Cathy and I got along wonderfully. The phone did not ring. I slept like a baby. That Sunday I preached better than ever. Lost people gave their lives to Christ.

Effective evangelism is a spiritual battle.

We Were the Battleground

As an infinite, omnipotent, omniscient, eternal being, God is a more formidable foe than can be imagined. As a warrior God is invincible. Yet surprisingly, God has a chosen "limitation" in this battle. He loves people. The only way to get at God is to attack those whom He loves, people. People are His weakness. Of course, Satan knows this, so Satan attacks people. Therefore, when it comes to spiritual warfare, we are the battleground.

Spiritual warfare begins at birth. At the time everyone on planet Earth is born, they have an enemy whose goal is to keep them from God. Regarding the plan of Satan, Paul wrote, "The god of this age has blinded the minds of unbelievers, so that they cannot see the light of the gospel of the glory of Christ, who is the image of God" (2 Cor 4:4 NIV).

Why Did You Never Tell Me This Before?

When I gave my life to God in high school, I naturally told my friends about it. One of my friends grew up in a home where his mother was Catholic and his father was Jewish. His parents chose to raise him as neither. Over my last couple of years in high school, I shared the gospel with him more than a dozen times. He did not respond.

After high school we went to different colleges. We got together when we both were home during Christmas break after our first semester.

"I want to tell you," he said with a big smile. "The guys across the hall in my dorm are born-again Christians like you. A few weeks ago they told me about Jesus, and I was born again," he said.

"That's great!" I said. "Welcome to the family."

"But there is something that has been bothering me," he continued. "Can I ask you a question?"

"Sure," I said. "What?"

"How come you never told me how to be saved?"

"What?" I said. "You have to be kidding. I shared the gospel with you a dozen times."

"Really?" he asked. "I don't remember ever hearing it."

What had happened? The enemy was trying to keep him from hearing. Therefore, he was blinding my friend's "spiritual eyes" from "seeing" the gospel and blocking his "spiritual ears" from "hearing" it. Effective evangelism is a spiritual battle.

We Are the Battleground

If you think that once a person gives his or her life to Jesus the battle is over, you are mistaken. In some ways it only intensifies. Once people are saved, the enemy works against them to keep them from telling others how to be free. The war continues.

For example, the apostle Paul had hoped to visit the Thessalonians in order to continue helping them mature in the Lord, in ministry, and in mission. Yet the enemy attacked. "Therefore we wanted to come to you—even I, Paul, time and again—but Satan hindered us" (1 Thess 2:18).

In Ephesians 6, Paul gave the most detailed explanation of spiritual warfare found in the Bible:

> Finally, my brethren, be strong in the Lord and in the power of His might. Put on the whole armor of God, that you may be able to stand against the wiles of the devil. For we do not wrestle against flesh and blood, but against principalities, against powers, against the rulers of the darkness of this age, against spiritual hosts of wickedness in the heavenly places. Therefore take up the whole armor of God that you may be able to withstand in the evil day, and having done all, to stand. (Eph 6:10–13)

In this passage Paul tells us that the nature of the war is not primarily physical, political, financial, legal, or educational. It is spiritual.

He also tells us that the proximity of the war is that it is here and now. It is not something involving someone else far away or long ago. It involves us today. It is *our* struggle.

Further in chapter 6, Paul tells us that the purpose of the war is to advance or stop the preaching of the gospel (vv. 19–20). If Paul had not given his life to take the gospel to people far from God, the enemy would have had no reason to attack him.

We also see that the intensity of the war is a life-or-death battle. The word "wrestle" used in verse 12 denotes "hand-to-hand combat to the death" in the original language. Paul wrote these words from a jail cell where he was imprisoned because of this warfare (see Eph 6:20) and eventually executed as a result of it!

The Devil Hates You

The Devil is a fallen angel who lives to exalt himself by opposing God. He opposes God by doing everything in his power to keep people out of the kingdom of God and cause Christians to become ineffective (Isa 14:12–17; Ezek 28:11–19; Rev 12:4,9; Matt 25:41; Eph 6:12; Mark 3:22; John 14:30; 16:12; Eph 2:2; 2 Cor 4:4; Rev 20:10).

The Devices of the Devil

In Eph 6:11, Paul refers to "the wiles of the devil." Satan uses several strategies to render Christians less effective at evangelism. In 2 Cor 2:11 Paul states that we can keep the enemy from having an advantage over us if we are not ignorant of his devices. What are some of those devices?

1. Denunciation/Accusation/Condemnation (1 Pet 5:8; Zech 3:1; Rev 12:10; Job 1:9–11)

Satan continually casts condemnation at us. When it comes to doing evangelism, he whispers in our ears such accusations as:

- You can't do it.
- No one will listen to you.
- You don't know what you are talking about.
- God won't use you.
- You aren't good enough to share your faith.

2. Defilement (1 Thess 3:5; Matt 4:1–11; Gen 3:1–6)

Satan is the original tempter. He strives to tempt us into sinning so we will feel too guilty to share the gospel with anyone else.

3. Deception (John 8:44)

The enemy will lie to us constantly with the goal of putting us in bondage and causing us to be inactive in sharing the gospel. When it comes to evangelism, he tells us such lies as:

- Those people don't need God.
- Why tell them? It won't make a difference anyway.
- It's not your job to win the world for Christ.
- There is plenty of time to do evangelism later.
- If you tell them about Jesus, they will never talk to you again.
- People will think you are some religious nut.

4. Distraction (Mark 8:31–33)

The enemy is content with our doing almost anything other than evangelism. He will persistently attempt to get our focus on noneternal things.

The Defeat of the Devil

Jesus Is Victorious

The war is real, but so is the victory available in Christ. Paul writes that followers of Jesus are supervictorious in Christ: "Yet in all these things we are more than conquerors through Him who loved us. For I am persuaded that neither death nor life, nor angels nor principalities nor powers, nor things present nor things to come, nor height nor depth, nor any other created thing, shall be able to separate us from the love of God which is in Christ Jesus our Lord" (Rom 8:37–39).

Prayer Is Powerful

The apostle Peter was a powerful evangelist. Three thousand people were saved as a result of his first sermon (Acts 2). He personally understood the spiritual battle that goes with aggressive evangelism. He was often arrested (Acts 4) and imprisoned (Acts 5, 12). He saw his church in Jerusalem scattered around the world through persecution (1 Pet 1:1).

It would have been easy for the enemy to intimidate him and eat him up with anxiety. But Peter understood that you fight a spiritual battle on your knees (Acts 1:12–14; 3:1; 6:4). He witnessed his own deliverance as the result of a prayer meeting (Acts 12:1–12). At the end of his letter to his scattered flock, Peter gave them a powerful key to winning against the attacks of the adversary—prayer: "Therefore humble yourselves under the mighty hand of God, that He may exalt you in due time, casting all your care upon Him, for He cares for you. Be sober, be vigilant; because your adversary the devil walks about like a roaring lion, seeking whom he may devour" (1 Pet 5:6–8).

The Word of God Gives Us Power to Overcome

The apostle John was a frontline warrior in spiritual warfare. His saw his brother martyred for his faith (Acts 12:1–2). In fact, when John wrote his letters, he was living in exile on a forsaken island. John keenly understood the power of the Word of God to defeat the enemy. "I have written to you, young men, because you are strong, and the word of God abides in you, and you have overcome the wicked one" (1 John 2:14).

The War Can Be Won Today!

On a Wednesday night several years ago, I had just walked in the door from a small-group meeting when the phone rang. It was Pastor Vik of the Columbus

Baptist Temple. He said, "I am sorry to bother you, but we have a problem, and we think you can help us."

"What is the problem?"

"It's the mother of a lady who is a member of our church. She's at Doctors' Hospital North."

"What's wrong with her?"

"Well," he paused, "I think she is demon possessed."

"How do you know?"

"She is hearing voices, and, uh, other stuff."

"What other stuff?"

"Can you help us?"

"I'll try."

"Good. We're just down the street on the phone. I'll pick you up in a minute."

We spent about an hour with the lady. We tried to share the gospel with her. No response. Finally I said, "Let's try something." I looked at her and said, "Repeat after me: Jesus is Lord, and I am washed in the blood of Jesus."

It worked. The countenance of this sweet little grandma totally changed. Then she curled back her lips and snarled at me. I said, "Repeat after me: the blood of Jesus cleanses me of all unrighteousness."

She growled.

For the next half hour we were talking with a male-voiced demon who was speaking through her. I could not get the demon to let go and could not get her to break through to God.

Finally we were exhausted, and the hospital staff was uneasy.

I was going to close our time in prayer. I raised my hand up in front of me and happened to have my Bible in my hand. Immediately she tightened up, and the demon voice said, "Get that knife out of here."

I stopped and looked around and said, "What knife?"

"That knife in your hand. There are knives all over this room."

"There are no knives here. How many knives do you see?"

"Four . . . no . . . five knives. Get those five knives out of here."

Then it hit me. I looked around. Pastor Vik had a Bible, the associate pastor had a Bible, the woman's daughter had a Bible, the woman's son-in-law had a Bible, and I had a Bible—five Bibles. I immediately thought of Eph 6:17 where we are commanded to "take . . . the sword of the Spirit, which is the word of God." The demon in the woman saw our Bibles as knives that threatened him.

No Doubt

If I ever doubted the power of the Word of God or that the Bible is the Word of God, I have never doubted since that moment. That woman sitting in the hospital bed with a man's voice crying out through her, "Get those knives out of here!" was blind! There was absolutely no human way she knew I had a Bible in my hand and that there were five Bibles in that room.

If I ever doubted the reality of demons and the importance of spiritual warfare, I have never doubted since then. Effective evangelism is spiritual warfare!

The Rest of the Story

Later that night the woman's daughter felt prompted of God to attempt one more time to win her mother to Christ. As they talked, the Lord worked, and the woman let go of the lie the enemy was using to hold her captive, and she got saved! The demon had to leave. The woman was no longer delusional and suicidal. Her doctor released her to go home the next day. That Sunday the woman attended Pastor Vik's church with her daughter and son-in-law. She never missed a Sunday for the next few years, until she went to heaven a few years ago.

⁓ Evangelism Is . . . ⁓

1. Evangelism is spiritual warfare.
2. Evangelism is often a battle fought on our knees.

⁓ Key Verse ⁓

For we do not wrestle against flesh and blood, but against principalities, against powers, against the rulers of the darkness of this age, against spiritual hosts of wickedness in the heavenly places. (Eph 6:12)

⁓ Good Quotes ⁓

Three eternal truths: things are not what they seem, the world is at war, and each of us has a crucial role to play. . . . The story of your life is the story of a long and brutal assault on your heart by the one who knows what you could be and fears it.

—JOHN ELDREDGE[1]

*I pray that when I die, all of hell will rejoice that
I am no longer in the fight.*

—C. T. STUDD[2]

*We are spiritual pacifists, non-militants, conscientious
objectors in this battle-to-the-death with principalities
and powers in high places. . . . We are "sideliners"—
coaching and criticizing the real wrestlers while content
to sit by and leave the enemies of God unchallenged.
The world cannot hate us, we are too much like its own.
Oh that God would make us dangerous!*

—JIM ELLIOT[3]

Notes

1. J. Eldredge, *Waking the Dead: The Glory of a Heart Fully Alive* (Nashville, TN: Thomas Nelson Publishers, 2003); and with Stasi Eldredge, *Captivating* (Nashville, TN: Thomas Nelson Publishers, 2005), 115.

2. C. T. Studd, quoted in Norman P. Grubb, *C. T. Studd: Cricketeer and Pioneer* (Fort Washington, PA: Christian Literature Crusade, 1985), 13.

3. J. Elliot, martyred missionary, at the age of 21, recorded in his journal November 28, 1948; online at http://www.seel.us/christian/Quotes-from-Jim-Eliot.htm; originally published by Elisabeth Elliot, *Shadow of the Almighty: The Life and Testament of Jim Elliot* (Grand Rapids, MI: Hendrickson Publishers, 2008).

20

Praying Prodigals Home

Dave Earley

It is possible to pray prodigal loved ones back home to God. Let me tell you our story.

My sister Carol fell in love with a young man named Don. She asked our pastor at the time if they could be married in our home church, but he refused. Our pastor felt that joining Carol, a Baptist, with Don, a Catholic, would create an unequal union (1 Cor 6:14). This made Carol bitter, and she dropped out of church.

A few years later the same pastor married his own son, a Baptist, to a Catholic girl in our church. This made my mom bitter, and she became a person who seemed barely to tolerate God. She attended church only on Sunday mornings, sat in the back, came late, and left early. I don't ever recall seeing her read her Bible during that time. I never heard her pray. She never spoke about spiritual things. In fact, when I told her I thought God was calling me to be a pastor, her reply was, "Oh, no. Not that."

Concerned for both of them, I put both of them on my daily prayer list. After over three years of daily calling my mom's name out to God, something happened. My wife Cathy and I were meeting my parents at a restaurant. My mom walked in with a new countenance. Her hard, heavily clouded-over expression was replaced with a bright, sunny smile. During the meal I was shocked to hear my ultraquiet mom speak with the waitress about her relationship with Christ. As we walked to the parking lot, my mother shocked me by putting gospel pamphlets on car windshields. My mom had turned into a spiritual fanatic!

"Mom," I asked, "what on earth has happened to you?"

She told us that she had been invited to a small-group women's Bible study. There she learned to let go of her bitterness and yield everything to God. She also learned to pray for my sister. When my mom came back to God, my dad stepped up his relationship with God. Soon we were all praying regularly for Carol.

Things Got Worse

Have you ever prayed for something or someone and things got worse before they got better? That's what happened with my sister. We had prayed for her consistently for nearly a decade when one day, out of the blue, she called a family meeting. She and Don sat on one side of the table; Mom, Dad, Cathy, and I sat on the other.

"From now on," Carol said, "I do not want to be considered part of this family."

We were dumbfounded to hear my sister tell us she disowned us as her family.

The next thing we knew, she and Don got up and left. Shortly after that, Carol left Don and moved to another state.

Maybe you are more spiritual than I am, but I have to admit that I quit praying for her because it did not seem to be working. Fortunately, Mom and Dad did not quit. Every day they called Carol's name out to God.

We did not see or hear from her for years. One day my youngest son, Luke, was looking at an old family photo album. He pointed to a picture of lady and asked, "Daddy, who is that lady with you and Mommy?"

It was Carol. He had never seen her.

A Christmas Surprise

One Christmas Eve I got up to lead one of several Christmas Eve services at our church, looked out in the audience, and was shocked by what I saw. About halfway back, on the middle aisle sat Carol, Don, and their two daughters. We spoke with them after the service and were surprised to find that they had recently gotten back together and had moved from a town 75 miles away to a town 15 minutes away.

Carol began to attend some of our family events and even began to come to our church about once a month. One Saturday while we watched my boys at a sporting event, she surprised me again.

"I think I would join your church," she stated, "except for three things."

After regaining my composure, I asked, "What are the three things?"

"I think abortion is all right; I think homosexuality is OK; and I hate Jerry Falwell."

I chuckled at her third excuse, but I could see that she was serious. "Well," I started, "you have been to our church enough times now to know that the big issue is Jesus Christ. What we focus on is a person's relationship with Jesus, not abortion, homosexuality, or Jerry Falwell. We believe that once you have a real relationship with Him, you can read the Bible and see what He thinks about abortion, homosexuality, or Jerry Falwell."

That seemed to satisfy her, and she began to come to church every Sunday morning.

"It Is Good to Be Home"

A few months later I walked up on the platform to lead a Sunday evening celebration of the Lord's table. When I looked out into the audience, I was shocked to see my sister sitting about halfway back on the middle aisle. We had an amazing time with the Lord that night as we seriously considered His death, burial, and resurrection for our sins. We confessed our sins and praised His name.

After the service I was walking down the aisle to go into the lobby to meet people. Carol grabbed me as I approached her and gave me a bear hug. I noticed tears on her face as she leaned in to whisper into my ear. I will never forget what she said: "It is good to be home," she said. "It has been 30 years since I celebrated the Lord's table, and it is so good finally to be home."

Like Mother like Daughter

A few years later my mom went to heaven. The last few years of her life, she had become a mighty prayer warrior. Less than five feet tall and weighing less than a hundred pounds, she prayed with a simple, direct faith that got amazing results. Now she was gone. I remember bemoaning the fact that my best prayer partner was no longer with us. I wondered who would ever take her place.

About a week later we had a family get-together at my sister's house. Exactly as my mom had done, she made us all grab hands and led us in a prayer. It was eerily familiar. She prayed with simple, direct faith exactly like Mom had done.

Beyond that, Carol has become a spiritual fireball in her own right. She has traveled the world on mission trips. She went from being in a small-group Bible study to leading one to now coaching 15 women's Bible study leaders.

I love to tell her story. It reminds us that it is possible to pray prodigal loved ones home.

The Rest of the Story

I was speaking at a church one Friday night, and I concluded the message by telling how prayer had brought Mom and Carol home to God. When I gave an opportunity for people to come and pray for prodigal loved ones, many responded. One couple especially caught my attention because they seemed especially broken as they wept at the prayer altar.

After the service they grabbed me and told me about their daughter, Ashley. Nineteen-year-old Ashley had run away from home six weeks earlier, and they did not know where she was. We prayed a special prayer for God to touch Ashley's heart and call her home. I looked at my watch and prayed, "Lord, we do not know where Ashley is, but You do. Right now, at 8:33 p.m., we ask that You speak to her heart. Make her hungry for home. Bring her to her senses and call her home to You."

They thanked me and told they would not be able to come back the next night because of a prior commitment but that they would be back on Sunday. I forgot about it, but God did not.

The next night as I was speaking, I noticed a young lady I had not seen the night before. I did not think anymore about it. After the service I was standing in the lobby, and that young lady ran up to me and hugged me.

Taken aback by her forwardness, I asked, "Who are you?"

"I'm Ashley," she said. "Last night at 8:33 p.m., I had an overwhelming longing to go home. I went home to Mom and Dad. Tonight I came home to God."

Don't Quit

Persistent, faith-based intercession produces results. No one symbolizes this better than George Muller. He was preaching in 1884 and testified that 40 years prior, in 1844, five individuals were laid upon his heart; and he began to intercede for them to come to Christ.

Eighteen months passed before one of them was converted. He prayed on for five years more, and another was converted. He continued to pray.

At the end of more than 12 years, the third was converted.

During his message given in 1884, Muller stated that he had continued to pray for the other two without missing a single day, but they were not yet converted. But he was encouraged that the answer would come.[1] In fact Muller said, "They are not converted yet, but they will be."[2]

Twelve years later, at his death, after interceding for them daily for a total of 52 years, they still were not yet converted. But one came to Christ at Muller's funeral and the other shortly thereafter![3] Resilient, persistent intercession makes a difference. It is possible to pray prodigals home to God.

Another Prodigal Comes Home

One of the greatest stories ever told is the narrative Jesus gave of the prodigal son. You know the tale of the young man who asked for his inheritance prematurely, then ran off and wasted it in wild living. (The word *prodigal* comes from the word for "wasted.") Finally he came to his senses and went home to his father's house. This story is a picture of the emptiness of running from God. It tells of the wayward coming home to God.

I especially love the statement Jesus made revealing the awesome love of the father. He was watching, waiting, and willing for his prodigal child to come home. "But while he was still a long way off, his father saw him and was filled with compassion for him; he ran to his son, threw his arms around him and kissed him" (Luke 15:20 NIV).

Prodigals do come home in response to prayer. Maybe you have loved ones who have wandered far from home. Luke 15 gives a good guide for praying for them.

Lord please:

- Bring them to a place of famine and need (Luke 15:14).
- Create within them holy hunger and homesickness (15:16–17).
- Cause them to come to their senses (15:17).
- Draw them home (15:18).
- Give them the gift of repentance (15:18–21).
- Give us welcoming grace (15:20).

More Prodigals Come Home

When I was a senior at Liberty University, I was a resident assistant giving leadership to dorm 8. I had an amazing group of prayer leaders. They began a nightly prayer meeting for guys on our hall who were not walking with God.

In those days the rule was that we were all to be in our rooms at 11:15 p.m. I had to check the rooms. A group of guys met to pray every night during room checks while I talked to the rest of the guys about their walk with God. The guys in room 22 were set hard against God and, as a result, against me.

One Saturday night they were all to be in their rooms because of an accumulation of discipline and/or academic breaches. I went to check their room, and they wouldn't let me in. In those days students were not allowed to play music other than Christian music in their dorm rooms. But the guys in room 22 were playing loudly some sort of vulgar, heavy-metal music. Finally they let me in, and we had a chat. The whole time I was talking with two of them, I thought the third was asleep. During this time the prayer leaders were heavy in their prayer meeting.

I cannot remember what I said, but God's presence came down in that room that night. The next thing I knew the guy I thought was asleep rolled out of bed, got on his knees, and said, "I don't know about you, but I'm tired of living like this. I want to get right with God." Then he grabbed me and pulled me down next to him.

Soon the other two joined us, and sinners turned from the error of their ways that night. After we were done, they started to hand me their stash—drugs, vulgar music tapes, and dirty books. The rest of the story is that the last time I heard from them, all three of those guys had become pastors.

Another Guide for Praying for the Lost and Backslidden

Sometimes I find it helpful to have an outline to guide me as I pray for others. Below is a suggested outline for praying for those who need Christ.

1. Lord, pour out Your Spirit upon (name of person) and:
2. Convict him/her of his/her sin, lack of righteousness, and deserved judgment (John 16:8).
3. Open their hearts (Acts 16:14).
4. Reveal to him/her who You are and what Christ has done for him/her.
5. Open the eyes of his/her understanding (Eph 1:18) and remove his/her spiritual blindness (2 Cor 4:4). Let there be light!
6. Draw him/her to Yourself in a powerful fashion (John 6:44).

7. Bind Satan from him/her. Keep Satan from stealing Your Word from his/her heart (Matt 12:19).
8. May Your grace and mercy surround him/her.
9. Grant him/her the gift of repentance (2 Tim 2:24–26).
10. Help me to be willing and anxious to be the means by which You save and deliver him/her. Lord, show me how to lead him/her to Christ.
11. Send people across his/her path to bring him/her a witness of Christ.[4]

— Evangelism Is . . . —

1. Praying prodigals home to God.
2. Continuing to pray even when things get worse.
3. Praying in faith that God is working even as we are praying.

— Key Verse —

My brothers, if one of you should wander from the truth and someone should bring him back, remember this: Whoever turns a sinner from the error of his way will save him from death and cover over a multitude of sins. (Jas 5:19–20 NIV)

— Good Quote —

It is possible to move men through God by prayer alone.

—HUDSON TAYLOR[5]

Notes

1. D. L. Moody, *Prevailing Prayer* (Chicago, IL: Moody Press, 1987), 100–101.
2. B. Miller, *George Muller: Man of Faith and Miracles* (Minneapolis, MN: Bethany House, 1943), 146.
3. Ibid., 146.
4. Adapted from G. Frizzell, *How to Develop a Powerful Prayer Life* (Memphis, TN: Master Design Ministries, 1999), 83.
5. H. Taylor as quoted in J. O. Sanders, *Spiritual Leadership* (Chicago, IL: Moody, 1974), 82.

21

Being Yourself

Dave Earley

D avid is an active and aggressive evangelist. He loves people and is determined to share his faith and see that no one goes to hell. He does not beat around the bush but cuts right to the heart of an issue or argument.

Ingrid is a fun-loving, talkative, persuasive, energetic people person. She seemingly has never met a stranger and has no problem sharing the gospel with people she has never met. Last week in the mall, she led to Christ two women she had never met before.

Steve is a servant. People say that he will give you the shirt off his back. He devotes every Saturday morning to cutting the grass of the elderly people in his neighborhood. Eventually he will ask them if he can pray for them. A month or two later he will share the gospel with them. After months of patiently mowing a widow's yard, he will finally be able to share Christ with her.

Curt likes to study apologetics, cults, and world religions. He has been known to get into interesting discussions at the local bookstore and enjoys witnessing over the Internet to spiritual seekers, agnostics, and atheists.

Which one is right? Which one is most like you?

You've Got Personality

Everyone is different. God has given each of us unique personalities. Of the four people mentioned above, as long as each one shares the gospel as part of his or her lifestyle, they all are right. They have different personalities, and, as a result, the way they share the gospel is somewhat different, but all are effective evangelists.

Christians most effective in evangelism learn to evangelize according to their personality *and* the personality of their listener. One thing that gives evangelism a bad name is the notion that there is only one right way to do it. That is not true. The right way is to share the gospel in a manner that fits your personality and that of the person you are trying to reach.

Four Common Personality Types

Perhaps the most common way of discussing and understanding common personalities is through the lens of four personality types. As best we can tell, this way of understanding personality goes back before the time of Christ to a man named Hippocrates.

Hippocrates was an ancient Greek physician (c. 460–c. 370 BC) who has been referred to as the "father of medicine." He has been credited as the author of the Hippocratic Oath, a document on the ethics of medical practice. Hippocrates believed certain human behaviors could be understood and related to the classical elements of air, water, earth, and fire. These are commonly referred to as the four temperaments: sanguine, phlegmatic, melancholic, and choleric, respectively.

As time progressed, numerous other paradigms were devised, which measured not only temperament but also various individual aspects of personality and behavior. Probably the most commonly used is called DISC. DISC is a four-quadrant behavioral model based on the work of William Moulton Marston, PhD (1893–1947), who examined the behavior of individuals in their environment or within a specific situation.[1] DISC looks at behavioral styles and behavioral preferences. D stands for Dominance, I for Influence, S for Steadiness, and C for Conscientiousness. The four people mentioned earlier in this chapter relate to the way the four personality types would do evangelism. David is a D. Ingrid is an I. Steve is an S. And Curt is a C.

What Is Your Personality Type?

Look over the charts below. Put a check by the characteristics that are most true of you. Try to pick only one per row. When you are finished, add up each column. Are you more of a D, I, S, or C?

D	I	S	C
Dominance	Influence	Steadiness	Conscientious-ness
Aggressive	Talkative	Security	Cautiousness
Willpower	Emotional	Unemotional	Perfectionist
Control and power	People and social situations	Patience and persistence	Rules and structure
Assertiveness	Communication	Thoughtfulness	Organization
Extroverted	Extroverted	Introverted	Introverted
Paul	Peter	Abraham	Moses
Lion	Otter	Golden Retriever	Beaver
Bear	Monkey	Dolphin	Owl
Intimidator	Poor Me	Aloof	Interrogator
Salsa	Swing Dance	Waltz	Tango
Total:	Total:	Total:	Total:

Put a check by every characteristic that is usually true regarding your personality.

D	I	S	C
Dominant	Expressive	Solid	Analytical
Choleric	Sanguine	Phlegmatic	Melancholy
Direct	Spirited	Considerate	Systematic
Powerful	Popular	Peaceful	Perfect
Self-propelled	Spirited	Solid	Systematic
Administrative	Active	Amiable	Analytical
Leader	Expresser	Dependable	Analyst
Production	Connection	Status Quo	Harmony

Dominance	Influencing	Steadiness	Cautiousness/ Compliance
Common Sense	Dynamic	Innovative	Analytic
Total:	Total:	Total:	Total:

Please put a check by the characteristic that is most often true of you.

D	I	S	C
Driver	Expressive	Amiable	Analytic
Guardian	Artisan	Philosopher	Scientist
Motivated	Messy	Casual	Compulsive
Controller	Promoter	Supporter	Analyst
Mastery	Belonging	Generosity	Independence
Achiever	Attached	Altruistic	Autonomous
Power	Significance	Virtue	Competence
Adventurer	Helper	Peacemaker	Asserter
Achiever	Romantic	Observer	Perfectionist
Total:	Total:	Total:	Total:

Now total up the findings from the three charts.

D	I	S	C
Chart 1:	Chart 1:	Chart 1:	Chart 1:
Chart 2:	Chart 2:	Chart 2:	Chart 2:
Chart 3:	Chart 3:	Chart 3:	Chart 3:
Total:	Total:	Total:	Total:

Which column is highest—D, I, S, or C? How has God wired you? What is your primary personality type? How will your primary personality type impact the ways you are most comfortable and effective in doing evangelism?

My wife, Cathy, is a high I. My youngest son, Luke, is mostly a C. My middle son, Andrew, is more of an S. My oldest son, Daniel, is primarily a D. I am a DC. All of us love God. All of us evangelize. All do it a little differently.

You Are Gifted

When you became born again, God took up residence in your life in the person of the Holy Spirit. One of the many benefits of having the Holy Spirit in your life is that He enables you to serve God with greater effectiveness. You have no reason to feel inadequate because the Bible promises that the Holy Spirit will give you dynamic power to be a witness and share the gospel (Acts 1:8). The Holy Spirit not only gives you power to be a witness in general, but He also gives each of us specific spiritual gifts by which we witness. The Bible clearly teaches several simple truths about spiritual gifts.

1. There are a variety of spiritual gifts (1 Cor 12:4–6).
2. Each believer has at least one gift (1 Cor 12:7).
3. Gifts are given by God's choice, not ours (1 Cor 12:11).
4. Gifts are to be honestly evaluated (Rom 12:3).
5. God uses different gifts to diversify His body (Rom 12:4–5).
6. Gifts are to be used (Rom 12:6–8).
7. There are seven primary spiritual gifts (Rom 12:6–8).

   - Prophecy: verbal proclamation of truth
   - Ministry/serving: ability actively to meet the needs of others
   - Teaching: ability to clarify and communicate truth
   - Exhortation: simple, practical spiritual encouragement
   - Giving: imparting earthly possessions to meet needs
   - Leadership: wise use of authority or superintendence; organization
   - Mercy: identifying with people in need

Every healthy Christian should consistently participate in all seven of these activities. Sometimes the right thing to do is to serve. Other times it is to give. On other occasions the best thing to do is to proclaim the truth. At other times we should offer encouragement or identify with someone who is hurting. These spiritual gifts reflect the ways God has wired us to be most comfortable and effective at serving in the church. They represent strengths God has given us. They also reveal how we feel most confident and have the greatest impact in evangelism. Let me explain.

My friend, Paul, has the spiritual gift of prophecy. His preferred way of evangelizing is boldly speaking to strangers on busy street corners. Every Friday night he hits the streets and attempts to engage lost people in conversations where he can proclaim biblical truth. Patti also has the gift of prophecy and uses it to debate atheists and Muslim students at her state university.

Sandy has the gift of servant. She is amazing at fixing meals for people who have been ill or who have family members in the hospital. Sam also has this gift.

Tom is a teacher. He works hard to get his coworkers to join him every day during lunch for a brief time of Bible study. Tim is also a teacher, but he is most comfortable dialoguing with spiritual seekers on chat boards over the Internet.

Elle is an encourager. She is gifted at encouraging lost people to come to church with her. Ernie also is an encourager, but his style is to encourage lost people to take the next step and cross the line of faith.

Grant is a successful businessman and a generous giver. He has personally given the money to build two orphanages in Africa. Jacob and Ashley also have this gift. They save up their money every week so they will have the funds to give and evangelize. Every Sunday they look for single moms who are visiting their church. Then they offer to treat them and their children to a nice lunch afterward. Over lunch they discern the young ladies' spiritual condition and look to share the gospel.

Leah is a leader. She completely organized the five-year-old children's ministry of her church so the teachers and helpers have reached all the children and their families with the gospel.

Marc is skilled at showing mercy. He goes out every Friday night to the homeless camps downtown. He feeds the men and takes them blankets, coats, and firewood in the winter. As a result he has shared the gospel with most of them and has seen several come to Christ.

All of these people do evangelism in different ways in accordance with their God-given spiritual gifts. All are active evangelists, and God has blessed their efforts.

How Has God Gifted You?

The way to discern how God has gifted you is to evaluate your past and present service for Christ. As you read through the above examples, which ones resonated most deeply? What are your strengths? Where has God obviously blessed your efforts? What type of service most appeals to you?

Look carefully through the list of primary gifts given in Romans 12 and circle one or two that would be most true of you.

1. Prophecy: verbal proclamation of truth
2. Ministry/serving: ability actively to meet the needs of others
3. Teaching: ability to clarify and communicate truth
4. Exhortation: simple, practical spiritual encouragement
5. Giving: imparting earthly possessions to meet needs
6. Leadership: wise use of authority or superintendence; organization
7. Mercy: identifying with people in need

You've Got Style

So far we have discussed personality types and spiritual gifts. There also is the matter of style. When you read the New Testament, you will see that different people had different styles when it came to bringing people to Christ.

- Peter was an out-there, up-front type of guy. He was bold and brash and preached to a huge crowd (see Acts 2).
- Andrew was more of a behind-the-scenes, quiet type. He consistently brought people to Jesus (John 1:25–42; 6:5–9; 12:20–22).
- Jesus' friend Mary served. She cooked the meals and cleaned up the messes (Luke 10:38–40).
- Matthew knew a lot of people and threw great parties. He invited sinners for dinner with Jesus (Matt 9:9–10).
- Paul was well educated, extremely intelligent, and an excellent teacher. He lectured in classrooms and synagogues (Acts 13:13–44; 14:1; 17:1–4,10,16–17; 18:4,19).
- The apostle John had a huge heart. He really loved people and repeatedly spoke to them of the love of God (1 John 4:8–11,16,19).
- James, the half brother of Jesus and pastor of the church in Jerusalem, was said to have "camel's knees" because he spent hours on his knees praying for others.[2]

What style is the right style? The one you will use.

Do It!

Everyone is called to evangelize, but too often we get the idea that we have to do it a certain way or not do it all. There is more than one way to share the gospel. The best way is the one that fits your personality, your giftedness, and your style. If you aren't sure which way best fits you, try them all!

Look back over this chapter and answer each of these four questions:

1. What is your primary personality type?
2. What are your primary gifts?
3. What is your favorite ministry style?
4. What will you do with it?

～ Evangelism Is . . . ～

1. Being yourself as you share the gospel.
2. Sharing the gospel in a way that best fits your personality and the person you are trying to reach.
3. Sharing the gospel in accord with your spiritual giftedness.

～ Good Quotes ～

Do you want to be a contagious Christian? Then stop apologizing for your God-given design. Quit trying to deny your individuality. . . . Somewhere in your community, there is probably a seeker who's one step from coming to faith but who needs to come in contact with someone like you—with your personality, your temperament, your passion, and your interests.

—BILL HYBELS AND MARK MITTELBERG[3]

God deliberately shaped and formed you to serve him in a way that makes your ministry unique. . . . God never wastes anything. He would not give you the abilities, interests, talents, gifts, personality, and life experiences unless he intended to use them for his glory.

—RICK WARREN[4]

Rejoice in your God-given temperament and use it for God's purposes.

—REBECCA MANLEY PIPPERT[5]

Notes

1. See W. M. Marston, *Emotions of Normal People* (New York: Harcourt, Brace, 1928).

2. R. Eisenman, *James the Brother of Jesus: The Key to Unlocking the Secrets of Early Christianity and the Dead Sea Scrolls* (New York: Penguin, 1998), 4.

3. B. Hybels and M. Mittelberg, *Becoming a Contagious Christian* (Grand Rapids, MI: Zondervan, 1994), 59.

4. R. Warren, *The Purpose Driven Life* (Grand Rapids, MI: Zondervan, 2002), 235.

5. R. M. Pippert, *Out of the Salt Shaker and Into the World: Evangelism as a Way of Life* (Downers Grove, IL: IVP, 1979), 121–22.

22

Evangelism Is . . .

A Lifestyle

Dave Earley

"H ello, Kim, what can I do for you?" Christie said, surprised to be getting a call from her coworker, Kim, this late at night.

"Yes," Kim said into the phone, "the answer is yes."

"Good," Christie answered, "but what is the question?"

"You invited Nick and me to come to a Bible study thing at your house on Thursday nights," Kim said. "We just had another discussion, and we both want to come tomorrow night. The Bible seems to have the answers that make your marriage to James work, so maybe it can help us."

Nick and Kim had been married only a few years, and they were struggling. Both worked high-pressure jobs. Neither had grown up in church. Both were on their second marriage. Neither wanted to continue their constant fighting over the bills. They loved each other and wanted help.

Fortunately, Kim worked with Christie. Christie lived an authentic Christian life and understood that evangelism is a lifestyle. She had built her worldview on the teachings of the Bible, and as a result she lived Jesus on her job. Christie also knew how prayerfully, patiently, casually, and naturally to work Jesus and the Bible into her lunchtime conversations with Kim. She went out of her way to show interest in Kim and was a patient listener when Kim shared her struggles and joys with Christie. She was careful to make occasions like Christie's birthday and the anniversary of her second year at work real celebrations. After six months of being the recipient of Christie's friendship and lifestyle evangelism, Kim was now ready to begin seriously to investigate Christianity.

After an especially heated argument with Nick, Kim reached out to Christie for help. Kim realized that Christie and her husband, James, had something that she and Nick needed. She knew that she could trust Christie to give her love and acceptance without judgment.

After a couple of months of coming to the weekly Bible study at Christie's house, Kim and Nick felt like they belonged. Their defenses came down. The other people in the Bible study treated Kim and Nick like friends, not like unclean pagans. To Nick and Kim the four other couples were normal young adults yet somehow different from most of the people they knew. Sometimes the guys got together on the weekends to watch football, and the ladies got together to go shopping. To Kim and Nick the people in the Bible study seemed to be genuinely happy but definitely not plastic. They showed true interest in Nick and Kim and even helped them move when they changed condos. Nick and Kim also noticed that the couples in the group based their life philosophy on the Bible and talked about Jesus like He was not only a real person but also a true friend.

Kim knew something was missing in her life, and she desperately wanted and needed what they had. One night after the Bible study, she stayed late to talk with Christie and gave her life to Christ. The change in her attitude was so noticeable Nick wanted what Kim had. A few weeks later James began weekly lunch appointments with Nick. Patiently he listened to Nick's concerns and tried to answer Nick's questions. On their fifth lunch together, Nick gave his life to Christ in a quiet booth in a corner of the restaurant.

Back to the Future

In the last several decades, America has shifted from a mostly Christian nation to a post-Christian nation. An ever-increasing majority of the population is secularized. According to Jim Petersen *secularized* describes "people who are not operating within a religious framework. Religion is not a vital aspect of their existence. Their personal philosophy of life is not based on religious concepts."[1] He continues, "They feel that religion has been exhausted as a valid basis for a personal philosophy. They are post-religious. They may have a traditional knowledge of religion but no personal religious life."[2]

Nick and Kim were secularized people. They had attended church only a few times as children, but religion had no place in their personal philosophies of life. They were uninterested in church and had been turned off by the judgmental attitudes of the few Christians they had met. Humanly speaking, if Christie had not become Kim's friend at work, Kim and Nick would still be far from God.

For decades Christians have counted on reaping events such as crusades, revivals, and church services to do their evangelism for them. This approach is no longer as effective, especially in an increasingly post-Christian culture. And make no mistake, America is an increasingly post-Christian nation. Church attendance in America continues to drop, going from 60 percent after WWII, to 49 percent in 1991, to just over 18 percent of the population attending church on any given Sunday today.[3] That means fewer than two out of 10 people you see at Walmart were in church last Sunday.

Seminary professor and consultant Aubrey Malphurs addressed the fact that America is changing when he said, "Essentially, what was a churched, supposedly Christian culture has become an unchurched, post-Christian culture. People in our culture are not antichurch; they simply view the church as irrelevant to their lives."[4]

If secularized people like Kim and Nick meet Christ, it will probably be as a result of Christians who view evangelism as a process and a lifestyle, not merely an event. They will be patiently willing to plow, plant, and water before they try to reap (1 Cor 3:6). They will be intentionally willing to build friendships with people far from God and live their Christianity in order to give a clear explanation of the gospel out of an authentic lifestyle and a genuine concern. They will reach people as they allow investigators to *belong* before they ask them to *believe*.

Peanut Butter and Jelly

Some things are better together than separate. Few people eat peanut butter sandwiches. Not many people eat jelly sandwiches. But nearly everyone enjoys peanut butter and jelly sandwiches. Why? They taste better together.

The peanut butter and jelly of effective evangelism is proclamation and affirmation. Proclamation describes the event of giving a clear explanation of the gospel to a non-Christian as an event (Mark 16:15). Affirmation describes living the character of Christ (John 20:21). Proclamation is preaching the gospel with our lips. Affirmation is preaching the gospel with our lives. Proclamation is doing. Affirmation is being. Proclamation is telling the truth. Affirmation is living the truth. Effective evangelism, especially of secularized people, requires both proclamation and affirmation.

In Eph 4:15 we are told to speak the truth in love. Truth without love destroys. Love without truth deceives. Truth combined with love draws people into a relationship with Christ. Truth and love are what lost people hunger to see. Truth and love are proclamation and affirmation joined in effective evangelism.

Jesus Was a Lifestyle Evangelist

In John 1:14, we read: "And the Word [Jesus, *logos*, message] became flesh and dwelt among us, and we beheld His glory, the glory as of the only begotten of the Father, full of grace and truth." The Greek term for "flesh" (*sarx*) is used when referring to "flesh, muscles, tissue and the like." The implication is that Jesus, who was born physically, was a human being through and through. The word *incarnation* is taken from the Greek *in carne* or, literally, "in the flesh." "Dwelt," used in John 1:14, is an Aramaic term that could be translated "pitching one's tent." Linking the two ideas together, we see that Jesus did not merely shout the good news at us from heaven. No, He literally became one of us and "pitched the tent" of His life among us so He could get the message of God to us in a manner that was "full of grace and truth."

We Should Be Lifestyle Evangelists

Richard Bond leads an organization dedicated to proclamation evangelism. Yet he sees the wisdom and biblical teaching of combining both proclamation and affirmation in order to reach the lost. In addressing the value of affirmation evangelism, he writes:

> As God personally brought the Good News to mankind, so we are to "incarnate" Christ to the lost, that is, to penetrate, (pitch our tent) significantly into the lives of the non-Christian for the purpose of not only verbalizing the Gospel but also to live it before them. As Christ lives His life through the believer, they see the "visible expression of the invisible God" as well as hearing the Word of salvation.[5]

Be Witnesses

Acts 1:8 gives the famous last words of Jesus when He told His followers, "You shall *be* My witnesses" (NASB). Note that His last command was to *be* witnesses, not merely *do* witnessing. *Doing* witnessing without *being* a witness tends to treat lost people as projects instead of friends.

While proclamation evangelism alone may reach some people, the people it reaches are usually already prepared. They have already heard the basic truths of Christianity a few times, and God has been working on their hearts. The seed of the gospel has already been planted and watered and is ready to be reaped.

As America becomes more and more secularized, most of the prepared people have already been reached. Secularized people are rarely reached through an initial encounter with the gospel and rarely through proclamation of the gospel alone. They require time to process the information and observe an affirmation of the message as seen in an authentic life. They have to *see* Jesus in us before they believe what we have to *say* about Him.

Stop and think what we expect when we proclaim the gospel to a nonbeliever. Let's say we approach a 20-year-old secularized man with the intent of proclaiming the gospel to him. He has rarely, if ever, been to church. Over the past 20 years, he has done primarily what he wanted to do, establishing habits and developing his own belief system. Almost everything he has fed into his mind is contrary to the Word of God.

Let's say we spend an hour explaining the gospel. Now what do we expect to happen? Often we expect him to conclude that the direction he is taking in his life is wrong. We expect him to turn his back on 20 years of living and say, "For 20 years I have been mistaken. In one hour you have shown me how to change everything I have ever believed. I repent of my sin and cry out to Jesus to save me."

To expect that to happen is to expect the practically impossible. Does it ever happen like that? Yes, but in America it is occurring less and less often than it did 30 years ago. Why? People are less prepared. They did not learn the Ten Commandments in public elementary school. They do not have a strong church background. They do not know many evangelical Christians as friends. The story of Jesus is new to them. They usually need time to process the decision.

The Rest of the Story

When I use the term *lifestyle evangelism*, I am speaking of intentionally combining both proclamation and affirmation over a period of time through a friendship relationship. Many have discovered that people who come to Christ as a result of lifestyle evangelism and who are born again after a lengthier gestation period have fewer spiritual problems, continue in the Lord more often, and usually become spiritual reproducers.

This is what happened with Nick and Kim. They had several secularized friends who were also struggling with their marriages and with life in general. As Nick and Kim began to reach out to their friends through intentional lifestyle evangelism, several responded and began attending the Bible study group. The prolonged study of the Scriptures backed up by the affirmation of the group in general, and Nick and Kim in specific, wore down their defenses. Two other couples gave their lives to Christ because of the intentional, patient, prayerful, loving lifestyles of Kim and Nick.

⚊ Evangelism Is . . . ⚊

1. Evangelism is a lifestyle, not merely an event. It takes time.
2. Evangelism that is effective with secularized people comes as a result of Christians who are willing to *be* witnesses, not merely *do* witnessing.
3. Lifestyle evangelism intentionally combines both proclamation and affirmation over a period of time through a friendship.
4. Evangelism is more than merely reaping. It is the result of plowing, planting, watering, and reaping.

⚊ Key Verse ⚊

And the Word became flesh and dwelt among us, and we beheld His glory, the glory as of the only begotten of the Father, full of grace and truth. (John 1:14)

⚊ Good Quotes ⚊

Evangelism is expressing what I possess in Christ and explaining how I came to possess it. In the truest sense, evangelism is displaying the universals of God's character— His love, His righteousness, His justice and His faithfulness— through the particulars of my everyday life.

—Joseph C. Aldrich[6]

Evangelism is a 24-hour-a-day activity for everyone. From home, to school, to work, to play, you are constantly sending out a message to those around you with your mouth and your mannerisms.

—Joseph C. Aldrich[7]

The best argument for Christianity is Christians:
their joy, their certainty, their completeness. But the strongest
argument against Christianity is also Christians—when they
are somber and joyless, when they are self-righteous and
smug in complacent conversation, then Christianity
dies a thousand deaths.

—SHELDON VANAUKEN[8]

It's been said that there are two reasons people do not go to
church: (1) They don't know a Christian, or (2) They do.

—GREG LAURIE[9]

Notes

1. J. Petersen, *Evangelism as a Lifestyle* (Colorado Springs, CO: NavPress, 1980), 18.

2. Ibid.

3. A. Malphurs, *Planting Growing Churches for the Twenty-first Century* (Grand Rapids, MI: Baker, 1992), 27.

4. http://www.theamericanchurch.org, accessed April 15, 2009.

5. R. Bond, "Understanding a Relational Model of Evangelism and How It Relates to Evangelism Explosion," http://www.youthee.org/articles/relmodelee. htm, accessed January 15, 2009.

6. J. C. Aldrich, *Life-Style Evangelism* (Portland, OR: Multnomah Press, 1981), 29.

7. Ibid.

8. S. Vanauken, *A Severe Mercy* (New York: Harper and Row, 1977), 77.

9. G. Laurie, *New Believer's Guide to How to Share Your Faith*, 11.

Evangelism Is . . .

23 Winning Three Battles so Jesus Can Win the War

Dave Earley

*Making a place in your life for non-Christian neighbors
demands effort, thought, and at times risk. Bridges are harder
to construct than walls. But that doesn't alter this reality:
Outsiders to the faith are first drawn to Christians, then
to Christ.*

—HADDON ROBINSON[1]

Building Relationships

Effective evangelism is all about building relationships with lost people. Dr. Elmer Towns writes, "A relationship between Christians and unsaved people has proven to be the most effective means of influencing unsaved people to get saved."[2]

Several times in the Gospels we see the power of relationship building in bringing lost people into a relationship with Jesus. For example, John the Baptist introduced Andrew, one of his own disciples, to Jesus (John 1:35–36). Then Andrew immediately introduced his brother, Simon Peter, to Christ (John 1:41–42). The day following, Jesus found Philip (John 1:43), a resident of the

188

same town as Andrew and Simon Peter (John 1:44). Friendships played some part in Philip's meeting the Savior. Philip applied the principle of networking by immediately finding his friend Nathanael and introducing him to Jesus (John 1:45–46). Regarding this powerful chain of redemptive relationships, Towns writes:

> In retrospect, three things become clear. 1). A relationship with God is the foundation to the Christian faith. 2). Human relationships are the most effective way of opening the door to reach people for Christ. 3). Working through existing relationships, or networking people for the gospel is a biblical approach to evangelism.[3]

Many people may not require a great deal of relationship building in order to create a productive atmosphere for sharing the gospel. However, vast numbers of people *do* require time and effort to establish a needed level of trust before they are willing to hear something they view as deeply personal as how to have an intimate faith in a personal God.

Winning Friends and Winning Souls

Some people like to refer to evangelism as "soul winning." The term *soul winning* comes from the book of Proverbs where King Solomon wrote, "The fruit of the righteous is *a* tree of life, and he who *wins souls* is wise" (Prov 11:30 NIV, italics added). I especially like the way the Amplified Bible renders this verse: "The fruit of the [uncompromisingly] righteous is a tree of life, and he who is wise captures human lives [for God, as a fisher of men—he gathers and receives them for eternity]" (Prov 11:30 AMP).

Evangelism is capturing human lives for God. Our family lived in the same town for 20 years. Over that time we led many people to a fruitful relationship with Jesus Christ. The process often took years and usually involved many small steps. Eventually we saw that the people we were reaching were won to Christ after two other victories were won first. This battle to capture human lives for eternity was usually the result of winning three victories.

1. Win them to yourself.
2. Win them to your church.
3. Win them to Christ.

1. Win People to Yourself

As I read and think about evangelism, one statistic has held firm over the decades: more lost people come to Christ as a result of family and friends than any other means.[4] We spend millions of dollars each year on television and radio outreach, crusades, campaigns, and special events. But just as it was in the first century, it is true in the twenty-first century: more people come to Jesus because of friends and family members than any other method. What that means is this: You are God's best method of evangelism!

Thom Rainer's research team interviewed several hundred unchurched persons. They were largely surprised by how receptive the unchurched were to genuine Christianity. Twyla Fagan, the leader of the research team, stated, "Most of the unchurched the team is interviewing would respond positively to a 'genuine' Christian who would spend time with them in a gentle, nonjudgmental relationship. . . . Most of the unchurched can easily tell the difference between drive-by evangelism and a person who really *cares*."[5]

Most people will gravitate to people who truly accept them, deeply love them, and strongly believe in them. People tend to like the people who like them, listen to the people who listen to them, and love the people who love them.

It is not hard to figure out. If lost people don't like you, they will not be interested in what you have to say about Jesus. If they do not trust you, they will not believe what you have to say about sin, eternity, and abundant life.

Jesus gave us the best advice when it comes to relational evangelism when He said, "You shall love your neighbor as yourself" (Matt 22:39)." If we are to be truly effective evangelists, we must love people as God loves them and see them as God sees them. This means we will have to love people for who they are, not as targets. We will need to take the time to get to know them as people.

Jim Petersen was an effective missionary to secularized college students of Brazil. With great wisdom he writes, "Our function is to accompany our acquaintances on the road to Christ, showing them the way. We must walk the road with them, a step at a time."[6] As you begin to win people to yourself, you should elicit from them several "preconversion decisions" about you:

1. He is OK.
2. I'd like to know him better.
3. I feel comfortable with him. He accepts me.
4. I want to find out why he is so different.
5. It seems that he gets his outlook on things from the Bible.

6. He's a Christian, but he's OK.
7. Being a Christian sure has its advantages.
8. I like his friends. I envy their confidence. I like his church. It seems relevant.
9. Looking at the Bible might be interesting someday.[7]

2. Win Them to Church

Eighty-two percent of the unchurched are at least "somewhat" likely to attend church if they are invited. . . . More than eight out of 10 of the unchurched said they would come to church if they were invited. . . . The process was pretty basic. If we invite them, they will come.[8]

After winning someone to yourself, usually the second major victory that must be won is winning the lost person to church. Now understand me clearly, when I use the word *church*, I am not talking about a building. Jesus did not pour out His life on the cross for some building with a steeple on the roof. Jesus died for a group of people who would be rescued from hell and be passionate about following Him. He died for His bride.

When I speak of winning a lost person to church, I am talking about leading the not-yet-believer to a gathering of God's people who are seriously studying the Bible and actively trying to obey it. Winning your friend to church may mean inviting your lost friend to check out Jesus by visiting a small group of believers who meet to study the Bible regularly, or to meet you at a Sunday morning worship experience that meets in a public school, or to ride with you to a gathering of a couple of your friends who weekly discuss life and the Bible in a coffee shop one morning a week.

The goal is simple: get the nonbeliever around other genuine Christians so the nonbeliever can see the love and power of God at work in human lives. The goal is also to get the lost person in an environment where God the Holy Spirit can speak to them through the Word of God. Often they simply must feel like they *belong* before they can *believe*.

Again, our job is helping the nonbeliever take ministeps toward full-on commitment to Jesus Christ. Along the way they will go through a process of thinking that will incorporate increased trust in the Bible and enhanced desire to have the same type of relationship with Jesus they are seeing in you and your Christian friends. Some of their preconversion steps may be as follows:

1. This gathering is OK.
2. I like the fact that these people are just people yet somehow positively different.

3. Jesus has made a difference in their lives.

4. I wonder if Jesus can make that type of difference in my life also.

5. I like the encouragement I get here to pursue a relationship with Jesus.

6. I feel accepted and even loved.

7. The Bible is not impossible to understand.

8. The Bible says some important things.

9. What the Bible says about life fits my experience.

3. Win Them to Christ

Once you have led your friend to start attending your group, it is usually not difficult to lead him or her into a personal relationship with Jesus Christ. Sometimes you can use the impetus of the gathering prayerfully to turn the conversation to the spiritual issues. In these situations I have said things such as:

- "Do you realize how much God loves you?"
- "What did God say to you during the meeting tonight?"
- "When the speaker spoke about eternity, how did you feel?"
- "If you died on the way home tonight, are you sure that you would be with God in heaven?"
- "May I show you what the Bible says about starting an eternal relationship with God?"
- "May I tell you how I gave my life to Jesus Christ?"
- "May I share with you the biblical road to a relationship with God?"

When Thom Rainer's team invited more than 300 unchurched people, they were surprised to find that few of the unchurched have had someone share with them how to become a Christian.[9] The reason most Christians have not led anyone to Christ is not because non-Christians aren't interested as much as it is because Christians haven't stepped out of their comfort zone and told them how to become a Christian. If you truly care about the lost person you have been befriending, you will reach a point in the process when it would be criminal to keep silent.

Help Them Cross the Finish Line of Faith

After having cultivated the relationship; after having won the lost person to myself and to church; after sharing the good news of the death, burial, and resurrection of Jesus for their sins, I try to win them to Christ. At this point I generally ask a lost person, "Is there any good reason you should not put your faith in Jesus right now?"

When the Holy Spirit is obviously working, the lost person will usually answer, "No."

Then I say, "Why not give your life to Jesus right now? If you would like, I can verbalize a prayer that summarizes what we have been talking about. Let's close our eyes, and I will say the prayer out loud slowly. If it expresses the deep desire of your heart, you can repeat each phrase after me."

At this point most people gulp and say, "Alright."

Then I pray a prayer like the one given below, pausing after each phrase to let them say it. Of course, often, if you have had several gospel conversations with the person, they know what they want to say to God without your help.

> Dear God,
> I admit that I have sinned.
> I admit that I do not deserve eternal life.
> I believe that Jesus never sinned.
> I believe that He died to pay for my sins.
> Right now I call on Jesus to be my Lord and Savior.
> I choose to commit the rest of my life to following Him as my King.
> From this moment on, I will try to do everything He asks me to do.
> Thanks for giving me eternal life.
> Amen.

If you read the prayer carefully, you will notice that the prayer has four key elements. They are called the ABCs of salvation. I have had the privilege of leading hundreds of people to a soul-saving, life-changing relationship with Jesus by leading them through this simple prayer.

> Dear God,
> I **admit** that I have sinned. I **admit** that I do not deserve eternal life.
> I **believe** that Jesus never sinned. I **believe** that He died to pay for my sins.
> Right now, I **call** on Jesus to be my Lord and Savior. I choose to **commit** the rest of my life to following Him as my King.
> With God's help, from this moment on, I will **do** everything He asks me to do.

— Evangelism Is . . . —

1. Capturing human lives for God.
2. Winning a few strategic battles so Jesus can win the war.
3. Building relationships with lost people.
4. Following the example of Jesus in leaving His comfort zone in order to build a redemptive bridge between us and the Father.
5. Soul-winning.
6. Usually the result of winning three victories.

— Key Verse —

*The fruit of the righteous is a tree of life,
and he who wins souls is wise. (Prov 11:30)*

— Good Quote —

*By and large, this generation will not be won to Christ
and assimilated into the church because of some crusade or
brilliant preacher, but due to a quality relationship that has
been built with them by an authentic follower of Christ.*

—T<small>IM</small> E<small>LMORE</small>[10]

Notes

1. H. Robinson, as quoted in J. C. Aldrich, *Life-Style Evangelism* (Portland, OR: Multnomah Press, 1981), 11.
2. E. Towns, *Winning the Winnable: Friendship Evangelism* (Lynchburg, VA: Church Leadership Institute, 1986), 6.
3. Ibid., 6.
4. According to W. C. Arn in *How to Reach the Unchurched Families in Your Community* (Monrovia, CA: Church Growth, n.d.), 75–90 percent of those who visit church do so because of friends or relatives. E. Towns gives the number as 86 percent who visit church as the result of family or friends: Towns, *Winning the Winnable*, 5.
5. T. Rainer, *The Unchurched Next Door* (Grand Rapids, MI: Zondervan, 2003), 28.
6. J. Petersen, *Living Proof* (Colorado Springs, CO: NavPress, 1989), 150.
7. Ibid., 151.

8. Rainer, *The Unchurched Next Door*, 24–25.

9. Ibid., 26.

10. Quoted by T. Elmore in "Spiritual Trends and Changing Values in Colleges," a lecture given at Liberty University to the campus leadership team, August 2006.

24
Reaching People Through Relationships

David Wheeler

If every believer reached his or her concentric circles, the whole world could be drawn to Christ.

—CLAUDE KING[1]

Concentric Circles of Concern

Oscar Thompson was a pastor for 20 years before joining the faculty at Southwestern Baptist Theological Seminary in Fort Worth, Texas, as professor of evangelism. Before dying of cancer in 1980, Oscar left a treasure of wisdom, at least in rough form, for those of us charged with sharing the gospel and making disciples. Shortly after Thompson's death, his wife, Carolyn, compiled his manuscript and published *Concentric Circles of Concern*.[2] In 1999 Claude King and Carolyn worked together to revise and expand the original text.

Thompson's notion of relational evangelism is a helpful way of understanding and explaining how God reaches people with the gospel through relationships. Simply put, "He [God] wants to love your world through you and to draw it to Him."[3]

The diagram below shows the radius of relationships in our lives. Each circle from the center represents a slightly more distant relationship.

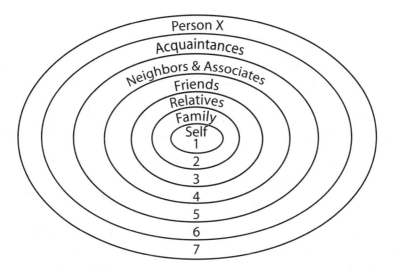

It Is Who You Know

As Christians, each of us occupies circle 1: "Self." We are surrounded by people we can influence with the message of Christ. These people fall into any of six concentric circles around us.

The closest circle to us is our "Immediate Family" in circle 2, followed by our "Relatives" in circle 3, and our "Friends" in circle 4. "If our relationship with the Lord is genuine," Thompson says, "we will want to share the good news of Christ with those closest to us." Circle 5 includes "Neighbors and Associates," followed by "Acquaintances" in circle 6. The outermost ring, circle 7, represents strangers, which the author refers to as Person X.

While the initial intended focus of Thompson's approach was to encourage Christians to seek out "Person X" intentionally, Thompson observed another more powerful phenomenon. More often those in his classes were reaching people in their first three circles—family, friends, and neighbors. He observed that this "happened only as God's people were led to share the gospel with the people they were closest to."[4] He found that we reach people through relationships.

Make Disciples

Thompson's second major emphasis aimed at explaining *how to* make genuine disciples of those individuals in the circles of influence. The process has seven stages:

Stage 1. Get Right with God, Self, and Others

Thompson said, "A person can never lead another closer to the Lord than he or she already is. Evangelism must flow from a life that is deeply in love with the Lord."[5]

This first stage of disciple-making emphasizes the critical importance of relationships. Thompson believed that the most important word in the English language was *relationship*—even more important than *love* because love is stalled without relationship. If love is the train, he says, "relationship is the track."[6] To Thompson, evangelism traveled down the track of relationships. He would say that evangelism is supremely relational.

We can almost always associate times of crisis or times of joy with the state of our relationships. Crisis situations like divorce, alienation from family or friends, divided churches, or failed business partnerships point to damaged relationships. On a larger scale, fractured relationships can result in war and death. Healthy or restored relationships produce the opposite effect—happy marriages and families, successful businesses and ministries, and strong alliances between nations.

The most important relationship, and the one we need to get right first, is our relationship with God. We must come to God on His terms, make Him Lord of our lives, and receive His gift of salvation. Having done that, if we have been disobedient to His direction, we need to repent and ask for God's forgiveness. First John 1:9 promises believers that God will not hold a grudge but is eager to restore fellowship with His children.

Once we are right with God, we need to examine our relationships with others and restore them if necessary. No one can be right with God and still be wounded by broken relationships. Matthew 5:23–24 reminds us of this: "Therefore if you bring your gift to the altar, and there remember that your brother has something against you, leave your gift there before the altar, and go your way. First be reconciled to your brother, and then come and offer your gift."

Thompson stated that "reconciled relationships with others will clean the channel in your life so that the love of God can flow through you to others around you. The gospel will move through these right relationships."[7]

Relationships may include the unlovable or those whom we don't particularly like. Thompson reminds us that part of following God's will is surrendering the right to choose whom we love.[8]

Stage 2. Survey Your Relationships

In this stage Christians are encouraged to examine their circles of relationships in order to identify individuals in need of Christ's love and salvation. Until we survey, we may not realize how many people God has put within our reach. Once we start to identify these individuals, we should gather basic information that will guide both our prayers and efforts to reach out to them.

Stage 3. Work with God Through Prayer

Prayer is not just a warm-up exercise before you do your spiritual work but intimate fellowship with a holy God who desires close and frequent prayer time with His children. Through these intimate times you will gain the wisdom and discernment to recognize opportunities for making disciples. According to Thompson, working with God through prayer will teach you to pray "that God engineer[s] circumstances in the lives of others to draw them to Himself and to his Son Jesus Christ. . . . You will pray about the people in your survey and watch to see where God is working in their lives. When you become aware of those needs that will be your invitation to join God and show his love to the needy person."[9]

Stage 4. Build Relationship Bridges to People

As you pray for those people in your concentric circles, you will learn to recognize unsaved individuals. In response you should intentionally begin to build bridges to those people that God has put in your path. This enables God's love to flow through you with the goal of leading them to Christ.

Bridges to others can be built a number of ways—through mutual interests or hobbies, by helping them through times of crisis, or even sharing moments of joy. Make no mistake; building relational bridges is the most effective way of leading others to Christ.

Stage 5. Show God's Love by Meeting Needs

When you show God's love to a needy world, it becomes visual evidence that He is working in your heart to love people you otherwise may not seek to know. Meanwhile, God is working in those you are praying for and connecting with, thus allowing His love to impact others. You literally become conduits of God's unending love as He draws hurting people to Himself. In the end, the people in your concentric circles "will know they have been loved by a heavenly Father, and they will begin to sense His invitation to become a part of His family by adoption and by the saving grace of His Son."[10]

At this point it is interesting to note the findings of Thom Rainer in *The Unexpected Journey*. He discovered that regardless of people's spiritual backgrounds (Muslim, Mormon, Wiccan, Jehovah's Witness, etc.), through coming to Christ in personal faith, they all had one experiential aspect in common: genuine Christian love, as demonstrated through genuine believers, is the most attractive component in effective evangelism.[11] That bears repeating: genuine Christian love, as demonstrated through genuine believers, is the most attractive component in effective evangelism.

Stage 6. Make Disciples and Help Them Grow

At some point, after praying for unbelievers, getting to know them, and showing them God's love, you will need to confront them with the claims of Jesus Christ. Once we see people as God does, helplessly lost without Christ, you will want prayerfully to share the good news with them and give them the opportunity to surrender their heart to Christ.[12]

In this stage Thompson outlined our responsibilities and that of the Holy Spirit. We are to be witnesses for Christ and to share our faith. The Holy Spirit's role is to convict them of sin and show them the truth of the gospel. Then, if they choose to yield to Christ, we (and other Christians) need to help them develop a personal relationship with Jesus Christ through consistent prayer and reading His Word.

Stage 7. Help New Christians Make Disciples

The final stage is the beginning of the cycle for new Christians. Once they have become Christ followers, encourage them to survey the people in their concentric circles. They should immediately begin praying for them, mending broken relationships, building relational bridges, and showing God's love in practical ways. The ultimate goal is to multiply through leading others to become authentic disciples.[13]

There's an old saying: Give a man a fish, and you feed him for a day; teach a man to fish, and you feed him for a lifetime. The first method shows addition; the second demonstrates exponential multiplication. The same can apply to building the kingdom of God. We can lead someone to Christ and add an individual to the kingdom. Or we can lead people to Christ, teach them to pass it on, and the result is exponential.

This God-given approach is both biblical and effective. It is, after all, the essence of the Great Commission!

> And Jesus came and spoke to them, saying, "All authority has been given to Me in heaven and on earth. Go therefore and *make disciples* of all the nations, baptizing them in the name of the Father and of the Son and of the Holy Spirit, teaching them to observe all things that I have commanded you; and lo, I am with you always, even to the end of the age." Amen. (Matt 28:18–20, italics added)

Internal Relationship-Building

Evangelism is lived out through intentional relationships. I recall partnering with the Billy Graham Association during the 1999 crusade in Indianapolis, Indiana. During one of the training sessions, the teams shared that after several decades of leading evangelistic events throughout the world, regardless of the preparation, the most important factor to assure success is intentional relationships! Without Christian foot soldiers leading the way by fostering relationships, praying, sharing Christ in the field, bringing friends to the crusade, and making a commitment to follow up, the other activities would be minimally effective. The bottom line is that while relationships can be elusive in contemporary culture, they are nonetheless essential!

Biblical Community

One of the requirements Jesus gave His followers was to love one another. He told them that by loving one another they would attract those who were not yet following Him. "By this all will know that you are My disciples, if you have love for one another" (John 13:35).

Evangelism is a living example of biblical community. The issue of genuine community is huge in the contemporary church. Everyone wants to feel accepted and loved, not condemned and prejudged, especially by the people who are supposed to represent Christian ideals. You may recall the old theme song to the television show *Cheers*, "Sometimes you want to go where everybody knows your name." If it is true at a fictional bar on television, it is certainly true in reference to the church and the process of evangelism!

The Eternal Process of Multiplication

Evangelism is an eternal process of multiplication. The gospel was never meant to be lived out in a vacuum. While one's faith is personal, it is not meant to be private. Christianity is a living process of multiplication that is prompted by the fact that believers claim to have a relationship with the living Savior, Jesus Christ. As part of Christ's body, Christians are expected naturally to multiply their faith just as one's body remains healthy through naturally multiplying cells.

⚊ Evangelism Is . . . ⚊

1. Supremely relational.
2. Cooperating with God in reaching people with the gospel through relationships.
3. Reaching your concentric circles of influence with the gospel.

⚊ Key Verse ⚊

*"By this all will know that you are My disciples,
if you have love for one another." (John 13:35)*

⚊ Good Quote ⚊

*I believe the most important word in the English language,
apart from proper nouns, is relationship. . . . The thing that
satisfies the deepest longing of your being is a relationship
with someone. . . . God wants to reveal His character through
a Christian's life. . . . He does this by loving through you in
your relationships with others.*

—Oscar Thompson[14]

⚊ Application ⚊

1. Start a list of people in your concentric circles who do not know Jesus Christ as personal Savior. Include at least one person in each of the following circles:
   - Circle 2: Family
   - Circle 3: Relatives
   - Circle 4: Friends
   - Circle 5: Neighbors and associates (work, school, community groups, etc.)
   - Circle 6: Acquaintances

2. Pray for those individuals on your list and ask God to begin working out circumstances in their lives to draw them to His Son.

3. Look for ways to build a bridge to those on your list by demonstrating God's love.

4. Ask God to make you aware of any relationships that are broken or in need of attention. Pray for reconciliation.

5. Seek to become more sensitive to the not-yet Christians (Person X) in your life. Start each day by asking God to bring someone into your life who needs a Christian witness.

Notes

1. W. O. Thompson Jr., C. King, and C. T. Ritzmann, *Witness to the World* (Nashville, TN: LifeWay, 2008), 5.

2. O. W. Thompson Jr., *Concentric Circles of Concern: Seven Stages for Making Disciples* (Nashville: B&H, 1999), 20.

3. Ibid., 9.

4. Ibid., 2.

5. Thompson, et al., *Witness to the World*, 9.

6. Ibid., 2.

7. Ibid., 8.

8. Ibid.

9. Ibid., 31.

10. Ibid., 32.

11. T. Rainer, *The Unexpected Journey* (Grand Rapids, MI: Zondervan, 2005).

12. Thompson, *Concentric Circles of Concern*, 33.

13. Ibid., 35.

14. Ibid., 8.

25

Evangelism Is . . .

Hanging Out
with a Purpose

David Wheeler

"Can We Do That?"

I was recently invited to attend the annual men's breakfast at a small country church in rural Virginia. As you might expect, they served grits, homemade biscuits, sausage gravy, scrambled eggs, lots of greasy pork, fried potatoes, pancakes, waffles, strong coffee, and best of all, strawberry freezer jam! I'm hungry just thinking about it.

After partaking in numerous servings of this fine meal, the men asked me if I was pleased with their efforts. Of course, my response was positive. I used words like *amazing* and *legendary*. I think I even suggested they should open their own restaurant!

However, my next response drew a collective sigh from the men. I simply asked if they ate breakfast most mornings with a group of friends. After all, we were in the country; they had to have a Hardee's somewhere. Sure enough, the men affirmed my suspicions that yes, they ate breakfast most mornings with a group of friends.

I then asked where their friends might be eating breakfast that Sunday morning. They were not sure, so I challenged them to imagine the possibilities if they had invited their friends to attend the men's breakfast. Think about it:

they could hang out, gorging themselves on some great food, followed up with a brief Bible study. Who knows what might have happened?

The response of the men's group was priceless. While looking a little confused, they asked, "Can we do that? You really think our friends would attend a church function?"

I could not help but laugh and cry at the same time. In the end the men caught the vision of what could happen when "hanging out" meets compassion for the lost souls.

Volleyball Evangelism

Beach volleyball is a popular pastime for those blessed to live in warmer climates. It is, in fact, the passion of one mid-20s single man named Chris. As a strong Christian, he was convinced that he could mix what he loved most, volleyball, with a chance for others to hang out or do evangelism. So he did both. He called it the Midnight Volleyball Club.

It started small with only a few friends showing interest the first month. Through word of mouth, it was not long before this tight-knit volleyball club had turned into a weekly social gathering that averaged more than 40 young professionals.

The club met on the campus of a local university. Some people came wanting to hang out and meet new friends. Others saw it as an opportunity to minister by inviting coworkers to get involved and have some fun. Most of the guests would never socialize with the stereotypical church crowd.

Eventually Chris and others from the club became accepted into the beach subculture. This gave them the opportunity to meet new people who shared similar interests. As it grew, the Midnight Volleyball Club became a way to integrate these new friends into a Christian environment without the fear and pressure associated with going to church.

Upon arriving at the courts on Thursday night, they were greeted by a variety of young professionals who enjoyed volleyball and loved the Lord. What started as a way for friends to play ball and hang out during the week turned into a sports-driven mission field. The club's motto soon became, "Always act like Jesus . . . because you never know who's watching!"

This continued to grow as local college students prioritized Thursday nights as an opportunity to unwind in a safe but competitive environment. It was not long before the basketball courts also became a place of fellowship while others played games like four square, or brought their dogs to run and play. Unlike many churches, laughter—not judgment and condemnation—became the Thursday night language around the courts.

Chris and the Midnight Volleyball Club members attended a local young adults group that held a Tuesday night worship service. As the Midnight Volleyball Club members invited the people they met on Thursdays, the Tuesday evening worship service grew to more than 200 singles meeting every week. The volleyball and basketball courts served as an opportunity for club members to invite their new friends to come and see what was happening at church.

As a result of adding purpose to their hanging out, the Midnight Volleyball Club members made an impact. Large numbers of students and young professionals were introduced to Christianity, attended the weekly services, and surrendered their lives to Christ.

You Can Do It

It really is a simple concept. Take something you and others enjoy like softball, volleyball, dodge ball, bowling, golf, or hiking. Then adapt the concept of hanging out by adding intentionality and purpose.

I learned this concept while attending seminary. When my wife went to the local K-Mart, I would often tag along. However, my intention was not to shop but to look for opportunities to engage in gospel conversations.

As an avid sports enthusiast, I would hang out in the sports department looking for divine appointments. As people shopped for sports equipment, I would listen carefully and chime in with suggestions based on past experiences with various items. I was many times able to share Christ after recommending a softball bat or glove.

Sound crazy? It isn't! After people expressed their appreciation for my assistance, as a courtesy they often asked about my story (job, family, etc.). While the initial connection was sports equipment, the purpose of hanging out was to engage in spiritual discussions. Through the leadership of the Holy Spirit, the key was to adopt an intentional lifestyle, thus creating opportunities to share my story in hopes of discussing spiritual matters.

What the Bible Says

In John 2:1–10 we find Jesus at one of the most common places of fellowship, a wedding. As He celebrated the union of two friends, He found Himself in the midst of His first public miracle. Mary, His mother, knew when crisis struck (the wine was gone) where to go for help. "On the third day there was a wedding in Cana of Galilee, and the mother of Jesus was there. Now both Jesus and His disciples were invited to the wedding. And when they ran out of wine, the mother of Jesus said to Him, 'They have no wine'" (John 2:1–3).

The idea of running out of wine being a crisis may seem odd to us. After all, why would this be a justifiable cause for a miracle? Furthermore, why would Jesus use this event to display publicly His prowess as the Messiah?

In biblical times wedding ceremonies were even more significant than today. The event often lasted a week or more. If the wine ran out during the celebration, the bride and groom were humiliated. Jesus was fully aware of this Jewish custom, thus He responded with compassion for the wedding party in hopes of seizing a ministry opportunity.

> His mother said to the servants, "Whatever He says to you, do it."
> Now there were set there six waterpots of stone, according to the manner of purification of the Jews, containing twenty or thirty gallons apiece. Jesus said to them, "Fill the waterpots with water." And they filled them up to the brim. And He said to them, "Draw some out now, and take it to the master of the feast." And they took it. When the master of the feast had tasted the water that was made wine, and did not know where it came from (but the servants who had drawn the water knew), the master of the feast called the bridegroom. And he said to him, "Every man at the beginning sets out the good wine, and when the guests have well drunk, then the inferior. You have kept the good wine until now!" (John 2:5–10)

Keep in mind that none of this would have been possible if Jesus had not been willing to be seen in society. He valued hanging out with the people He came to serve.

The same was true with Chris and his friends. They may not perform miracles in order to display their faith, but they understand the power of taking everyday opportunities and interests and creating ministry moments. If Jesus could use water and wine at a wedding feast, they could certainly use midnight volleyball on a university campus.

When we further look at the story of Jesus in John 2, we see that He did not attend the wedding solely to perform miracles. Instead, Jesus came as a guest, as a friend. He wasn't there to boast or to show off in order to force others to believe. Jesus' only concern was to glorify His Father.

The bottom line is that Jesus often ministered through hanging out. He never avoided people or situations for fear of harming His reputation. Whether attending a wedding feast or simply hanging out at a Samaritan well with a woman of shady character, Jesus set the ultimate example for His children to follow in their daily lives. The issue is never self-gratification or gaining public attention; it is rather the imperative to "go" into the world seizing divine moments, always directing people back to Him!

Hanging Out with a Purpose

There are several keys to make hanging out with a purpose most effective.

1. Be Fully Present as You Walk Through Daily Life

To be fully present means that you are always on the lookout for opportunities to exalt Christ through ministering to others. Jesus practiced this in His daily life. He noticed and healed a woman who had been suffering from a hemorrhage for 12 years (Matt 9:20–22). He made time for a nobleman's son who needed healing (John 4:46–54). He took the opportunity to minister to a crippled man waiting at the pool of Bethesda (John 5:1–9).

All of these miracles happened because Jesus was present among the people He came to serve. He was never blind to the multitudes. On the contrary, Jesus saw beyond the masses of humanity and felt compassion for their individual needs. To put it another way, Jesus did not just casually hang out among the people; rather He hung out with a purpose, always being fully present with them.

2. Be Intentional About Seeking Witnessing Relationships

Hanging out can become an act of intentional ministry leading to evangelism as one walks through daily life. A good example of this occurred when Jesus met Zacchaeus (Luke 19:1–10). Even though Zacchaeus was despised by society for being a dishonest tax collector, Jesus intentionally sought to build a relationship. He was not deterred by negative comments from the local people. As a result, a man's life was changed!

3. Be Available to Seize Divine Moments

You never know when a divine moment is about to occur. The key is to be available and willing to respond. A good example is recorded in John 6:1–14 when Jesus fed 5,000 men. While the disciples wanted to send the multitudes home for lack of food, Jesus wanted to teach the disciples how to seize divine moments. The Bible says that He tested the disciples to see how they would respond. Sadly the disciples were predictable and saw the opportunity as insurmountable. Jesus took a few loaves and fishes from a young boy, multiplied them, and fed the massive crowd with "twelve baskets with the pieces of the five barley loaves left over by those who had eaten" (v. 13 NIV). Availability is the key to seizing divine moments.

4. Be Prepared to Respond to Ministry Opportunities

Paul wrote in 2 Tim 2:15, "Be diligent to present yourself approved to God, a worker who does not need to be ashamed, rightly dividing the word of truth." In other words, if you intentionally begin to hang out looking for evangelistic opportunities, you must be well prepared to handle the Word of God effectively and present the gospel. The Bible teaches that a workman must count the cost before pursuing a direction in life or ministry (Luke 14:28–33). For instance, if you are targeting a heavily Muslim or Mormon area in which to minister, know what they believe. More importantly, know what you believe and be able to communicate it clearly.

5. Be Bold with the Message of Christ

It is one thing to be prepared to share Christ; it is something totally different when the opportunity arises. You must be sensitive to the Holy Spirit and bold in your response. This does not mean you need to be overly aggressive, brash, or pushy, but rather deliberate, sensitive, and consistent with the gospel message. Just like the K-Mart example given earlier, the idea is not to pounce on unsuspecting people. The key is to be obedient and intentional when people open the spiritual door to their lives. When this occurs, be bold and share your spiritual story, then point the person to the cross.

It Worked!

God taught our family how to hang out with a purpose and impact others. My daughter Dana loves sports, especially softball. By the time she was 10 years old, she clearly had a gift as a left-handed pitcher. When coaches began to ask if she could participate on their travel teams, we initially said no because we did not want her to miss church several weekends in the summer.

All of this changed when we surrendered her gift as an offering back to God. After much prayer we decided as a family to use softball as a bridge to doing evangelism. I prayed with Dana's teams before each game while my wife, Debbi, provided snacks and TLC for players and their parents. When the team played on Sunday mornings, we also led a brief Bible study for anyone desiring to attend.

Over the years several coaches and players responded to the call of Christ. Countless others were encouraged and remain as close friends. To some softball is just a game. By hanging out with a purpose, we made it a ministry!

How You Can Do It

You can turn any activity into an evangelistic ministry. Make a list of activities you enjoy, anything from sports to crafts. Imagine how God could use that hobby or interest to exalt His kingdom.

Begin to hang out in places and with people who have the same interests. Ask God to give you a vision for how He can use it. Be intentional.

When appropriate, ask your church for support. Recruit volunteers while making plans to launch the ministry. The ministry can reach the masses or one person at a time. It all begins with a willingness to surrender everything to Christ.

⚊ Evangelism Is . . . ⚊

1. Hanging out with a purpose.
2. Being on the lookout for opportunities to exalt Christ through ministering to others.
3. Seizing divine moments to share the gospel.

⚊ Key Verse ⚊

"For if you remain completely silent at this time, relief and deliverance will arise for the Jews from another place, but you and your father's house will perish. Yet who knows whether you have come to the kingdom for such a time as this?" (Esth 4:14)

⚊ Good Quotes ⚊

My own false perceptions about non-Christians had convinced me at one point that only the lowest forms of life on the planet hang around bars. . . . God has shown me a different kind of love, a fertile love that reaches out towards everyone. For years I loved the lost in obedience to God and His Word. In recent years something has shifted in my heart. I feel I've grown. Now I don't just love the lost, I even like them.

—Steve Sjogren[1]

This statement was made after hanging out and serving people at a local bar with the intent of sharing Christ. Sjogren met one interested lady who asked the question, "Do you think people like us would fit into a church like yours?"

> *Once some religious leaders wanted to sting Jesus with the*
> *most devastating insult they could conjure up. . . .*
> *After wracking their brains, they finally sputtered,*
> *"You . . . You . . . You friend with sinners. . . . He pleaded*
> *guilty to attending raucous weddings, hanging around with*
> *crooked tax-gatherers, talking with women of ill repute, and*
> *mingling with riffraff from the wrong side of town.*
> *His motive was simple: Jesus befriended sinners because*
> *they mattered to His Father!*
>
> —BILL HYBELS[2]

> *Christianity doesn't get more basic. . . . It is seeing value in,*
> *and loving and caring for, and reaching out to, and spending*
> *time with "the least of these."*
>
> —CHUCK SWINDOLL[3]

⚊ Application ⚊

Where can you start hanging out today with the intent of building witnessing relationships? What gifts or interests has God given you that could become a budding ministry if mixed with some intentionality of purpose and evangelistic direction? Start now by writing down a list of your interests or hobbies. Give them to God along with your time, and be ready for your life to change!

Notes

1. S. Sjogren, *Conspiracy of Kindness* (Ventura, CA: Regal Books, 2003), 98–99.

2. L. and B. Hybels, *Rediscovering Church* (Grand Rapids, MI: Zondervan, 1995), 169.

3. C. Swindoll, *Compassion* (Waco, TX: Word Books, 1984), 60.

26

Evangelism Is . . .

Incarnational Living

David Wheeler

K aren and Steve Rogers drove past the Sandhills Mobile Home Park every Sunday on their way to church. It was hidden behind a rickety, unpainted privacy fence. Like many Christians, the Rogers were oblivious to the needs in the trailer park because they were consumed with the demands of daily life.

The Sandhills Mobile Home Park was brought to the Rogers' attention when the local news carried a story of the police busting a drug ring that operated out of the mobile home park. After finally noticing the small community, they began to pray for ministry opportunities. In turn, God began to call the Rogers to invade the community with the love and message of Christ. They discovered the area was known for drugs, alcohol, pornography, domestic violence, and other types of crime.

Nevertheless, the Rogers were hooked. In a few short weeks God gave them a passion and love for the people of this closed community. They could no longer drive past and ignore the cries of hurting families. The more they visited, the more God gave them a vision to stay and serve.

After some initial trepidation, their church began to go into the community and invite the residents to Sunday school and worship. They even offered free transportation. However, after three Sundays with no response, the church abandoned the project. Although this became a time of deep discouragement, God enlightened the Rogers one night during family devotions. They discovered a profound truth: "'Go therefore and make disciples of all the nations, baptizing them in the name of the Father and of the Son and of the Holy Spirit, teaching them to observe all things that I have commanded you; and lo, I am with you always, even to the end of the age.' Amen" (Matt 28:19–20).

"We've got it all backwards," they proclaimed. "We've been asking them to come to church with us when the Great Commission does not say '*come*' but '*go*' . . . make disciples!"

This revolutionary thought turned their outreach into a new lifestyle of community involvement. While they continued to invite people to their church, their focus changed to building relationships with the people of the Sandhills community. As much as possible, the Rogers tried to experience life through the eyes of the local residents.

Eventually the Rogers, along with two other families from the church, rented a mobile home in the community to act as a ministry base. After developing trust and deeper relationships with the residents, the ministries started to multiply. Soon the mobile home ministry trailer launched a children's club, free food and clothing for the unemployed, assistance for unwed teenage mothers, and weekly jail visitation with incarcerated family members from the community. As a result, Sandhills Chapel of Faith developed in the tiny living room of the ministry center.[1]

Going

Stories like these can be multiplied countless times across North America. For example, a stay-at-home mother in a middle-class Midwestern community used her college degree in science to assist neighborhood children in completing difficult school projects. She provided free child care, snacks, and meals, and then shared simple tidbits of the gospel eventually resulting in several neighbors coming to Christ.

Another family in an upper-class community in the deep South reached out to a recently divorced mother. They organized the neighborhood to provide much-needed stability for her children by assisting in daily child care when the mother was forced back into the workplace. The mother and her children surrendered their lives to Christ.

Like Jesus we must be willing to go. We must learn to live like Jesus. But even more importantly, we should be Jesus to a hurting world.

Living the Incarnational Life

Theology speaks of the incarnation of Jesus Christ, describing God's taking on human flesh. It is succinctly expressed in the Gospel of John: "The Word

[Jesus] became flesh and blood, and moved into the neighborhood. We saw the glory with our own eyes, the one-of-a-kind glory, like Father, like Son, generous inside and out, true from start to finish" (John 1:14 *The Message*).

Jesus, the Son of God, took human flesh so He could show us what God was like up close and personal. Yet He did not merely leave the glory of deity in heaven to stoop down to be one of us; He stepped even lower and became our servant! "Yet it shall not be so among you; but whoever desires to become great among you shall be your servant. And whoever of you desires to be first shall be slave of all. For even the Son of Man did not come to be served, but to serve, and to give His life a ransom for many" (Mark 10:43–45).

For a Christian to live an incarnational lifestyle is to be like Jesus in identifying with lost people and humbly serving them. Paul tells us that this life of humble service is expected for the obedient Christian. "Let this mind be in you which was also in Christ Jesus, who, being in the form of God, did not consider it robbery to be equal with God, but made Himself of no reputation, taking the form of a bondservant, and coming in the likeness of men" (Phil 2:5–7).

Living an incarnational life demands surrender not only to the words of Christ but to His actions as well. Regardless of the circumstances the world may present as stumbling blocks to our faith, we must always yield our actions and attitudes under Christ's authority.

The essence of this lifestyle is wrapping our faith in the flesh of daily living! Specifically, it is authentically living out our faith in every situation.

May Christ Be Exalted Through My Pain!

I recall a former seminary professor who was diagnosed with prostate cancer in his early 50s. When it became apparent that the cancer was resistant to chemotherapy and would take his life within months, he refused to become bitter and angry with God. His earthly testimony concluded with multiple stories of how he joyously lived out his final days by sharing his faith with everyone who entered his world. Nurses, doctors, and orderlies testified to his amazing spirit of love for Christ and for them. You could not help but smile at his funeral when his son quoted some of his father's final words. "I may be on my way out," he said, "but I want to take every soul I can with me. . . . May Christ be exalted through my pain!"

It's in Our DNA

As we mentioned in chapter 12, John's Gospel records the account of Jesus' meeting with a Pharisee named Nicodemus, a well-respected ruler of the Jews. He came to Jesus by night out of curiosity in order to discuss matters of faith. Three times Jesus told Nicodemus that he had to be born again.

> "Most assuredly, I say to you, unless one is born again, he cannot see the kingdom of God." (John 3:3)

> "Most assuredly, I say to you, unless one is born of water and the Spirit, he cannot enter the kingdom of God. That which is born of the flesh is flesh, and that which is born of the Spirit is spirit." (John 3:5–6)

> "Do not marvel that I said to you, 'You must be born again.'" (John 3:7)

Jesus' contrast between the natural birth through the flesh and being "born of the Spirit" has eternal ramifications as to how we should interpret the process of salvation and how we should live out the new life in the world. In other words, our Christian life is to be much more than simply committing ourselves to a set of rules. Through the new birth we are expected to represent Christ as if He were standing in our place.

Just as this passage compares the physical birth with the spiritual birth, we can do the same in order to understand the incarnational life into which we are called as Christians. All of us carry certain characteristics that are passed down through physical DNA. The same is true in a spiritual sense. When we are born again into Christ, we become recipients of His spiritual DNA. Therefore, we should live out the ways of Christ in our actions, attitudes, words, and deeds.

Put another way, I cannot help that I am short in stature, prematurely gray, and slowly going bald. All of that is passed along through the DNA of my parents. In the same way, the overwhelming love and compassion that Christ demonstrated for people should naturally run through my spiritual veins and be evident to the world. Since He obviously cared for lost people as evidenced by His sacrifice on the cross, we must incarnationally do the same in our daily lives.

Principles of Incarnational Living

1. Incarnational Living Is an Expression of Our New Birth

Because we are reborn as Christians into the image of Christ and have become genuine members of His family, we are given a new nature. The new nature, which is our spiritual DNA, is the nature of Christ being revealed through our new desires and attitudes. This expression of our spiritual DNA is especially true when it comes to evangelism and the desire to reach the unsaved. God's desire is that all men come to Him in personal relationship (2 Pet 3:9; 2 Tim 2:3–6). Therefore we should also desire to be used of God in this process. In other words, there should always be a family resemblance between Christ and His children!

2. Christ Followers Should Be the Incarnation of the Gospel They Proclaim

Steve Sjogren, author of *Conspiracy of Kindness*, in speaking of our approach to lost people poses the question, "How do you see them?" He responds by presenting several ineffective ways Christians may view and respond to lost people.

Evade. Many Christians willfully choose to evade the unsaved. This is a deceptive response. If Christians never encounter unsaved people, they feel little responsibility for a person's eternal condition. This appears to be the most popular approach.[2]

Pervade. Armed with an oversized Bible and the proverbial soapbox, these individuals prefer the message of condemnation over compassion. As a result, healthy dialogue is usually sacrificed on the altar of legalistic dogmatism.

Masquerade. Many so-called believers masquerade as Christians with little understanding of how their hypocritical behavior damages the kingdom of God. People will not believe the truth of Christ until that same truth is accurately demonstrated through the lives of genuine believers.

Lemonade. In a day of tolerance and pluralism, a growing number of church people are choosing to use the lemonade approach. That is, do not speak about personal sin or the exclusivity of Christ in salvation for fear of offending someone. Just keep everything sweet and refreshing, kind of like a glass of cold lemonade on a hot day.

Invade. Sjogren's solution is to "invade" society through incarnational living. This combines intentional personal evangelism with the genuine spirit of a Christlike servant. As incarnations of the gospel, we become Christ's hands and feet, thus wrapping our faith in the flesh of daily living.[3]

3. Christ Followers Should Be Agents of Social Justice and Spiritual Transformation

God's love for hurting humanity has both a personal and a social dimension. Christians should confront sinful attitudes and structures that oppress human beings. Injustice in society is an affront to God. Jesus proclaimed the gospel to oppressed and disadvantaged groups such as minorities, people with disabilities, migrant laborers, and the poor. He also sought to change the social structures and attitudes that marginalize and dehumanize His creation. Note Isa 58:6–12 in *The Message*:

> "This is the kind of fast day I'm after:
>> to break the chains of injustice,
>> get rid of exploitation in the workplace,
>> free the oppressed,
>> cancel debts.
> What I'm interested in seeing you do is:
>> sharing your food with the hungry,
>> inviting the homeless poor into your homes,
>> putting clothes on the shivering ill-clad,
>> being available to your own families.
>
> Do this and the lights will turn on,
>> and your lives will turn around at once.
>
> Your righteousness will pave your way.
>> The God of glory will secure your passage.
>
> Then when you pray, God will answer.
>> You'll call out for help and I'll say, 'Here I am.'"

Jesus was a master at challenging the prejudiced attitudes of his day. Nevertheless, Christians must recognize that His primary message was redeeming sinful humanity to a loving Savior. Believers should always be concerned with social justice and meeting needs but never to the exclusion of loving people enough to verbalize the gospel.[4]

4. Christ Followers Should Love Everyone, Including Social Outcasts

In *Fresh Wind, Fresh Fire*, Jim Cymbala, pastor of the Brooklyn Tabernacle in New York City, shares about an encounter he had one Easter evening with a homeless man named David. His first impression was that the man only wanted money. He would soon be surprised. Cymbala recalls:

> When he came close, I saw that his two front teeth were missing. But more striking was his odor—the mixture of alcohol, sweat, urine, and garbage took my breath away. I have been around many street people,

but this was the strongest stench I have ever encountered. I instinctively had to turn my head sideways to inhale, then looked back in his direction while breathing out.

I asked his name.

"David," he said softly.

"How long have you been homeless, David?"

"Six years."

"Where did you sleep last night?"

"In an abandoned truck."

I heard enough and wanted to get this over quickly. I reached for my money clip in my back pocket.

At that moment David put his finger in front of my face and said, "No, you don't understand—I don't want your money. I'm going to die out there. I just want that Jesus the red-haired girl talked about."

I hesitated, then closed my eyes. *God, forgive me,* I begged. I felt soiled and cheap. Me, a minister of the gospel. . . . I had wanted simply to get rid of him, when he was crying out for the help of Christ I had just preached about. I swallowed hard and God's love flooded my soul. . . .

And that smell . . . I don't know how to explain it. It had almost made me sick, but now it became the most beautiful fragrance to me. . . . The Lord seemed to say to me in that instant, *Jim, if you and your wife have any value to me, if you have any purpose in my work—it has to do with this odor. This is the smell of the world I died for.*[5]

Jesus obviously has a special place in His heart for those shunned and rejected by society regardless of their socioeconomic level. We should do the same.

— Key Verses —

Then He also said to him who invited Him, "When you give
a dinner or a supper, do not ask your friends, your brothers,
your relatives, nor rich neighbors, lest they also invite you
back, and you be repaid. But when you give a feast, invite
the poor, the maimed, the lame, the blind. And you will be
blessed, because they cannot repay you; for you shall be repaid
at the resurrection of the just." (Luke 14:12–14)

"For the Son of Man has come to seek and to save that which
was lost." (Luke 19:10)

— Good Quote —

*Need is the trigger which activates God's call to minister if we
have the heart to hear and respond.*

—ALBERT L. MEIBURG, *CALLED TO MINISTER*[6]

Notes

1. *His Heart, Our Hands* (Alpharetta, GA: North American Mission Board, 2000), 1.

2. "Evade," "Pervade," and "Invade" come from S. Sjogren, Servant Evangelism meeting, May 16, 1995, held at the Vineyard Community Church, Cincinnati, OH.

3. Ibid.

4. *His Heart, Our Hands*, 3.

5. J. Cymbala and D. Merrill, *Fresh Wind, Fresh Fire* (Grand Rapids, MI: Zondervan, 1997), 142–43. Used by permission of Zondervan Publishing House as it appears in *His Heart, Our Hands*, 4–5.

6. A. L. Meiburg, *Called to Minister* (Nashville: Convention Press, 1968), 39.

27

Being the Change You Wish to See in the World

David Wheeler

You must be the change you wish to see in the world.

—MOHANDAS GANDHI

Young Professionals Are Being the Change

A group of young professionals and graduate students in Lynchburg, Virginia, call themselves "Life Group." They want to make a difference.

Recently more than a dozen young adults from Life Group gathered on a cold and rainy day to tear down ceilings, gut interior walls, and to clean up a yard filled with trash and debris from years of neglect. After hours of labor, they shared Christ with the appreciative homeowner. She was delighted to find people who cared for others in need.

As she told of her failing health and a near-death experience, the door was opened to share the gospel. Eventually one of the young adults asked her, "If you died then, where would you have spent eternity?" The group shifted gears from being a group of humanitarians to a team of caring evangelists. Although the woman knew the group had come from a local church, she was now connecting the dots between their honest compassion for her physical well-being and the loving message of Christ and the cross.

This type of ministry in action breaks down the walls of resistance in communities everywhere. The homeless are being fed and prison inmates are receiving love from visitors committed to sharing the gospel in both word and deed. Our communities are filled with hurting people, especially in times of financial recession. We can make a difference if we will get to know our neighbors, the people we work with, and anyone outside of our Christian comfort zones.

Angel Tree

Every Christmas thousands of churches and local businesses collect gifts for children of incarcerated parents through a ministry of Prison Fellowship called "Angel Tree" (www.pfm.org). One church who regularly participated in Angel Tree decided to do something extra for the kids. Instead of just collecting gifts from church members and their families, this local fellowship brought a group of volunteers together and created a carnival-like atmosphere for the hurting children. Church members provided special events for the day's festivities.

Children were brought to a location where they could play games, have their faces painted, shoot basketball hoops, and eat lots of goodies. They also received Christmas gifts based on their requests. By doing this, the church was able to personalize their love for the children, the foster parents, and their incarcerated parents. It was as if Jesus physically walked into the prison and hugged everyone in His path!

Ministry After Hurricane Katrina

On August 23, 2005, Hurricane Katrina formed in the Atlantic Ocean over the Bahamas and crossed into southern Florida causing damage and death. After going out into the Gulf of Mexico and gaining strength, Katrina crashed into southeast Louisiana and tore its way to central Texas. By the time it had finished, 1,836 people lost their lives in the hurricane and in subsequent floods, making Katrina one of the deadliest hurricanes in history. Katrina was the largest natural disaster in the history of the United States causing over $100 billion in damage. The most severe loss of life and costliest damage was in the city of New Orleans, Louisiana.

A disaster relief worker from Ohio told the inspiring story of a man and his family who were displaced by the hurricane. The man, a longtime resident of the New Orleans area, was forced to flee New Orleans like thousands of other people. He and his family packed up the few possessions that were left and moved to northern Louisiana.

There the man was greeted by Southern Baptist Disaster Relief ministry teams offering hot meals, clothing, showers, and other amenities. The government provided shelter for his family in a small trailer.

Within a couple of days of arriving, the family was invited by a disaster relief worker to attend an evening Bible study. The man and his family were not accustomed to worship services and admitted they rarely attended church. Nevertheless, because of the genuine love they had been shown through the disaster relief ministry, they went. Over the next several weeks the man and his family surrendered their lives to Christ. The father was later quoted as stating, "I know it sounds crazy, but I praise the Lord for Katrina. . . . If not for the hurricane, I would never have met Christ. . . . I have lost everything of material value but gained much more in return!"[1]

"You Must Be Angels"

Violent tornados ravaged a community outside of Akron, Ohio. Chain-saw and feeding units were deployed from local churches to a small town to assist the residents. The teams spent several weeks providing free cleanup and meals. The ministry workers walked the streets making sure physical and spiritual needs were being met and community residents were encouraged. It was not long before the residents started asking questions that opened doors for the gospel. In one instance a man bluntly made the observation, "My [Catholic] church has done nothing to help me in my time of need. Exactly who are you people? You must be angels sent by God!"[2]

Putting Feet to Your faith

By putting ministry into action, evangelism becomes a natural byproduct. Consider the possibilities. Someone with carpentry skills can update a kitchen for a single mom or build a wheelchair ramp, repair drywall, or paint a house for an elderly person. An accountant could donate his or her time to assist struggling workers to file their annual tax returns. A teacher could provide free math or science tutoring after school. High school athletes could lead sports camps in low-income neighborhoods. Church members could volunteer to provide free English as a second language classes or free transportation for people needing rides to the grocery store or doctors visits. If you are willing to be used, the possibilities are endless.

Consider one small church who responded to a need when their community received over 12 inches of ice and snow. When the electricity went out, the men gathered together with their chain saws and assisted (for free) the local power companies in removing fallen trees. While others were charging exorbitant fees to assist vehicles stuck in the snow, church members took their four-wheel-drive trucks and pulled vehicles out of snowdrifts for free!

The key to ministry evangelism is getting to know your community and finding ways to use your resources and talents to meet perceived needs and to build relationships. The end result is changed lives both inside the church and out in the community!

"You Did It to Me"

In Matt 25:31–46 Jesus tells of the future judgment on humankind, separating the righteous from the cursed. This passage is often used at homeless shelters and ministry boards to remind believers that reaching the world through ministry is glorifying to Christ. He states:

> Then the King will say to those on His right hand, "Come, you blessed of My Father, inherit the kingdom prepared for you from the foundation of the world: for I was hungry and you gave Me food; I was thirsty and you gave Me drink; I was a stranger and you took Me in; I was naked and you clothed Me; I was sick and you visited Me; I was in prison and you came to Me."
>
> Then the righteous will answer Him, saying, "Lord, when did we see You hungry and feed You, or thirsty and give You drink? When did we see You a stranger and take You in, or naked and clothe You? Or when did we see You sick, or in prison, and come to You?" And the King will answer and say to them, "Assuredly, I say to you, inasmuch as you did it to one of the least of these My brethren, you did it to Me." (Matt 25:34–40)

Notice the last five words in this passage: "You did it to Me." When they fed the hungry, clothed the needy, cared for the sick, and visited the prisoner, they were serving Jesus! The righteous were unaware they had done these things for Jesus. Instead, it was a way of life for them to go out and love their neighbor as commanded. The humility and kindness of the righteous was a direct reflection of their hearts for ministry and their desire to love others. This is never far from the heart of God.

Do It with Love

Agnes Bojaxhiu spent her adult life ministering to the poor, the sick, the orphaned, and the dying among the poorest of the poor in the horrific slums of Calcutta, India. When she started an open-air school for slum children, she was joined by voluntary helpers. Financial support began to come in as she loved and cared for those persons nobody was prepared to look after.

Later known as Mother Teresa, she was given the Nobel Peace Prize in 1979 "for work undertaken in the struggle to overcome poverty and distress." Not surprisingly, she refused the conventional ceremonial banquet given to laureates and asked that the $192,000 funds be given to the poor in India.

In speaking about what it took to love poor, sick, orphaned beggars, she always spoke of the love involved in giving. Her example makes her words more powerful. She said, "Intense love does not measure; it just gives." She also said, "It is not how much we do but how much love we put in the doing. It is not how much we give but how much love we put in the giving."

In speaking of serving lowly people, she said, "We can do no great things, only small things with great love." When asked about why she could serve so tirelessly, she replied, "Love cannot remain by itself; it has no meaning. Love has to be put into action, and that action is service."

My favorite quote is the one she made when asked how she could love such filthy, stinking, mean, helpless, hopeless people. She simply answered, "Each one of them is Jesus in disguise."[3]

Not Far from the Kingdom

One day a scribe attempted to trick Jesus by asking Him which of all the commands was the greatest. Jesus quoted the Old Testament when He replied: "'And you shall love the LORD your God with all your heart, with all your soul, with all your mind, and with all your strength.' This is the first commandment. And the second, like it, is this: 'You shall love your neighbor as yourself.' There is no other commandment greater than these" (Mark 12:30–31).

The man to whom Jesus had spoken understood His words. He comprehended that love was more valuable than offerings and sacrifices. Jesus agreed.

So the scribe said to Him, "Well said, Teacher. You have spoken the truth, for there is one God, and there is no other but He. And to love Him with all the heart, with all the understanding, with all the soul, and with all the strength, and to love one's neighbor as oneself, is more than all the whole burnt offerings and sacrifices."

Now when Jesus saw that he answered wisely, He said to him, "You are not far from the kingdom of God." (Mark 12:32–34)

No amount of sacrifice or tradition (church attendance, tithing, religious practices, etc.) can compare to the second greatest commandment to "love your neighbor as yourself." This means to meet needs and find ways to engage in the lives of unreached neighbors. The command to love is a call to action. In doing so, "You are not far from the kingdom of God."

Open Your Eyes, Meet Needs, and Share Christ

We can easily close our eyes to others' needs. I often challenge my classes to put their iPods away, shut off their cell phones, and relieve themselves of Facebook for 24 hours with the intent of seeing the world through unobstructed eyes. One student, Kristina, followed the instructions and was able to lead a construction worker to Christ. She later admitted, "This person was in my life every day, but I never noticed until I was able to see without distraction."

Once we become aware of needs, we must do what we can to meet those needs. This can require food, medicine, or hard work. The key is a willingness to sacrifice time, energy, or money.

Once we have built a ministry bridge to the heart of the person we are serving, we need to share Christ. Do not hesitate to share your testimony and the gospel with those you serve. People are usually more open to spiritual matters when they are hurting or humbled.

⚊ Evangelism Is . . . ⚊

1. Being the change you wish to see in the world.
2. Opening your eyes to the needs of others.
3. Serving Jesus by feeding the hungry, clothing the needy, caring for the sick, and visiting the prisoners.

⌒ Key Verse ⌒

"And the King will answer and say to them, 'Assuredly, I say to you, inasmuch as you did it to one of the least of these My brethren, you did it to Me.'" (Matt 25:34–40)

⌒ Good Quotes ⌒

Each one of them is Jesus in disguise.
—AGNES BOJAXHIU, MOTHER TERESA[4]

Often we are blind. We act as if those around us were not really people like us. If we see them bleed, we pretend they aren't really hurting. If we see them alone, we tell ourselves that they like it that way. . . . But Jesus wants to heal our sight.
—REBECCA MANLEY PIPPERT[5]

When action-oriented compassion is absent, it's a tell-tale sign that something's spiritually amiss.
—BILL HYBELS[6]

⌒ Application ⌒

1. Spend at least 30 minutes praying and researching the various ways to put ministry into action immediately in your life. Take time to walk through your community and ask God to reveal how you can serve and reach your unsaved neighbors. Do the same at your school, workplace, dorm, or where you engage in leisure activities. Make a list to follow up. You can make a difference!

2. Go to your local school or chamber of commerce and ask about community needs. One suggestion is to sponsor local teachers by helping them secure needed classroom supplies. I surveyed several teachers a few years ago; this was their number one request. With budget cuts, most teachers are spending hundreds of dollars of their own funds to provide essential supplies. You might also adopt a park or assist with local kids' sports leagues. You can provide weekly help for the concession stand or help mow the playing fields, etc.

Notes

1. Taken from personal conversations with D. Floro, ministry evangelism strategist for the State Convention of Baptists in Ohio, September 2005. The disaster relief ministry falls under his supervision.

2. Ibid.

3. Brainyquotes, http://www.brainyquote.com/quotes/authors/m/mother_teresa_2.html.

4. Ibid.

5. Ibid.

6. R. M. Pippert, *Out of the Saltshaker and into the World* (Downers Grove, IL: InterVarsity, 1979), 114.

7. B. Hybels and M. Mittelberg, *Becoming a Contagious Christian* (Grand Rapids, MI: Zondervan, 1994), 67.

28

Learning to Listen

David Wheeler

Kyle recently came up to me after class expressing concern for a good friend in his dorm. Evidently, they had known each other for several months before either one of them surrendered their lives to Christ. Kyle had recently become a Christian and now desperately wanted his friend to make the same decision.

At first his passionate gospel presentations overwhelmed his friend. Frustrated, he came up to me after class and told me that he was close to giving up. He said, "I have tried everything, but he still will not respond to Christ. He seems indifferent and turned off. What can I do to help him?"

My answer surprised the student. I did not teach him another way to share Christ, nor did I hand him a gospel tract. I did not give him a slick DVD presentation or direct him to a helpful Web site. I simply told him, "Learn how to listen to your friend."

At first he was unimpressed. He questioned, "What is the point of listening without sharing the gospel?" To him evangelism was merely the act of sharing information, even if the other person tuned you out.

I reiterated my initial advice, "Learn to listen to your friend!" I sent him back to the dorm with strict instructions to be a good friend, learn to relax, trust the Holy Spirit, and most of all, start listening!

I did not hear from Kyle for about a month and forgot about the incident until he walked up to me after class with a big smile on his face. He said, "I can't believe how such a simple act of love could produce eternal fruit. When I stopped putting my friend on the defensive and started enjoying his company, he opened up. When he talked, I listened. He shared his concerns about becoming a Christian." He continued, "Eventually, he surrendered his life to Christ."

No Advice, Just Listening!

While driving home from work one day a few years ago, I heard about a new business opportunity that was becoming popular on the West Coast. Understanding that people crave attention and value genuine listening, a small group of entrepreneurs launched a listening service. They would set up in malls and other public arenas charging 25 dollars for 30 minutes of giving the customer their undivided attention. No advice, just listening! There were no limits on what the customer could share, and the entrepreneurs swore total secrecy.

The business exploded as long lines accumulated at each location. However, this should not surprise anyone. The skill of listening has always been a misunderstood expression of love. The same is true today. In a culture where distractions and being impersonal have become art forms, nothing is valued more as an expression of intimacy and compassion than good listening skills. This is especially vital when it comes to evangelism in today's world.

Jesus Was a Good Listener

As you read through the Gospels and study the encounters Jesus had with people, you quickly see that He was a good listener. Jesus always practiced active listening skills. That may not sound like much, but in contemporary culture listening equals love!

One of my favorite stories from the ministry of Jesus is when He evangelized the woman at the well. The reason Jesus connected with this woman was not only because He talked to her but because He took the time to listen. If we want to have successful relationships and be effective evangelists, we need to develop our listening skills.

Listening Can Be Learned

This is something Dr. Jerry Pipes points out in his book *Building a Successful Family*. Under the assumption that communication is one key to a happy home, he makes several observations in reference to the importance of learning to listen.[1]

Levels of Listening

According to Pipes, there are five basic levels of listing. They are:

1. Ignoring.[2] This is obviously not a desirable level for effective ministry. It is, however, by simple observation, the level that seems to be most common in society. Consider the fact that we live in a world of constant noise and interruptions. As a result, it is easy to walk through life without connecting with the people in our spheres of influence. We may justify our disinterest as being too busy with pressing matters or simply troubled by life's challenges. The truth is, we have allowed Satan to blind us to a hurting world. Rather than investing our lives into eternal issues as Christ desires, it is much easier to disconnect and to rationalize our disobedience to the Great Commission.

2. Pretend Listening.[3] Considering the need for genuine community and authenticity in contemporary culture, this is an especially damaging level of listening in relation to effective evangelism. With the constant distractions of cell phones and handheld computers, modern society has perfected the craft of pretend listening. We justify our rude behavior under the banner of multitasking, thus minimizing the real needs of other people as less than a meaningless text message. Do not fool yourself: people know if you are genuinely listening . . . or just pretending to care!

3. Selective Listening.[4] My wife tells me this concept is inbred into the mind of every male. I don't know if that is true, but I do recall that my father never forgot the pastor's sermon if it dealt with a wife's being submissive to her husband! It was comical. Dad might have fallen asleep the previous week but never when this subject was discussed. So there may be something to my wife's assumption. At any rate, selective listening is not a good way to build lasting relationships for evangelism.

4. Attentive Listening.[5] By nature this level indicates that one is connected and tuned in to the person who is speaking. This means good eye contact and a singular focus upon what the person is sharing. Keep in mind that *attentive* means both verbal and nonverbal. People know if you are genuine. Effective evangelism always requires one's total attention.

5. Empathetic Listening.[6] This is the deepest level of listening and authentic ministry. At this point witnesses are not just hearing noise or listening with their ears. Rather, they are listening with their hearts!

Key Listening Mistakes

If the goal is "attentive" and eventually "empathetic" listening, you will want to avoid the five key listening mistakes. They are:

1. Make-Believe Listening.[7] This is similar to "pretend" listening. If listening is equated to caring, people will eventually know that you care by the way you value their words!

2. One-up Listening.[8] This reminds me of a group of people sitting around at a senior citizens' home arguing over who has the worst health. Rather than listening and empathetically relating to the other person's pain, the temptation is to minimize that person's story with a more impressive experience. This will not lead to effective evangelism.

3. Barney Fife Listening.[9] You can stop laughing now. We all know about this mistake. It relates to one of Barney's most famous lines on *The Andy Griffith Show,* "Nip it in the bud." As my wife always tells me, "Sometimes it is better to listen and to keep our solutions to ourselves." She's right. The heart of "empathetic" listening is not arriving at a solution. It is, rather, the compassion it takes to be fully connected, even if that means remaining silent.

4. Dr. Phil Listening. This is listening that can easily become a show, or worse, your job. There is little empathy here, just a disconnected string of trite suggestions. It is listening with your mind but not your heart!

5. iPod Listening. In my opinion this is one of the greatest afflictions of modern culture. That is, we deify ourselves by walking through life in our own little world with little concern about the needs of hurting people. After all, how can we listen to the cries of the needy if our hearts, minds, and ears are closed and we are consumed by the desire for personal gratification? Think about it. How often have you walked through a crowded area with little concern for others because you are distracted by some form of technology? I could never imagine Christ walking through that same room with His fingers in His ears, His head down, and His eyes closed to hurting people.[10]

Hints for Listening for Understanding

The story of the woman at the well is fully explained in two other chapters of this book. However, for the sake of this important lesson on listening, we will make some quick references back to the story found in John 4. You can learn to listen for understanding by taking these steps:

1. Seek to determine the other person's perspective.[11] This is true with Christ as He used a series of responses to establish the woman's deeper life issues. Unlike many of us, Jesus was not so quick to speak His mind and usurp the woman's perspective by trying to force His perspective. His approach was genuine and elevated compassion over condemnation.

2. Ask good strategic questions and respond with well-placed statements.[12] Jesus did this with the Samaritan woman when He asked for a drink. He also did it when He transitioned the conversation from physical water to spiritual water. He did it again when He commented about her going to get her husband. In contemporary culture a good leading question is simply, "Will you tell me your story?" Believe me, it works. Just be ready to listen.

3. Give the other person space.[13] Once again Jesus did this with the woman at the well. He did not attack her with a barrage of information. He wisely gave the woman room to consider Christ. This principle is sometimes called "continuing the conversation." It means that we should meet people where they are and, if needed, be willing to continue the conversation through later encounters. Be sensitive to the Spirit and never close the door. Who knows, that next opportunity may be the appointed time.

The Response of the Woman

The woman at the well did not have to be honest when she responded to Jesus' questions. After all, at that time in their conversation, she did not know she was speaking with the Messiah. So what made the woman trust Christ? It was the fact that He listened and rewarded her honesty by revealing His deity.

Jesus accepted the woman regardless of her shady past. As a result, His non-judgmental conversation about sin, grace, and everlasting life gave the woman a new kind of confidence. She responded by going into town and boldly proclaiming, "Come, see a Man who told me everything I ever did. Could this be the Christ?" (John 4:29 NIV).

Jesus is the ultimate example of effective evangelism. His bold actions and ability to listen and engage in relationship with the woman at the well give us the challenge to do the same. Had Jesus ignored her because she was living in sin with her male companion or because she had lived a life full of sin prior to their meeting, He would not have had the opportunity to bring the others into relationship with Him as well. Jesus knew the woman's lifestyle, and He went straight to her heart. He did not sit as a male Jew worthy of respect; instead He sat with her and spoke to her as a person in need of a friend and Savior. Jesus did not dominate the conversation; He did not confuse her with big words or judge her for past mistakes. He also did not shame her into accepting His living water. He simply listened to her heart and responded to her greatest need . . . salvation!

⁓ Evangelism Is . . . ⁓

1. Both verbal and nonverbal. True evangelism is expressed with the whole being, both verbally and nonverbally. From a nonverbal perspective, learning to listen is essential to expressing love in a contemporary culture. While one must be bold and verbally proclaim the message of truth to a hurting world, receptivity to the gospel is often predetermined by harnessing the nonverbal expressions related to listening and building relationships.

2. Knowing the difference between hearing and listening. The difference between hearing and listening is similar to the concepts of random noise and genuine communication. It is common to walk through daily life hearing but not truly listening. For instance, if you live in the city, car horns are a normal occurrence. Simply hearing a horn as background noise while walking down the street is totally different than if you strolled out into traffic and listened to the horn of an approaching car before putting your life in danger. The same is true in reference to evangelism. If listening is an expression of love that can open the door for a witnessing opportunity, you must move beyond merely hearing and ignoring the noise of people around you and begin intently listening. This occurs when we slow down and begin comprehending the needs of the people God has placed in our lives.

3. Denying self. The act of listening is always an expression of self-denial and humility. The prudent witness is always a willing participant as God reveals His redemptive plan. As Jesus said, "If anyone would come after me, he must deny himself and take up his cross and follow me" (Mark 8:34 NIV).

4. Being ready to share when the right time arises. Listening should always be active and intentional. The ultimate end of all evangelism is to share the redemptive story of Christ.

⁓ Key Verse ⁓

*"For whoever wants to save his life will lose it,
but whoever loses his life for me and for the gospel will save
it." (Mark 8:35 NIV)*

~ Good Quotes ~

Listening means we are willing to learn from others.
Listening means we are not threatened in our own Christian
beliefs by hearing what someone else believes. Listening
means we really care for the person.

—THOM RAINER[14]

Sometimes I think the only people who stay with me and
really listen are people I hire, people I pay.

—MARILYN MONROE[15]

Imagine what might have happened with Ms. Monroe if someone, preferably a Christian, had really cared and taken the time to listen. Would she have
taken her life through suicide? Unfortunately, we will never know!

Notes

1. For a full explanation of the issues related to the importance of listening, see J.
Pipes, *Building a Successful Family* (self-published, 2002), 55–62.
2. Ibid., 56.
3. Ibid., 57.
4. Ibid.
5. Ibid., 58.
6. Ibid.
7. Ibid., 59.
8. Ibid.
9. Ibid., 60.
10. Dr. Phil and iPod Listening are not found in Pipes' book. Both points are
personal observations by the author.
11. Pipes, *Building a Successful Family*, 61.
12. Ibid.
13. Ibid., 62.
14. T. S. Rainer, *The Unexpected Journey* (Grand Rapids, MI: Zondervan, 2005),
200.
15. Quote taken from W. J. Weatherby, *Conversations with Marilyn*, as found
in R. J. Morgan, compiler, *Nelson's Complete Book of Stories, Illustrations, and
Quotes* (Nashville, TN: Thomas Nelson, 2000), 516.

29

Empathy with Action

David Wheeler

S ara Tucholsky was a five-foot two-inch, seldom used, senior outfielder for the Western Oregon University softball team. She became nationally known after slugging her only career home run in a key conference game against Central Washington. However, it was not the home run that prompted ESPN.com to display her picture on their splash page or to memorialize the event with a coveted ESPY for Great Sportsmanship. Rather it was the unique response of empathy from two players on the opposing team.

While rounding first base, Sara inadvertently missed the bag. When she turned to go back, her anterior cruciate ligament (ACL) gave out, leaving her writhing on the ground in pain. Unfortunately, softball rules would not allow her coaches or trainers to touch her while on the base path, even after a home run. The only solution was to credit Tucholsky with a single, thus nullifying her home run, and give her a pinch runner.

Knowing that the rules allowed defensive players to touch base runners, senior first baseman Mallory Holtman stepped in and shocked everyone by stating, "Excuse me, would it be OK if we carried her around and she touched each bag?"

Holtman and shortstop Liz Wallace picked up Tucholsky and carried her around the bases, eventually handing her to her coaches and teammates after passing home plate. Even more incredible is that a bid to the Division II National Tournament was on the line!

Holtman and Wallace's reponse is a perfect example of empathy in action. Their willingness to elevate the painful situation of Tucholsky over the need to win shows that they personally identified with the unfortunate situation. They actively empathized with Tucholsky.

Herein lies the difference between sympathy and empathy. If Holtman and Wallace simply felt sorry for Tucholsky, that is sympathy. No doubt many people in the stands and on the field felt sympathy for her plight. However, when the girls began to feel Tucholsky's pain to the point they responded by assisting her around the bases, they moved from sympathy to empathy.

Definitions of *Empathy*

Empathy is a powerful perspective and tool in the tool kit of any effective evangelist. But what is it?

- "The action of understanding, being aware of, being sensitive to, and vicariously experiencing the feelings, thoughts, and experience of another of either the past or present without having the feelings, thoughts, and experience fully communicated in an objectively explicit manner" (*Merriam-Webster*).[1]
- "Identification with and understanding of another's situation, feelings, and motives; the attribution of one's own feelings to an object; sympathetic, sad concern for someone in misfortune. Synonym is also pity" (Answers.com).[2]
- "Ability to imagine oneself in another's place and understand the other's feelings, desires, ideas, and actions. The empathic actor or singer is one who genuinely feels the part he or she is performing. The spectator of a work of art or the reader of a piece of literature may similarly become involved in what he or she observes or contemplates. The use of empathy was an important part of the psychological counseling technique developed by Carl R. Rodgers" (Britannica Concise Encyclopedia).[3]
- Empathy (from the Greek *empatheia*, "to suffer with") is commonly defined as one's ability to recognize, perceive, and directly and experientially feel the emotion of another. As the states of mind, beliefs, and desires of others are intertwined with their emotions, one with empathy for another may often be able to define more effectively another's modes of thought and mood. Empathy is often characterized as the ability to 'put oneself into another's shoes' or experiencing the outlook or emotions of another being within oneself, a sort of emotional resonance" (*Wikipedia*).[4]

Steve Is Changed

Steve was my daughter Dana's coach for her traveling softball team. He was also the proud father of two beautiful daughters, one who suffers from severe cerebral palsy. Her name is Emily.

Like most fathers with disabled children, Steve struggled with the concept of a God who would allow children to be afflicted with such maladies. Because he lived with Emily's pain and challenges to survive on a daily basis, he slowly became calloused toward God. This is not to say that Steve was hard-hearted or bitter because of Emily. He obviously loved her as any father would care for his child. Yet over time he drifted away from God.

At this point God placed our family into Steve's life. Coincidentally, we also have two beautiful daughters, one who struggles with mild cerebral palsy. Her name is Kara.

Because of Kara, we could empathetically relate to Steve's struggles with God. We experienced the anger, frustration, and fatigue that are part of raising a special-needs child. We also know the amazing love and rewards that come with every small victory our daughter has experienced.

Over time we intentionally loved on Steve, Emily, and the rest of the family. Steve later told me that our positive interaction with Kara and the way she responded to him was part of the pilgrimage that inspired him to begin seeking God again. Three years of active Christian empathy passed before Steve finally professed faith in Christ.

Lessons from the Tragedy at Virginia Tech

In the wake of the shootings at Virginia Tech in April 2007, many churches and Christian organizations converged on the Blacksburg, Virginia, campus in hopes of providing much-needed emotional and spiritual assistance. The result was generally positive, but many still had much to learn about the power of empathy.

During that time a mother of a Virginia Tech student approached me after a church service and handed me a letter from her son. It was entitled "Update on the Climate of Virginia Tech."

As a believer himself, his insights into how other Christians responded to the tragedy are both discouraging and convicting. His words reveal the negative influence that results from lacking empathy and understanding. Under the advice of "please be a thermometer before trying to be a thermostat," he explained an experience barely 24 hours after the tragedy:

There are many Christians here right now who are doing much, and it has been very encouraging. At the same time, however, we have people on campus right now who are here in the name of Christ who try to point out blame and have a message that nothing was learned from Columbine. I personally sought out some counseling today and unfortunately before I could get some decent help, a group from a church in North Carolina came into the Baptist Collegiate Ministries (BCM) building where I was and approached with their own agenda uninvited. They recorded the conversation on a digital voice recorder without asking our permission, and they handed out a flyer that was almost like a battle plan for showing us why such evil exists. It was so general [in] purpose and showed no individual care at all for the people's suffering.

He then gave some empathetic solutions he believed would have yielded eternal fruit. In one brief paragraph he explained what to do if you want to be effective:

Listen much, touch gently, and speak when needed. Words are hard to come by to describe these days in Blacksburg. Words can be encouraging, but really what we desire is your concern and to know that you love us. . . . A gentle touch on the shoulder as we cry, a message of "I'm thinking of you" or "We are praying for Tech," and a bear hug go much farther than any speech could ever cover."

He believed that people "need to see that Christ is love in the truest and noblest sense, a love that desires our personal faith and provides companionship and one that binds us in community."

His final empathetic decree is to "invest in people!" If you want to reach people for Christ, do not just view them as potential church members or pre-verbal notches on your Bible. Put yourself in their shoes, be patient and walk with them, then tell them about the One who understands their pain and will save their souls.

Empathy Was Needed

In John 11:1–44 we discover an example of empathy in action. The story begins as Jesus hears the news that a dear friend, Lazarus, has fallen sick. Lazarus's sisters, Mary and Martha, sent word to Jesus because they knew He could heal their brother. Martha met Jesus when He arrived. She was mourning the loss of her brother Lazarus who had died a few days earlier.

Jesus already knew about Lazarus's death. He asked to see Mary so that He could pay His respects. When she came out to meet Him, many others from the city followed. It was a Jewish custom to go to the home and mourn with those who had lost someone to death. When Jesus saw Mary weeping, He was deeply moved.

> Therefore, when Jesus saw her weeping, and the Jews who came with her weeping, He groaned in the spirit and was troubled. And He said, "Where have you laid him?"
> They said to Him, "Lord, come and see."
> Jesus wept. Then the Jews said, "See how He loved him!" (John 11:33–36)

"Jesus Wept"

"Jesus wept" is often quoted and pushed aside as the Bible's shortest verse. But how incredible is it that God used two simple words to reveal the heart of Christ. Within these two words is more emotion, love, and compassion than contained in some novels. True to form, Jesus takes something small and seemingly insignificant to teach an amazing lesson. He leads by example, instructing us that empathy, putting ourselves in someone else's shoes, is essential to effective ministry.

Some may say Jesus was mourning the loss of His friend. That is only partially true. According to John 11:13–15, Jesus, being God, already knew Lazarus was dead. He was not caught off guard by the news of his friend's death. Instead He was moved by the emotion of Lazarus's sisters and friends and felt their pain enough to draw tears. His tears were not a reflection of sadness and loss but rather a way to relate and communicate to those who were with Him.

The Bible does not tell us how Mary and Martha responded to Jesus' empathy, but it does tell us that others were witnesses of His love for Lazarus. Seeing Him get on Mary and Martha's level and experience their pain made an impact on the lives of those around Him.

Throughout the story Mary and Martha never lose touch of the fact that Jesus is Lord and can do all things. They knew of His awesome power but for a moment were blessed to see His authentic expression of emotion and love.

Empathetic Living

It is easy to read John 11 and lose sight of the two insightful words, *"Jesus wept."* After all, Christ does eventually raise Lazarus from the dead! It is understandable that such a miraculous event would steal the thunder for the moment.

The problem is that it is too easy to celebrate the supernatural acts of Christ without seeing His humanity. Here we are encouraged to feel and hurt for those we serve. This is especially true when it comes to being effective in evangelism.

When I was in seminary, we were warned about becoming too engaged in others' pain for fear of being consumed by emotions that might cloud our discretion. The result was a generation of ministerial robots who lost touch with society and the people they were called to serve.

Jesus' example should encourage us to live empathetic lives. Contemporary culture is crying out for genuine Christianity, not lifeless religion.

Empathetic living is never forgetting how it feels to be lost. It is hard to empathize with the unsaved if you have forgotten what your life was like before you surrendered to Christ. For a glimpse of this concept, go to Rev 5:4. John is in heaven kneeling before the throne of God. He notices several scrolls being grasped by the One sitting on the throne. He then realizes that if no one steps out to open the scrolls containing the redemptive history of humankind, then everyone is destined to spend eternity in hell. John's response was to cry uncontrollably for fear of a lost eternity! We must display the same urgency in our daily lives for the unsaved in our spheres of influence.

Empathetic living is taking what Satan means for destruction and turning it around for the glory of God. Everyone has a testimony of God's grace and love. It may be the loss of a friend, personal illness, loss of a job, or the challenge of a disability. Being the liar that he is, Satan will try to use difficult times to pull you away from God. In reality God is sufficient and wants to use your testimony to celebrate His wonders and empathetically to point people to Him!

Empathetic living is relating to the emotional pain of hurting people. Learn to relate to the pain of others. Hurt with them. Pray for them. Share Christ with them!

Empathetic living is living an authentic life, not hiding your warts. Part of living an empathetic life is learning to live with your personal struggles and shortcomings (warts). People in today's culture are not looking for perfect examples to follow. Rather, they would prefer that you identify with them as flawed human beings. In doing so, people are more comfortable developing relationships, thus it is easier to open the door for gospel conversations. Remember, accepting and loving people is not the same as condoning their sinful behavior!

Empathetic living is proclaiming complete restoration through Christ. The ultimate outcome of putting empathy into action is to see hurting and unsaved people restored through the power of the gospel. By becoming vulnerable enough to feel a person's pain, you are living out the message of Christ to people in need of a Savior.

⌐ Evangelism Is . . . ⌐

1. Empathetic living.
2. Loving as Jesus loved.
3. Weeping with those who weep.
4. Actively recognizing, perceiving, and experientially feeling the emotion of another with the purpose of sharing the love of God and the gospel of Christ with them.

⌐ Key Verse ⌐

Jesus wept. (John 11:35)

⌐ Heed the Warning ⌐

*When I was in seminary, we were warned about becoming
too engaged in the pain of others for fear of being consumed
by emotions that might cloud our discretion. The result was
a generation of ministerial robots who lost touch with society
and the people they were called to serve!*
—DAVID WHEELER

⌐ Good Quotes ⌐

*There is no use trying to do church work without
[empathetic] love. A doctor, a lawyer, may do good work
without love, but God's work cannot be done without love.*
—D. L. MOODY[5]

We who are Christians can win many to Christ if we just
demonstrate the love that Christ commanded us to show.
The hurting world waits for people just like that.

—THOM RAINER[6]

Notes

1. http://hubpages.com/hub/Sympathy_vs_Empathy.
2. Ibid.
3. Ibid.
4. Ibid.
5. Quote found in A. Strauch, *Leading with Love* (Littleton, CO: Lewis and Roth Publishers, 2006), 9.
6. T. Rainer, *The Unexpected Journey* (Grand Rapids, MI: Zondervan, 2005), 204.

Part 4

Methods

30

Evangelism Is . . .

Sharing Your Story

Dave Earley

One day during Christmas break after my first semester in college, I had spent the morning working out with my high school wrestling team. Our high school coach was always glad to have any of his former athletes come back from college and show his prep school students what we had learned by wrestling with the big boys in college.

I had left practice a little early that day because I needed to get to work. The only one in the locker room with me was the current captain of the high school team who also had to leave early that day. He had to go to a doctor's appointment. He asked me a few questions about wrestling and a couple about college. He told me that he was not sure what he was going to do after he graduated.

Then I whispered a quick prayer, took a deep breath, and took the plunge.

"So Eddie, do you ever think about God?" I asked him.

"My grandma used to take me to church when I was little. I thought about God a lot then," he said.

"I used to not think of God much," I said, "but that all changed a couple of years ago. God has changed my life."

"How did God change your life?" he asked.

"Let me tell you my story," I said. Then I gave him the one-minute version of my testimony, tailored to scratch him where he itched.

"The short version is, until my junior year of high school, my life was empty; and I was frustrated. I was drinking a lot and headed in the wrong direction. I was worried about the future and had no idea what I was going to do after I got out of high school."

"Wow," he said. "Sounds like me."

"A couple of my friends were real Christians, and I wanted what they had. They told me I needed to give my life to Jesus," I said. He was glued to every word.

"So I did," I continued. "Everything has changed since then. I have peace in my heart. I don't need to drink to feel happy or confident, and God is guiding me one step at a time."

"That's what I need," he said as he stared into my eyes. "Tell me more."

So I did. I told him of the death, burial, and resurrection of Jesus for his sins. I talked to him about faith and repentance. God was with us in that locker room. A few minutes later he was on his knees next to me on the floor of that locker room, giving his life to Jesus Christ.

Share Your Story

For many of us, the hardest part of evangelism is building a bridge so we can get into the gospel in an unoffensive way. One of the easiest ways to do so is by sharing your testimony. Giving a testimony is nothing new. People have been doing it since Jesus began changing people's lives.

A Demon-Possessed Man Shares His Story

I love the salvation story of the man who lived in the graveyard. This poor guy was full of so many demons that even binding him in chains and shackles could not keep him under control. He was in such misery he would yell, scream, and cut himself with sharp stones.

What an awesome day it was in his life when Jesus appeared on the scene and cast out the demons. The demons took up residence in a nearby heard of pigs. It must have been wild as the newly crazed pigs ran off a cliff and drowned in the water below.

The freshly freed man was so excited that he wanted to travel with Jesus on His journeys. But Jesus knew the man's greater ministry was going to share his story with friends. "However, Jesus did not permit him, but said to him, 'Go home to your friends, and tell them what great things the Lord has done for you, and how He has had compassion on you.' And he departed and began to proclaim in Decapolis all that Jesus had done for him; and all marveled" (Mark 5:19–20).

The Lord has done great things for all of us who are saved. Like this man, we need to tell our friends about it.

A Woman Tells Her Story

One day Jesus met a Samaritan woman as He paused to get a drink by a well. In talking with her, He led her to a personal recognition that He was the promised Messiah. She was so excited that she told people all over town her story. "And many of the Samaritans of that city believed in Him because of the word of the woman who testified, "He told me all that I ever did" (John 4:39).

Other people believed in Jesus because of her testimony. Other people will also believe in Jesus because of our testimonies.

A Blind Man Tells His Story

No one's story is exactly the same. Jesus healed dozens of people, many of blindness, often in slightly different ways. Some He simply touched and they were healed. For one man Jesus made mud, rubbed it in the man's eyes, and told him to wash in a nearby pool. When the man did as Jesus said, he was healed of his blindness and could see.

The happy man told his neighbors about what Jesus had done for him. Word got back to the Pharisees who brought the man in for questioning because the healing had occurred on the Sabbath, a no-no in their book.

The man told them that as far as he was concerned Jesus was at least a prophet because He had healed him. They did not like that and proceeded to call Jesus a sinner. To this the man gave a simple yet wise answer: "He answered and said, 'Whether He is a sinner or not I do not know. One thing I know: that though I was blind, now I see'" (John 9:25).

I love it! The man did not claim to be an expert in theology. He was not a Bible scholar. He was not a famous philosopher or apologist who had all the answers and all of the evidence for the skeptical Pharisees. But he had the one thing they could not refute. Jesus had changed his life.

An Intellectual Tells His Story

The apostle Paul was a highly educated intellectual who was well schooled in Hebrew, Greek, Aramaic, and Latin. He was an expert on the Old Testament law and also was current with the great philosophers and poets of his day. Yet, when given audiences with persons of great power such as the Roman political leaders, Paul did not debate theological or philosophical issues. He simply gave his testimony. He told them how he came to know Jesus as his Lord. He shared about his life before Christ, how he met Christ, and of his life since meeting Christ (see Acts 22:3–21; 26:4–23).

Benefits of Sharing Your Testimony

1. Sharing your salvation story builds a relationship bridge of understanding that Jesus can walk across into the heart of a lost person.
2. Sharing your testimony is a convenient and effective way to bypass intellectual defenses. It is difficult to argue with the evidence of a changed life.
3. Sharing your story often holds the hearer's interest longer than if you were quoting the words of great theologians. People will listen to you because instead of being a professional salesman, you are a satisfied customer.
4. Sharing your story can be done in any time span you are given from a minute to an hour.
5. Sharing your story is not reserved for the highly educated or spiritually mature. It can be done by a newly saved believer.
6. Sharing your story makes evangelism personal and relational.

If You Have Been Saved, You Have a Story

When we speak of sharing your story or telling your testimony, we are talking about proclaiming to others how you came to Christ. You are giving a witness. "In a courtroom, a witness isn't expected to argue a case, prove the truth or press for a verdict; that is the job of the attorneys. Witnesses simply report what happened to them or what they saw."[1]

Every believer has a testimony. If you have been saved, you have a salvation story. Granted, some may be more dramatic than others, yet there are people who need to hear *your* story. No one else's story is exactly like yours, so you need to share it, or it will be lost forever.

One, Two, Three

In our evangelism training courses, David Wheeler and I have our students write their testimony out using three main points.

1. What my life was like before Christ
2. How I met Christ as Savior
3. How Christ changed my life

I have students practice sharing their stories in a minute—three 20-second sections. We also have them write their testimonies in a paper. They can do it in less than a thousand words. Many love this project because in writing their testimony they realize what God has done for them. They realize that they do have a story and, after writing it down, feel much more confident in sharing it.

Tell Your Story

Before I Met Jesus

Tell about your life before you came to Christ. Make known your perspective of how you viewed your life spiritually before you came to Christ. For example, did you feel you were going to heaven and why? Or did you feel you were a good person and didn't need God? Or were you searching for something more?

Use adjectives to describe your life before Jesus. They may be words such as *lonely*, *empty*, *proud*, *confused*, *religious*, or *broken*. Maybe you will say, "I just knew something was missing in my life." Tell of activities that filled your life before Christ such as, "I was trying to climb the ladder of success," or "I was a faithful church attender," or "I was on my way to becoming an alcoholic."

In the story I told at the beginning of this chapter about sharing with my friend Eddie, I described my life before Christ with these words: "The short version is, until my junior year my life was empty, and I was frustrated. I was drinking a lot and headed in the wrong direction. I was worried about the future and had no idea what I was going to do after I got out of high school."

How I Met Jesus

Here you will talk about the circumstances surrounding your conversion. For example, where were you when you received Christ? Were you with your friends, at a church camp, in a church service, or in your room? Talk about exactly what truth gripped your heart when you realized you needed Christ. Talk about what you thought or felt when you accepted Christ as your Savior.

With my friend Eddie, I said, "A couple of my friends were real Christians, and I knew I wanted what they had. They told me I needed to give my life to Jesus. So I did."

Later, as I had Eddie's permission to share more, I clarified how I meet Jesus by talking about the gospel—the death, burial, and resurrection of Jesus for my sins. I quoted a few Bible verses from the book of Romans. I talked about faith and repentance. But in the short version, I simply said, "I needed to give my life to Jesus."

Since I Met Jesus

This is where you talk about the changes Jesus has made in your life. How would you describe your spiritual growth from the time you accepted Christ to today? This is the time honestly to assess and describe your spiritual growth, challenges, and victories, since you accepted Christ.

When I gave my testimony to Eddie, I described in three short sentences the changes Jesus made in my life: "Everything has changed since then. I have peace in my heart. I don't need to drink to feel happy or confident, and God is guiding me one step at a time."

Advice

Don't exaggerate or glorify your past. Dishonesty will only stifle the work of the Holy Spirit. You are not the star of this story; Jesus is. Spend less time talking about what you did and more time talking about what He has done for you.

Don't belittle the power of coming to Jesus at a young age and being spared a life of sin and wickedness. If you are living the Spirit-filled life full of love, joy, and peace, you have something any lost person will crave.

~ Evangelism Is . . . ~

1. Telling your friends what great things the Lord has done for you and how He had compassion on you.
2. Giving your testimony.
3. Sharing your salvation story so as to build a relationship bridge of understanding that Jesus can walk across into the heart of a lost person.
4. Being a witness—not arguing the case, proving the truth, or pressing for a verdict as much as simply reporting what happened to you.

⁓ Good Quotes ⁓

One of the best ways to "build a bridge" with a person who does not have a relationship with Christ is through your personal testimony.

—GREG LAURIE[2]

God has given you a life message to share. When you become a believer, you also become God's messenger. God wants to speak to the world through you. . . . You may feel like you have nothing to share, but that's the devil trying to keep you silent. You have a storehouse of experiences God wants to use to bring others into his family.

—RICK WARREN[3]

⁓ Application ⁓

Write your testimony.

1. What my life was like before Christ
2. How I met Christ as Savior
3. How Christ changed my life

Notes

1. R. Warren, *The Purpose Driven Life* (Grand Rapids, MI: Zondervan, 2002), 290.

2. G. Laurie, *New Believer's Guide to How to Share Your Faith* (Wheaton, IL: Tyndale House, 1999), 45.

3. Warren, *The Purpose Driven Life*, 289.

31 Sharing Jesus Without Fear

David Wheeler

W illiam (Bill) Fay is not your typical evangelist. Once the president and CEO of a multimillion-dollar international corporation, Bill also owned one of the larger houses of prostitution in the United States. Not surprisingly, he also had ties with the mob and was involved in racketeering, bookmaking, and gambling. To the world and Fay, he had it all. He created a successful business, owned nice cars and homes, and went on extravagant vacations. Bill thought he didn't need God. Anyone who had faith and dared share that faith to him was on the receiving end of Fay's cynicism, sarcasm, and scorn.

The day his second business, a house of prostitution, was raided, he began to feel himself losing control. At a baccarat table in Las Vegas, Bill received a phone call that would change his life. Fantasy Island, the house of prostitution he built in Lakewood, Colorado, had just been raided. His attorney informed him a warrant had been issued for his arrest. While he received probation, Bill admits he considered it a warning. That is, he could not get caught again, or he would be facing a six- to eight-year prison stint.

Almost immediately his face was plastered across the local news channels in Denver. Fired from his CEO position, he promptly became employed in an executive search business. On his fourth marriage, Bill recognized that something was missing in his life. During a retreat at Lost Valley Ranch in Colorado, he heard an Easter sermon about the difference between happiness and inner peace. Disgusted, he returned home.

A short time later he met Dr. Paul Grant. They became racquetball partners and quick friends. In fact, Fay recalls hearing the gospel from him the first day they met outside the courts. Knowing that Dr. Grant was Jewish, Fay obnoxiously approached him with the question, "What are you doing here on Yom Kippur [a day set aside for Jews to pray for forgiveness of sins]?" Without fear or hesitation, Dr. Grant let him know that he is a Christian Jew, thus nullifying the need to seek forgiveness because he'd already been redeemed by the blood of Jesus Christ. This simple and quick conversation was the foundation of a friendship that would change Fay's life.[1] The events that followed offered a new beginning for Fay, for he describes how "God chose to take my life and flip it over."[2]

Bill became a fervent evangelist. Within days of his conversion, by a series of divine circumstances, he met his daughter from a previous marriage for the first time. After Bill shared Jesus with her, she came to faith in Christ.

Since then Bill has shared his faith personally with more than 25,000 people on a one-to-one basis. He graduated from Denver Seminary in 1987 and has written the series Share Jesus Without Fear for Lifeway Christian Resources and the notes in the *Share Jesus Without Fear* New Testament. His pamphlet *How to Share Jesus Without an Argument* has 3.5 million copies in print, and his radio program *Let's Go with Bill Fay* is heard on more than 100 radio stations.

His message is simple: "If God can change my life, He can change yours."[3]

It's All About Obedience

Bill Fay will be the first to tell you that he rarely responded to Christians in a positive manner. He often sneered and rolled his eyes at people who tried to share Jesus with him. He was often abusive and arrogant in expressing his distaste for Christianity. Nevertheless, today Bill is adamant that these people did not fail in their attempts. He states:

> Through the years, many people came into my life to share their faith,
> but I would not receive it. I sent these people away, discouraged, because
> I either insulted them, antagonized them, or persecuted them. And if they
> walked away from me believing they had failed, they believed a lie. For I
> never forgot the name, the face, the person, or the words of anyone who
> ever told me about Jesus.[4]

The moral of this story is that you should never give up but should keep on sharing regardless of the immediate results or perceived fears. Real Christians will share Jesus. Bill believes that the key to a successful Christian life is faithfulness in sharing about Christ *regardless of the results*. He states, "Success is sharing your faith and living your life for Jesus Christ. It has nothing whatsoever to do with bringing anyone to the Lord. It has everything to do with obedience."[5]

Sharing Jesus Without Fear

Bill Fay's book, *Share Jesus Without Fear*, introduces an evangelism method that is focused on Christians asking non-Christians a series of questions and trusting the Holy Spirit for the results. Once you learn the questions, you too can share Jesus without fear.

Introductory Questions

Fay's method is simple and easy to learn. You begin with five questions:

1. Do you have any kind of spiritual beliefs?
2. To you, who is Jesus Christ?
3. Do you think there's a heaven or a hell?
4. If you died, where would you go? If heaven, why?
5. If what you believe is not true, would you want to know?[6]

The unsaved person's answers to the questions above are somewhat irrelevant to the larger aim of sharing Jesus without fear. Obviously, one's beliefs about Jesus as well as heaven and hell are significant, but rarely are people convinced through heated discussions about these issues. The goal of sharing Jesus without fear is to avoid an argument and to help the person get into the Scriptures.[7] "For the word of God is living and powerful, and sharper than any two-edged sword, piercing even to the division of soul and spirit, and of joints and marrow, and is a discerner of the thoughts and intents of the heart" (Heb 4:12).

Getting into the Bible

Once you have asked a person the five introductory questions and they have answered yes to question 5—If what you believe is not true, would you want to know?—you now have the opportunity to open your Bible and share Scripture. Fay believes that the key to this part is having the person, not you, read the Scripture out loud.[8]

After the person reads each verse aloud, the Christian witness asks one simple question following each verse: "What does this say to you?" There's no need to argue; the key is to let the Holy Spirit work through His Word. The seven verses to be read aloud in order are:

1. "For all have sinned and fall short of the glory of God" (Rom 3:23).
2. "For the wages of sin is death, but the gift of God is eternal life in Christ Jesus our Lord" (Rom 6:23).
3. "Jesus answered and said to him, 'Most assuredly, I say to you, unless one is born again, he cannot see the kingdom of God'" (John 3:3).
4. "Jesus said to him, 'I am the way, the truth, and the life. No one comes to the Father except through Me'" (John 14:6).
5. "That if you confess with your mouth the Lord Jesus and believe in your heart that God has raised Him from the dead, you will be saved. For with the heart one believes unto righteousness, and with the mouth confession is made unto salvation. For the Scripture says, 'Whoever believes on Him will not be put to shame'" (Rom 10:9–11).
6. "And He died for all, that those who live should live no longer for themselves, but for Him who died for them and rose again" (2 Cor 5:15).
7. "Behold, I stand at the door and knock. If anyone hears My voice and opens the door, I will come in to him and dine with him, and he with Me" (Rev 3:20).[9]

Write the Scripture references in your Bible for quick recall. After the person reads each verse aloud, the Christian witness asks one question, "What does this say to you?" Do not argue; just let the Holy Spirit work through His Word.

Bringing the Witnessing Encounter to a Decision

After you have led the person to read the Scriptures aloud and the Holy Spirit is moving in the person's life convicting of sin and the need of forgiveness, you can move to the last phase of sharing Jesus without fear. The biblical process closes with five final questions that are intended to lead the person to a decision.

1. Are you a sinner?
2. Do you want forgiveness of sins?
3. Do you believe Jesus died on the cross for you and rose again?
4. Are you willing to surrender your life to Jesus Christ?
5. Are you willing to invite Jesus into your life and into your heart?[10]

Remain completely silent at this point and let the person answer so that he will fully understand the type of decision he is making.[11] Our job is not to convince or to convict the person of his need for salvation. That is the job of the Holy Spirit. Be patient and prayerfully wait for an answer.

On the other hand, if the person gives an excuse, it is fair to ask why. He may have a simple misunderstanding or may be afraid of the unknown.[12] However, if the person says no and means it, let him go and immediately begin to pray for God to create other divine opportunities in the person's life.

If the person says yes and the Holy Spirit is clearly working and drawing the person to Christ, do not hesitate to ask for a response by leading the person in a simple prayer similar to this one:

> Heavenly Father, I have sinned against You. I want forgiveness for all my sins. I believe that Jesus died on the cross for me and rose again. Thus, I am willing to turn away from my sinful life and to follow You. Father, I give You my life to do with as You wish. I want Jesus to come into my life and into my heart. This I ask in Jesus' name. Amen.

It Really Works

A few years ago I had in my class two freshmen students who happened to be sisters. We will call them Brenda and Julie. After hearing the "Share Jesus Without Fear" presentation in class, they began to pray for their family. After a few days God impressed Brenda to contact an aunt over the phone and to present the first five questions. At the same time Julie was led to contact a cousin with the same intent. Admittedly, they were petrified and feared being rejected. Yet they asked God for the strength to obey. Both the aunt and the cousin surrendered their lives to Christ.

In another instance a 17-year-old young man named Shawn was texting a female friend. His father asked him if the friend was a Christian. Shawn responded that he was not sure but immediately texted the question to his friend. She admitted that she was unsaved.

Shawn then began to text her the first five introductory questions. When she affirmed that she wanted to know more, he requested that she get a Bible and read the verses out loud to herself. Shawn asked, "What does this say to you?" She responded to each verse by texting back an answer. The Holy Spirit worked as she began to fall under conviction for her sin.

Shawn continued the witnessing opportunity by texting her the final five questions. She responded by asking for some time to discuss her situation with her Christian grandparents. Later that night she called Shawn, and he was able to lead her in a prayer surrendering her life to Christ.

The Fearless Apostles

The book of Acts is the story of Christ followers' boldly sharing their faith in the midst of intense persecution. For example, after being arrested, beaten, and warned not to say anything else about Jesus, Peter and John asked the church to join them in prayer. Did they pray that the persecution would lessen? No. Instead they prayed for more boldness to share Jesus. "Now, Lord, look on their threats, and grant to Your servants that with all boldness they may speak Your word" (Acts 4:29).

In the next chapter Luke tells us that the apostles were again facing persecution for sharing the gospel. These men were unafraid to obey the command to share Jesus regardless of the circumstances.

Again they were imprisoned, but this time the Lord sent an angel to open the doors and let them go free. The angel's message to them was to continue telling people about Jesus regardless of persecution. So the next day that is exactly what they did. "But at night an angel of the Lord opened the prison doors and brought them out, and said, 'Go, stand in the temple and speak to the people all the words of this life.' And when they heard that, they entered the temple early in the morning and taught" (Acts 5:19–21).

When they got up the next morning, they went to the temple courts looking for opportunities to share Christ. As always, the courts were crowded, the Grand Central Station of the New Testament. These men were not hiding from the people who imprisoned them the day before; instead they remained faithful to their call as evangelists. Like the apostles we may also face persecution. Also like the apostles, nothing should keep us from sharing the gospel with the people around us.

Later the apostles were again taken and questioned by the Sanhedrin. God used an unlikely ally within the Sanhedrin to keep them from death. Instead of cowering in fear, the apostles rejoiced to be considered worthy to suffer for the cause of Christ. To them persecution and spiritual warfare were proof that the message of Christ was being communicated. Despite their difficulties and unplanned persecutions, they never ceased telling of Jesus' love. "And daily in the temple, and in every house, they did not cease teaching and preaching Jesus as the Christ" (Acts 5:42).

Can we say we have the same boldness and passion to reach the lost and guide them to Christ? Do you have a pre-Christian William Fay in your life that needs to hear the gospel today? If so, do not be shy. Be faithful to trust God. In doing so, you *can* share Jesus without fear!

⚊ Evangelism Is . . . ⚊

1. Sharing Jesus without fear.
2. Asking questions and listening.
3. Leading lost people to read the Word of God and letting the Holy Spirit use God's Word to reach them.
4. Being sensitive to the Holy Spirit and letting God give the increase.

⚊ Key Verse ⚊

"Now, Lord, look on their threats, and grant to Your servants that with all boldness they may speak Your word." (Acts 4:29)

⚊ Good Quotes ⚊

If you wish to experience the level of joy that so many others have found, you will have to drop those excuses for not sharing your faith.

—Bill Fay[13]

Realizing that God has empowered every Christian to witness helps us focus on sharing Jesus with every person.

—Darrell Robinson[14]

I find that almost everyone I have ever talked with has been willing and often eager to talk about spiritual things if he can do it in a relaxed, nonthreatening situation.

—Leighton Ford[15]

— Application —

Look for opportunities to share the first five questions with at least two unsaved people during the next week. As the Holy Spirit leads, if they respond positively to question 5, prayerfully walk through the rest of the Share Jesus Without Fear presentation.

Notes

1. W. Fay, *Share Jesus Without Fear* (Nashville, TN: B&H, 1999), 1–2.
2. http://bhpublishinggroup.com/truthquest/static/fay.asp.
3. Ibid.
4. Fay, *Share Jesus Without Fear*, 2.
5. Ibid., 3.
6. Ibid., 33.
7. Ibid., 34–36.
8. Ibid., 45
9. Ibid., 44.
10. Ibid., 61.
11. Ibid., 63.
12. Ibid., 65.
13. Ibid., 27.
14. D. W. Robinson, *People Sharing Jesus* (Nashville, TN: Thomas Nelson, 1995), 19.
15. L. Ford, *Good News Is for Sharing* (Elgin, IL: David C. Cook, 1977), 12.

32

Sharing Your Recovery Testimony

David Wheeler

A Miracle Changed My Life

My recovery testimony begins the week before Thanksgiving 1989. I walked into our apartment after returning home from speaking at a local church. I was astounded to find my wife, Debbi, bent over a trash can coughing up blood. She was almost six months pregnant with our second child.

I took her to the hospital early the next morning. At first they thought it was a blood clot, among other conditions. As Debbi grew weaker, the doctors were puzzled as to why a healthy 28-year-old woman would suddenly and uncontrollably begin to bleed from her lungs. She had no warning signs or previous ailments to explain her grave condition.

After only a few days the medical team was forced to put Debbi into a chemically induced coma. To my horror the doctor explained that her condition was critical and that if she did not stop bleeding soon, "she would first grow weak and lose the baby and eventually she would die." I was petrified.

The following days were long and draining, contrary to the normal excitement of the holidays. To be honest, I had a hard time praying or even reading the Bible. After all, how could God allow this to occur? We had committed our lives to serving Him. The obvious question was, Why? For the time being God remained oddly silent.

It took almost two weeks before the doctors returned with an official diagnosis. Debbi had a rare autoimmune illness called Wegener's Disease. The malady usually attacks men over 45. Up until the early 1970s, those suffering from Wegener's had a life expectancy of less than two years. The only proven treatment was large doses of steroids combined with immediate and ongoing chemotherapy to reduce the amount of antibodies in her system.

While the doctors were relieved finally to have a diagnosis, was it too late? By this point Debbi was given less than a 25 percent chance of living through the next few hours. In addition, we were concerned about the baby. The doctors were concerned that the chemicals used to treat Debbi's illness might be too much for the baby to ingest in the womb. There was a strong possibility that mom and baby would soon die!

I recall the night that Debbi received her first dose of chemotherapy. All I could do was stand next to her bed and place my hands on her stomach. I was finally able to pray out loud, just hoping to feel the baby move. After all, at that moment I did not know if I would ever speak with Debbi again or have the joy of holding our baby alive.

The drama continued with little change, other than Debbi's hair began to fall out. All of this came to a climax after three days when Debbi's body grew so weak that she spontaneously gave birth to the baby. The attending nurse was immediately on the scene and called the neonatal care unit.

After hearing an emergency announcement over the hospital intercom, I ran into the ICU and stood outside Debbi's room. Not knowing what had occurred, I feared the worst.

A few minutes later I was blown away by the sight of a one-pound fifteen-ounce baby girl! I felt like Mary and Martha at Lazarus's tomb, but to everyone's amazement, she was alive! We named the baby Kara, meaning "God's gracious gift."

After Kara's birth, Debbi slowly recuperated and was allowed to return home three weeks later. Because of atrophy in her muscles, she had to learn basic skills again like how to walk and feed herself.

Kara arrived home on February 15, 1990, weighing almost five pounds. She had a severe breathing disorder that required around-the-clock care. What a challenging beginning for a newborn.

Learning to Trust God

Several months after Debbi came home from the hospital, we were asked to visit with an older professor/pastor friend, Dr. Jimmie Nelson. After exchanging pleasantries, I can still remember his reaching out and gently taking our hands. God began to use Dr. Nelson to answer the why I asked in my heart.

He first encouraged us to remain firmly in the Word and to devote ourselves daily to prayer. In fact, he smiled as I shared with him about my questions during the early days of our experience. I admitted that I was puzzled by God's silence.

As a man of great wisdom, Dr. Nelson looked intently into our eyes, squeezed our hands, and implored us to let God use this "recovery" experience for His glory. He reminded us that Satan would try to pervert our hearts by making us angry toward God and each other.

He then cautioned us to protect our marriage relationship. After several decades in ministry, Dr. Nelson knew that the pressures of paying exorbitant medical bills and dealing with a chronic illness could easily make us bitter and even undo our marriage.

Like a father exhorting his children, he said, "Do not be deceived, you may not understand this now, but God has a plan for you. If you allow Him, He will empower you and use you to tell His story through the brokenness of what you have experienced." He further stated, "Trust me, God is never shy about advancing His kingdom. You are a living testimony to His grace and power. Now that you have experienced His mercy, go tell the world that He is alive!"

What Does the Bible Say?

As I wrestled with God and worked through what we were facing, I turned to the Bible. I found numerous examples and teachers who also had to learn to trust God.

The Apostle Paul

As Dr. Nelson shared, I was immediately reminded of Jesus' words as recorded by the apostle Paul in 2 Cor 12:9: "My grace is sufficient for you, for my power is made perfect in weakness" (NIV). At that moment I understood the reason for God's silence during the early days of Debbi's hospitalization. It was not because He was unconcerned or disconnected from us, His children. He was simply waiting on me to become weak.

John the Baptist

God was waiting for me to acknowledge my position as a surrendered disciple in need of Him. I could finally relate with John the Baptist, who boldly shared,

"He must increase, but I must decrease" (John 3:30). Even though he was facing death, John the Baptist was not bitter about his circumstances, and he never stopped proclaiming the message of Christ.

Joseph

I could also relate to Joseph. Even though he was left for dead and sold into slavery by his brothers, he refused to become bitter. Many years later he proclaimed to the same brothers who had sold him into slavery, "You meant evil against me; but God meant it for good" (Gen 50:20). To his credit Joseph went on to forgive his brothers, realizing that God allowed his discomfort and pain in order to fulfill His greater plan for the nations.

Moses

I also considered the plight of Moses in Exodus 3. After 40 years of running away from the hurts of his past, Moses found himself before a burning bush listening to God. As God shared His plan to rescue the Jews, Moses had to be elated to know that God was finally going to intervene and deliver His people from the bondage of slavery in Egypt. On the other hand, he would have been petrified to find out that God had chosen him to be the deliverer.

After all, how could Moses go back to Egypt? He fled in disgrace after losing his temper and killing an Egyptian guard. What if they met him at the gates and made him pay for his past indiscretions? In the end God used a more humble and obedient (weaker) Moses. Little did he know that God was preparing him through the struggles of life in order to develop the character he would need as a leader.

I wondered, could it be that God was doing the same in me?

Jesus

I believe everything eventually comes back to Christ. Was it fair that He suffered the indignity of leaving heaven to become a mere human, even being tempted by Satan? Was it fair that He was beaten, spat upon, and cursed in order to become the eternal sacrifice for our sins?

Yet He never complained about His humble past or became embittered against His Father. He simply stated in Luke 22:42, "Not My will, but Yours, be done." Jesus could have made a similar observation as Joseph, "What Satan meant for evil in reference to pain and suffering on the cross, God used for His eternal glory!" When we suffer, we must do the same.

Boldly Sharing the Testimony of God's Recovery

Since the initial diagnosis and the meeting with Dr. Nelson, Debbi and I have seen God use our recovery testimony to encourage thousands of believers to persevere and not give up! At the same time we have been able to share the gospel with many unsaved people who are discouraged and feel defeated by life.

Unfortunately for Debbi, Wegener's Disease is chronic and requires ongoing radical care. She has remained on periodic doses of chemotherapy and debilitating steroids since the original diagnosis in 1989 and has never experienced remission.

Yet she boldly proclaims her recovery story to a hurting world. After all, she understands the challenge of losing everything as our medical bills soared to over $500,000, totally exhausting all of our funds. We lost everything. She understands the lasting effects of chemotherapy and the indignity of being a human guinea pig for insensitive doctors trying to understand a rare disease. Rather than being bitter, Debbi understands the connection and uses it to share Christ.

As for Kara, in the years since her unbelievable birth, she has experienced life-threatening seizures and a diagnosis of mild cerebral palsy. Even though we were told by experts that she would never be able to function properly in school or to experience a normal life, Kara recently graduated high school as a member of the National Honor Society. Kara, too, trusted God and chose to share her recovery story with everyone who would listen. She was even featured by her public high school in a recent yearbook. The story was entitled "God Made Me to Share My Testimony." Kara will soon be a college freshman!

What Is a Recovery Testimony

In over 30 years of ministry experience, I have observed that since Satan cannot steal a person's salvation he will always try to render the Christian ineffective. Aside from creating the fear of sharing one's faith, he deceives the believer by keeping the person in bondage to the past.

The mistakes and tough times in our past open the door to the enemy's intimidation and fear. Therefore, we play it safe, pretending that we are perfect people. To be frank, those outside the church have seen enough of the "perfect people" in the church. Those who are honest about their shortcomings become a breath of life to those searching for life themselves. However, when we allow Satan to intimidate us or make us fearful, we remain silent.

Once I realized Satan's lie, I started requiring my classes to write their recovery testimonies. I was shocked by the emotional responses as many of the students verbalized publically their specific need to be released from Satan's bondage to past sins. In addition to the following stories, students have also spoken of abuse, molestation, drug addiction, and cultic activity.

In one instance a young man—we will call him John—tearfully shared with the class that he was formerly addicted to pornography. He was brokenhearted by his ongoing hesitation to share his faith because of his feelings of unworthiness. After all, he recalled, "Who am I to share about Christ? Look who I used to be!" When he was finally able to share his recovery testimony, he realized the power to break Satan's bondage. John is now a bold witness who can especially relate to young men struggling with pornography.

In another example a young woman—we will call her Amy—shared with the class in vivid terms about her eating disorder. After years of struggling with anorexia and bulimia, Amy barely weighed 75 pounds. Even though she was a young woman in her early 20s, she had resolved in her mind that she would soon die. When she heard a Christian artist on the radio share about the deliverance found in Christ, Amy surrendered her life to Christ and was eventually delivered from the idol of food. As she read her recovery testimony to the class, it was evident that she suffered from the same bondage as John in the previous story. Every time she began to share about Christ, Satan intervened with the charge, "What makes you so holy? Who are you to tell people about Christ?" But just like John, when Amy publically shared her recovery testimony, she exposed the lies of Satan, and the bondage was broken! She is now an amazing witness, specializing with young women struggling with eating disorders.

A recovery testimony is living out the words of Joseph shared earlier in this chapter from Gen 50:20, "You meant evil against me; but God meant it for good." Rather than allowing Satan to silence the followers of Christ through lies and deceit, we must admit our past indiscretions and forgive ourselves just as we are forgiven by Christ. In addition, we must use those past experiences as points of entry into the lives of fellow strugglers in need of salvation.

How to Prepare a Recovery Testimony

The focus of a recovery testimony is how Jesus helped you with a particular problem or need in your life. In writing a recovery testimony, follow a simple outline to prepare your story. Briefly explain:

1. My Life Seemed Normal Until . . .

Explain the occurrence(s) in your life where you were discouraged or challenged by a great burden. It can be something like a past addition to drugs, alcohol, or pornography. It can also be an event like the death of a friend or family member, an illness, depression, or maybe the divorce of your parents. It does not have to be anything catastrophic or impressive, just an important event to you. To be honest, this is not the time to be self-righteous. It is, rather, a time to be vulnerable and transparent.

2. I Discovered Hope and Help in Jesus When . . .

As you recall the past occurrence in your life, explain in detail how God intervened. Use phrases that express emotions and feelings. Also recall Scripture verses and biblical stories that were helpful in meeting your needs.

3. I Am Glad I Have a Personal Relationship with Jesus Today Because . . .

This is when you brag on Jesus! Explain how your life has changed for the better. However, be careful not to overexaggerate or to come off as if you have obtained perfection. The purpose of the recovery testimony is to gain victory over past indiscretions and to use those experiences to identify with unbelievers and create bridges to the gospel.

4. May I Share How Something like This Can Happen to You?

The point of this question is to remain intentional about building bridges in order to share Christ. Unless the other person is unresponsive, depending on the leadership of the Holy Spirit, one should always be inviting unbelievers to follow Christ.

⁓ Evangelism Is . . . ⁓

1. Sharing your recovery testimony with the unsaved.
2. Connecting your recovery testimony back to the gospel message.
3. Being vulnerable and transparent with the unsaved.

⁓ Key Verse ⁓

"My grace is sufficient for you, for my power is made perfect in weakness." (2 Cor 12:9 NIV)

⁓ Good Quotes ⁓

*As fellow members of the human race, we all deal
with life's hurts, habits, and hang-ups.*

—Rick Warren[1]

*There is no truth more generally admitted among earnest
Christians than that of their utter weakness.*

—Andrew Murray[2]

⁓ Immediate Application ⁓

Write your recovery testimony by using the guidelines below:

1. My life seemed normal until . . .
2. I discovered hope and help in Jesus when . . .
3. I am glad I have a personal relationship with Jesus today because . . .

⁓ Why Is a Recovery Testimony Important? ⁓

1. Your recovery testimony is a bridge to rescuing hurting people through the gospel.
2. Your recovery testimony validates your witness with a skeptical culture.
3. Your recovery testimony is a daily reminder of God's grace.
4. Your recovery testimony is a tool for spiritual warfare. . . . You are forgiven!

Notes

1. R. Warren, quoted in foreword of J. Baker, *Life's Healing Choices: Freedom from Your Hurts, Hang-ups, and Habits* (West Monroe, LA: Howard Books, 2007), 14.

2. A. Murray, *Abide in Christ* (Springdale, PA: Whitaker House, 1979), 179.

33 Answering Common Questions Seekers Ask

Dave Earley

"Tonight's Going to Be My Spiritual Birthday!"

Those were Jeff's words. Jeff was an intelligent young adult who grew up in an atheistic home. Both of his parents were professors at Ohio State University. One of his friends had challenged him to consider Christianity and attend a Bible study group I led for spiritual seekers. It ran for eight to 12 weeks, one night a week. We called it Christianity 101. We told seekers they could ask any question they wanted. Those who attended had to be unsaved, or if they were saved, they had to bring an unsaved person if they wished to attend.

The night Jeff called me, he had already gone through the Christianity 101 study three times and was halfway through for the fourth time. Each time he had more and more of his questions answered and was drawn closer to Christ. Each time he saw others get their questions answered and give their lives to Christ.

Late one night after I had put my boys to bed, the phone rang. It was Jeff. "Tonight's going to be my spiritual birthday!" he said eagerly into the phone. "This is my physical birthday, and I am tired of running from God. I want to give my life to Jesus tonight. This will be both my physical *and* my spiritual birthday."

"Great," I said. "By now you know what to do."

"But I want you to be here," Jeff said.

"Jeff, it is kind of late," I teased.

"Don't worry," Jeff said. "I'm already on my way. I'll be at your house real soon."

In just a couple of minutes, Jeff was at the door. I invited him into the living room. He bypassed the chair and got down on his knees. He pulled me down next to him. The next thing I knew, he was offering an amazing prayer of repentance and faith in the Lord Jesus Christ. He got up, and we both had tears in our eyes. He gave me a hug and then was gone to tell some of his friends that he had just been born again. A few weeks later Jeff was baptized and became vitally involved in our church life. Since then Jeff has lived for God. His big smile is a huge blessing to everyone who knows him.

Jeff's questions were not any different or more difficult than the basic questions many seekers have about Christianity. He needed a few years to reach the point where he truly trusted us. Then, when he was given intelligent answers to his questions in the context of loving gentleness and respect, the Holy Spirit made the truth of the gospel real to him.

Although most seekers don't take as long as Jeff, I have seen hundreds of people go through the same process. I have seen seekers come to a life-changing faith in Jesus when we loved them as people, respected their opinions, patiently answered their questions, and lived a genuine Christian life that they wished they were experiencing.

Evangelism Is Patiently Answering Common Questions About Christianity

When I first began sharing Jesus with lost people, I would occasionally run into someone who was older and more intelligent than I am. When they asked a few tough questions about Christianity, I was stumped as to what to say. Some skeptics made me feel like Christians were anti-intellectual, like we had to leave our brains at the door when we went to church.

But every time someone asked me a question or hit me with an argument I could not answer, I went back and tried to find the answer. Soon I discovered that there is plenty of evidence for the existence of God, the reliability and validity of the Bible, the historicity and deity of Jesus Christ, and His resurrection from the grave. I learned that Christianity was not just one of many religions but was the only logical and valid faith system and that only Christianity led to positive, lasting, and eternal life change.

When I began offering the Christianity 101 class based on the questions of skeptics and filled with nonbelievers, people thought I was crazy. But I had discovered that all of their questions revolved around a few basic areas and a handful of common issues. When the seeking skeptics were treated with prayer, gentleness, respect, love, and patience, God would wear down their defenses. Of the hundreds of people who have taken the class over the years, all of them who stayed with it gave their lives to Jesus Christ.

Reminders Before You Get into an Argument

Win the Heart, Then Win the Argument

The key to effectively evangelizing skeptics and seekers is not only knowing what you believe and why but also being careful first to win the heart and then to win the argument.

Aristotle was an ancient Greek philosopher. He was the first to create a comprehensive system of Western philosophy, encompassing morality and aesthetics, logic and science, politics and metaphysics. In training future philosophers to win others to their perspective, he taught that they should *first* earn trust, *then* give arguments or evidence. They were not to begin by trying to prove the other view was incorrect. Rather, they would first prove themselves trustworthy. Only after earning the trust of the skeptic, they were next to consider the questions/issues/problems facing those they hoped to reach. Then Aristotle's students were to show that their view was the right view.[1]

Abraham Lincoln was the sixteenth president of the United States. He is famous for being able to win his opponents over to his point of view and making his enemies become his most loyal friends. He shared his secret.

> If you want to win a man to your cause, first convince him that you are his true friend. Therein is the drop of honey that will catch his heart—which, say what you will, is the greater high road to his reason. When you have gained his heart, you will have little trouble convincing his judgment of the justices of your cause, if indeed your cause is really just.[2]

"I Have Never Argued Anyone into Heaven"

Dr. Gary Habermas is the distinguished professor of apologetics and philosophy and chairman of the Department of Philosophy and Theology for Liberty University and Liberty Baptist Theological Seminary. He is a prolific author, lecturer, and is considered the leading expert on the reliability of the resurrection of Jesus Christ. He has debated atheists in such lofty academic settings as Oxford, Edinburgh, and Cambridge universities. He also is my colleague and friend.

Recently I asked Gary, as a gifted debater, about the role of argument and apologetics in evangelism. "Let one thing be quite clear," he said. "I have never argued anyone into heaven. Arguments alone will only build walls. The people I have helped come to Christ have been first won through love, *then* answering their questions."

Paul

The great apostle Paul tells us how we are to respond to those who are still outside the faith. He suggests graciousness, love, and integrity.

> Use your heads as you live and work among outsiders. Don't miss a trick. Make the most of every opportunity. Be gracious in your speech. The goal is to bring out the best in others in a conversation, not put them down, not cut them out. (Col 4:5–6 *The Message*)

> Rather, let our lives lovingly express truth [in all things, speaking truly, dealing truly, living truly]. (Eph 4:15 AMP)

Responses to Common Questions Skeptics Ask

This book is not a book about Christian apologetics (the defense of the Christian faith). It is a book on evangelism. However, over the years I have found that in order to evangelize effectively, I often need to do a little apologetics first. In other words, I have had to do preevangelism by offering at least brief answers to the questions raised by the serious seekers and skeptics. In the rest of this chapter, I will offer some answers to common questions about God and the Bible. In the next chapter I'll give some answers to questions about Jesus and religion.

Usually a short answer is enough for most seekers. I suggest that after learning these short answers, you dig deeper to be able to give more thorough answers to these questions.

What Evidence Do You Have That There Is a God?

The existence of the universe is itself evidence that there is a God. Only three options can be offered to explain the existence of the universe: (1) The universe has always been. (2) It came into being by itself. (3) It was created.

Option 1. "The universe is eternal" has been utterly rejected by the scientific community. The motion of the galaxies, the background radiation echo, and other evidences overwhelmingly point to the fact that the universe sprang into existence at a particular point in time, something scientists call the big bang.

Option 2. "The universe created itself" is philosophically impossible. Before the universe existed, it would not have been around to do the creating. Obviously, a nonexistent universe could not have done anything! It did not exist. Nothing cannot produce something. Nothing is nothing. Nothing cannot see, smell, act, think, or create. So options 1 and 2 can be thrown out on scientific and philosophical grounds.

Option 3. "Something or someone outside the universe created the universe." This is the only reasonable option. For example, let's imagine I am holding up a painting. When you see a painting, what proof do you need to establish the fact that a painter exists? The only proof needed is the painting itself. The painting is absolute proof that there was a painter. You do not need to see the painter to believe that he or she exists. The painting is all the evidence you need. It would not be there if the painter did not exist, and so it is with the universe. The existence of the universe itself proves absolutely that there is a creator.[3]

What Evidence Do You Have That the Bible Is actually True?"

I have found a dozen good reasons to trust the Bible as the Word of God. For example, I have always been impressed with the outlandish number of fulfilled prophecies, the incredible scientific accuracy, the undeniable unity, the absolute honesty, the unbelievable indestructibility, the positive influence, and the life-changing power of the Bible.

The Bible, unlike any other religious book, has demonstrated itself to be the Word of God through its ability rightly to predict the future. Literally hundreds of specific prophecies in the Bible that were spoken hundreds of years before their fulfillment have already come to pass. No other religious book can verify itself in this way. For example, the specifics of the life and death of Jesus were predicted in detail hundreds of years before He was born in Bethlehem of Judea.

Beyond that, the Bible has also been proven to be historically reliable by numerous archaeological discoveries. To date, more than 25,000 archaeological discoveries have verified the names of persons, places, events, and customs mentioned in the Bible.

My favorite evidence for the unusual validity of the Bible is its unbelievable indestructibility. For example, the Roman emperor Diocletian fiercely attacked the Bible. He killed so many Christians and burned so many Bibles that in AD 303 he erected a pillar inscribed, "The name of Christians has been extinguished."

I don't think so.

A mere 20 years later, Rome had a new emperor, Constantine. Although his motives are debated, Christianity had become so prevalent in his kingdom that he declared Christianity the official religion of Rome. When he asked for a copy of the Bible, the book Diocletian had supposedly wiped out, he was stunned when within 24 hours, 50 copies of the Bible were delivered at his feet. Where had they come from? All 50 had been hidden in Diocletian's own palace!

Two hundred years ago the French atheist Voltaire declared, "Fifty years from now the world will hear no more of the Bible."

I don't think so.

In 1828, 50 years after Voltaire's death, the Geneva Bible Society bought his house and his printing press in order to begin printing Bibles. In 1933, just over 150 years after his death, during the same year that a first edition copy of Voltaire's book was selling for eights cents in Paris bookshops, the British Museum bought a copy of the New Testament from Russia for $500,000! Two hundred years after Voltaire's death, the Bible exceeded half a billion copies in print!

The Bible, the world's most indestructible book, is also the world's most popular book. It is far and away the most printed, sold, and read book on the planet. It has been printed in 1,500 languages, more than any other 100 books combined. It was the first book printed on a printing press. Today no one has any idea how many billions of copies of the Bible are in print. On top of that, it remains a best seller year after year.

Hasn't the Bible Undergone Corruption as It Was Translated Hundreds of Times Through the Centuries?

Yes, the Bible has been translated into hundreds of languages through the centuries. But the actual text of the Bible has been accurately preserved. How do we know?

First, there is the manuscript evidence. Simply put, we have many more copies that go much farther back than any other ancient piece of literature. Today several thousand partial and complete, ancient, handwritten manuscript copies of the Bible exist, some dating as far back as the third century BC. In comparison the next best piece of literature regarding manuscript evidence is

Homer's *Illiad* with only 643 copies dated 500 years after the original. The biblical manuscripts have allowed textual critics and scholars to verify that the Bible we have today is the same Bible the early church had.

A second evidence for the reliability of the Bible comes from the writings of the church fathers. By church fathers I am referring to leaders in the early church within a few generations of the apostles of Christ. In their commentaries on the Bible, their letters to one another, and their letters to other churches, these men quoted the New Testament Scriptures more than 86,000 times. Their quotations have allowed scholars to reconstruct 99.86 percent of the New Testament. There are only 11 verses in the New Testament that the church fathers apparently never cited. These two evidences, the manuscript evidence and the writings of the church fathers, verify conclusively that the original text of the Bible has been accurately preserved.

Haven't Certain Books of the Bible Been Lost?

No. The supposedly "lost books" of the Bible—the so-called gospels of Thomas, Philip, and Mary Magdalene—were not gospels. They are/were "pseudo-gospels" the early church rejected as spurious writings that did not qualify as being included in the Word of God. The Christian church was familiar with these documents but purposely left them out of the Bible, easily recognizing that they did not pass the test for whether a piece of writing met the criteria of being included in the Bible:

First, they were not written by any of the apostles (like Matthew or John) or their close associates (like the Gospel of Mark or Luke). Second, scholars date these spurious gospels to the second and third centuries, too long after the time of Christ to be considered credible. Third, these writings contradict authentic revelation. You can be absolutely confident that God, who inspired (2 Tim 3:16) men to pen the words of the Bible (2 Pet 1:21), saw to it that none of the inspired writings were lost. It would be foolish for us to think that an all-knowing, all-powerful God could lose track of books He intended to put in the Bible, or anything else for that matter.

⚊ Evangelism Is . . . ⚊

1. Patiently answering common questions.
2. Aided by being able to do some simple apologetics.
3. Not arguing people into heaven.
4. Earning trust, then presenting evidence.

～ Good Quotes ～

*I must say, that having for many years made the evidences
of Christianity the subject of close study, the result has
been a firm and increasing conviction of the authenticity
and plenary [complete] inspiration of the Bible.
It is indeed the Word of God.*

—Simon Greenleaf (1783–1853), founder of Harvard Law School

*A college student once told me I satisfactorily answered his
questions. "Are you going to become a Christian?" I asked.*

"No," he replied.

*Puzzled, I asked, "Why not?"
He admitted, "Frankly it would mess up the way I am
living." He realized that the real issue for him was not
intellectual but moral.*

—Paul Little[4]

Notes

1. See Aristotle's classic work, *Rhetoric,* or C. Carey, "Rhetorical Means of Persuasion," *Persuasion: Greek Rhetoric in Action,* ed. I. Worthington (London: Routledge, 1994), 26–45.

2. A. Lincoln, quoted in K. Boa and L. Moody, *I'm Glad You Asked* (Colorado Springs, CO: Cook Communications, 2005), 19.

3. For this brief answer I am indebted to C. Campbell, "Answers to Your Questions," www.ARB.com, http://www.alwaysbeready.com/index.php?option=com_content&task=view&id=51&Itemid=71, accessed June 1, 2009.

4. P. Little, *Know Why You Believe* (Downers Grove, IL: InterVarsity, 1988), 19.

34

Giving a Logical Defense of Your Faith

Dave Earley

Several years ago, I was sharing Christ with a man in a park in Dover, England. As he sat on his park bench, he smiled a smug little smile and said, "Well son, I think going to heaven is a lot like going to the post office in this town. There are several ways to get there from here, yet regardless of which way you take, they'll all lead you to the same place. It's like that with religion. You may take Christianity Street, and your friend may take Buddhist Boulevard, and someone else may take Hindu Road and somebody else Islam Road. As long as you all are good and sincere, they'll all take you to heaven. All religions are basically the same."

Is he right? Are all religions basically the same? Do they all point to the same God? Are they all paths leading to the same destination?

Whenever the subject of religion comes up in public settings, tension often arises. As I have engaged people in conversations about Jesus Christ, I have frequently heard them quickly jump to sharing with me their views on religion. Over the years I have had an ever-increasing number of people say to me things like:

- What makes Jesus so special? How can you say He is God?
- All religions are simply different paths up the same mountain.
- All religions have only partial truth. They need to be combined to get the complete picture.
- As long as people live a good life, no matter what they believe, they will go to heaven.

- It does not matter what you believe as long as you are sincere.
- We should tolerate the views of others even when they differ from our own. To say Jesus is the only way to heaven is wrong because it is intolerant of those who believe differently.
- Right and wrong is a matter of what is right and wrong for you. One religion or another doesn't matter. What does matter is finding the right belief system for you.
- Religion is religion. All religions are basically the same. So what's the big difference?

Don't Leave Your Brain at the Door

Peter encouraged us to know why we believe and to be ready to share it properly while carefully showing gentleness and respect. "But in your hearts set Christ apart as holy [and acknowledge Him] as Lord. Always be ready to give a logical defense to anyone who asks you to account for the hope that is in you, but do it courteously and respectfully" (1 Pet 3:15 AMP).

Too many believe that in order to become a genuine follower of Jesus Christ you must leave your brain at the door. They think Christianity is an irrational, anti-intellectual, sentimental, purely emotional leap into the dark.

True Christianity is not a blind leap in the dark. It is faith based on sound evidence and good reason. Christianity is rational and the only belief system that is both logically sensible and spiritually powerful. Be assured, by placing faith in Jesus, one is not committing intellectual suicide. You do not have to commit a lobotomy in order to be saved. Jesus died to take away our sins, not our brains. Christians do not have to leave their brains at the door until they get to heaven. We can give a reason for the hope that is within us.

Reasons for the Hope That Is in Us

How Can You Say Jesus Is God?

One reason I believe Jesus is God is that Jesus, a man of unquestioned integrity and sanity, clearly claimed to be God. In his famous book *Mere Christianity*, Oxford professor and former skeptic C. S. Lewis makes this statement:

> A man who was merely a man and said the sort of things Jesus said would not be a great moral teacher. He would either be a lunatic—on the level with a man who says he is a poached egg—or he would be the devil of hell. You must take your choice. Either this was, and is, the Son

of God, or else a madman or something worse. You can shut him up for a fool or you can fall at his feet and call him Lord and God. But let us not come with any patronizing nonsense about his being a great human teacher. He has not left that open to us.[1]

After studying the facts for himself, Lewis concluded that Jesus was indeed God. He spent the rest of his life using his gift of writing to tell the world about Jesus.

Another reason to believe that Jesus is God is because He allowed Himself to be killed because of this claim. What a dumb thing to do if He really was not God! Notice why the Jews wanted to kill Jesus: "Therefore the Jews sought all the more to kill Him, because He . . . also said that God was His Father, making Himself equal with God" (John 5:18).

Beyond that, I love the fact that Jesus had uniquely fulfilled the prophecies about God, the Messiah. His birth, life, death, and resurrection were described in amazing details hundreds and, in some instances, thousands of years prior to their occurrence.

The name of His great, great, great-grandfather was predicted. The place of His birth was predicted. So was the visit by the wise men, the gifts the wise men brought, the appearance of the star, and Herod's attempt to kill him. Jesus' trip to Egypt to avoid Herod was predicted. Those are merely several of the fulfilled prophecies about Jesus' birth.

In the Old Testament there are as many as 332 distinct predictions which are literally fulfilled in Christ.[2] Astronomer and mathematician Peter Stoner, in his book *Science Speaks*, offers a mathematical analysis showing that it is impossible that the precise statements about the Messiah could be fulfilled in a single person by mere coincidence. He estimates that the chance of *only eight* of these prophecies being fulfilled in the life of one man at 1 in 10 to the seventeenth power.[3] That is 1 followed by 17 zeroes or one chance in 100,000,000,000,000,000! (Compare this to winning the lottery with odds of "one in a million" as 1 followed by only six zeroes).

In order to understand how amazing it is that one man fulfilled just eight of the prophecies Jesus fulfilled, consider this example.

Take 100,000,000,000,000,000 silver dollars and lay them on the face of Texas [with its approximate land area of 262,000 square miles]. They will cover all of the state two feet deep. Now mark one of these silver dollars and stir the whole mass thoroughly, all over the state. Blindfold a man and tell him that he can travel as far as he wishes, but he must pick up one silver dollar and say that this is the right one.

What chance would he have of getting the right one? Just the same chance that the prophets would have had of writing these eight prophecies and having them all come true in any one man.[4]

That is one man fulfilling only *eight* of the prophecies regarding the Messiah. Jesus fulfilled 332!

Aren't All Religions Basically the Same?

My answer to that question is no. Even though the golden rule ("Do to others as you would have them do to you," Luke 6:31 NIV) runs through most religions, they sharply contradict one another on many major points.

Consider some of the major differences between the major religions and Christianity.

The Issue of God. Many other religions view God as one with the universe and/or impersonal. Eastern religions, like Buddhism, are pantheistic and say God is impersonal and permeates everything. God is everything. Everything is god. There is no real difference between god and the universe. As a result some, such as Hinduism, have millions of deities (Brahma, Shiva, Krishna, etc.).

Christianity and Judaism say that God is independent of His creation. Genesis 1:1 states, "In the beginning God created the heavens and the earth." The Bible teaches that God existed *before* creation and is independent of it. Just as a painter is not his painting, God is not His creation.

Christianity worships a personal God. Psalm 103:13 tells us that the God of Christianity has personal feelings: "As a father pities his children, so the LORD pities those who fear Him." Jesus taught us to pray to a personal God: "Our Father who art in heaven" (see Matt 6:9). John 1:14 tells us that our God became one of us: "And the Word became flesh and dwelt among us." You can't get anymore personal than that!

Islam says there is one God (Allah), but he is impersonal. Nowhere in the Koran are Muslims instructed to call Allah, "Father."

The Issue of Obtaining Merit with God. Other religions teach that it is entirely up to man to do something to merit favor with God. Christianity clearly teaches that man, in himself, is totally incapable of meriting favor with God.

A pastor named Harry Ironside was asked why all the religions in the world think theirs is right. Ironside replied, "'Hundreds of religions in the world? That's strange. I've only found two."

"Oh sir," the skeptic replied. "You must know that there are more than that?"

"Not at all, sir," Ironside answered. "While I admit varying shades of opinions of those comparing the two schools, there are still only two. The one covers all those who expect to be saved by *doing*. The other says you have been saved by something *done*. The whole question is this: 'Can you save yourself?' or 'Must you be saved by another?' If you can save yourself, you need not listen to my message. If you cannot save yourself, you had better listen closely."

The Issue of Assurance of Going to Heaven. Other religions can never assure one's salvation because they are based on good works. One can never know when he's done enough good works. Christianity can and does offer assurance of salvation because salvation is the result of the work of a perfect God instead of the efforts of an imperfect man. My salvation is not based on what I do but rather on what Jesus did. What He was and did was perfect. Therefore, I can be confident—not in imperfect me but in the perfect Jesus.

Isn't Living a Good Life Enough? Aren't Good People Going to Heaven?

When asked these questions, I point out two simple facts that almost everyone agrees with: (1) Heaven is a perfect place. (2) None of us are perfect. Then I generally ask people, "When you die, would you like to go to heaven?"

Nearly all say, "Yes, I would."

Then I may say, "That poses a problem if heaven is perfect and you aren't. If God let you into heaven as you are, imperfect, would heaven still be perfect?"

At this point the lightbulbs start going off for them so I share the gospel from Rom 6:23: "For the wages of sin is death, but the gift of God is eternal life in Christ Jesus our Lord."

As we discussed in a previous chapter, there are no "good enough" people in heaven, only perfect ones. Heaven is perfect. We are not perfect. Therefore, getting into heaven and having eternal life is a gift that must be accepted by faith. "For by grace you have been saved through faith and that not of yourselves; it is the gift of God" (Eph 2:8).

The difference between Christianity and other world religions is simple. In other religions heaven is a reward to be earned, and in Christianity it is a gift to be received.

Shouldn't We Tolerate Others' Views? Does It Really Matter What You Believe as Long as You Are Sincere?

Regarding Tolerance. I say, "Yes, we should tolerate others' views but only *until* those views conflict with the truth." Tolerance sounds kind and open-minded. But too often tolerance is used as a cover for shortcomings. ("If everything is right, then nothing is wrong. I can ignore the issue of sin and salvation.")

The biggest problem with "tolerance for tolerance's sake" is that tolerance is actually cruel when it conflicts with the truth. Truth by its own nature is intolerant of error.

Let's say a blind man stands on the edge of a cliff, and he turns to you to ask, "Which way should I step?"

I would be cruel to say to him, "Oh, it really doesn't matter. Just be sincere and do the best you can." The truth says that if he steps in the wrong direction, he will plunge to his death. But if he'll turn in another direction, away from the cliff or onto the bridge, he'll live. Tolerance is no virtue when it ignores reality.

Let's say a cancer specialist knows you have a malignant tumor in your body that will kill you in a matter of weeks if it isn't removed. Yet he doesn't want to seem narrow-minded and intolerant. Of course, he'd certainly hate to offend you, so he says, "If you sincerely believe that the tumor is no problem and you are a pretty good guy, I am sure it will all be OK."

What would you think of that doctor? How long do you think he would keep his license to practice medicine?

I would rather have a doctor tell me some narrow-minded, offensive truth than some nice little tolerant lie.

By the way, if something is not true, what is it? It is a lie.

Regarding Sincerity. I say, "What you believe does make a big difference. It is possible to be sincere and yet be sincerely wrong."

Every year dozens of people in this country are accidentally killed.[5] Someone jokingly points a gun at them, sincerely believing that the gun is empty. When the trigger is pulled, the gun goes off, and the other individual is killed, even though the one who pulled the trigger was sincere in not intending to shoot the other person. They sincerely believed something that was not true. Sincerity was not enough. All the sincerity in the world would not overrule or change the facts. The gun was loaded. The trigger was pulled, and the person was killed.

Sincerity, no matter how great the amount, does not change the facts. Believing something doesn't make something true anymore than failing to believe something makes it false. I can sincerely believe that my son's 1994 Honda Accord is really a 2010 Jaguar. Yet when I go to trade it in, no amount of sincerity will change the fact that it's just a 1994 Honda Accord.

I can sincerely believe that the law of gravity isn't real because I can't see it. I can believe so sincerely that the law of gravity isn't real that I jump off the top of a skyscraper. No amount of sincerity will change the fact that the law of gravity is real, and no amount of sincerity can stop me from falling to the pavement below.

Faith, no matter how sincere, is only as good as its object. It's not the amount of faith but the object of faith that truly matters. When electricity was first put in homes, some people had more confidence in it than others. When it came time to flip the switch, the amount of faith made no difference. For the person with a great amount of faith in electricity and the person with little faith, it does not matter. Both will have the light come on when they flip the switch.

The emphasis of the Scriptures is not so much on the one trusting but rather on the one being trusted. Paul wrote, "Believe on the Lord Jesus Christ and you will be saved" (Acts 16:31). Our faith is in Jesus Christ who is completely trustworthy.

⁓ Evangelism Is . . . ⁓

1. Boldly giving a reason for the hope that is within you.
2. Helping people grasp the unique truth of Christianity.

⁓ Key Verse ⁓

But sanctify the Lord God in your hearts, and always be ready to give a defense to everyone who asks you a reason for the hope that is in you, with meekness and fear. (1 Pet 3:15)

Notes

1. C. S. Lewis, *Mere Christianity* (New York: MacMillian, 1952), 41.
2. F. Hamilton, *The Basis of Christian Faith* (New York: Harper and Row, 1964), 160.
3. P. Stoner, *Science Speaks* (Chicago: Moody Press, 1963), 100.
4. Ibid., 107.
5. According to the Center for Injury Prevention and Control, the number of accidental deaths in the United States through the use (misuse) of a firearm was 642 in 2006. http://webapp.cdc.gov/cgi-bin/broker.exe, accessed July 5, 2009.

35

Asking for a Response

David Wheeler

Disciples Are to Catch Fish

A pastor friend of mine went on a fishing trip every spring with a professional fisherman. The professional fisherman obviously loved Christ and was not shy about boldly proclaiming his faith, as he put it, "with everyone who sat in his boat."

After two days of listening to exciting stories about his obvious evangelistic prowess, the pastor chimed in and made a simple observation. He said, "I am encouraged to hear about all the people who have heard the message of Christ while sitting in your boat; however, you have yet to mention if any of the people ever repented and surrendered their lives to follow Christ." Then the pastor asked, "What kind of professional fisherman would you be if you refused to cast your line and bait into the water; after all, is not the purpose of fishing eventually to *catch* fish?!"

The professional fisherman responded by stating, "What do you mean? I am, after all, being obedient by sharing my faith with unsaved people."

The pastor replied, "Yes, that is true, but like fishing, you cannot just show up at the lake and expect the fish to jump into the boat. Evangelism is more than merely sharing information and telling inspirational stories. Through the leadership of the Holy Spirit, it is also being intentional about *inviting* people to follow Christ!"

The pastor's words cut deep into the heart of the professional fisherman. He responded by promising the pastor that he would have a different testimony when they met again the next spring. The professional fisherman kept a journal of all the people he took on his boat over the next year. By asking for a genuine response to the gospel, the fisherman led more than 200 people to Christ in a single year!

Jonah Called for a Response

Jonah is known as the man who ran from God when God called him to go and call the city of Nineveh to repentance. "Now the word of the LORD came to Jonah the son of Amittai, saying, 'Arise, go to Nineveh, that great city, and cry out against it; for their wickedness has come up before Me'" (Jonah 1:1–2).

Jonah hated the people of Nineveh because they were wicked, idolatrous, baby killers. But after being rerouted in the belly of a whale, Jonah eventually obeyed God and called the people of Nineveh to repent. They did. "'Yet forty days, and Nineveh shall be overthrown!' So the people of Nineveh believed God, proclaimed a fast, and put on sackcloth, from the greatest to the least of them" (Jonah 3:4–5).

As you read the story of Jonah, don't lose sight of the fact that the reason Jonah ran was because he feared his preaching would be effective (see Jonah 4:1–2). Calling for a response is a powerful way to impact lives.

Elijah Called for a Response

Elijah was upset because wicked King Ahab was trying to lead Israel down the path to idolatry. Rather than stand by and let it happen, Elijah extended an opportunity for the nation to make a choice. With the entire nation gathered on Mount Carmel, Elijah gave them a public invitation: "And Elijah came to all the people, and said, 'How long will you falter between two opinions? If the LORD is God, follow Him; but if Baal, follow him'" (1 Kgs 18:21).

Initially the people were hesitant to choose. But after God miraculously sent fire from heaven, the people eagerly responded to Elijah's invitation.

> And it came to pass, at the time of the offering of the evening sacrifice, that Elijah the prophet came near and said, . . . "Hear me, O LORD, hear me, that this people may know that You are the LORD God, and that You have turned their hearts back to You again."
> Then the fire of the LORD fell and consumed the burnt sacrifice, and the wood and the stones and the dust, and it licked up the water that was in the trench.

Now when all the people saw it, they fell on their faces; and they said, "The LORD, He is God! The LORD, He is God!" (1 Kgs 18:36–39)

Jesus Extended Public Invitations

Jesus' first sermon was a public call to repentance.

Now when Jesus heard that John had been put in prison, He departed to Galilee. And leaving Nazareth, He came and dwelt in Capernaum, which is by the sea, in the regions of Zebulun and Naphtali, that it might be fulfilled which was spoken by Isaiah the prophet, saying:
"The land of Zebulun and the land of Naphtali,
By the way of the sea, beyond the Jordan,
Galilee of the Gentiles:
The people who sat in darkness have seen a great light,
And upon those who sat in the region and shadow of death
Light has dawned.
From that time Jesus began to preach and to say, "Repent, for the kingdom of heaven is at hand." (Matt 4:12–17)

Throughout Jesus' earthly ministry, He publically called people to make a decision to follow Him. Peter, Andrew, James, and John received public invitations as they were fishing.

And Jesus, walking by the Sea of Galilee, saw two brothers, Simon called Peter, and Andrew his brother, casting a net into the sea; for they were fishermen. Then He said to them, "Follow Me, and I will make you fishers of men." They immediately left their nets and followed Him. Going on from there, He saw two other brothers, James the son of Zebedee, and John his brother, in the boat with Zebedee their father, mending their nets. He called them, and immediately they left the boat and their father, and followed Him. (Matt 4:18–22)

Levi (Matthew) was also given a public invitation to follow Christ. "Then He went out again by the sea; and all the multitude came to Him, and He taught them. As He passed by, He saw Levi the son of Alphaeus sitting at the tax office. And He said to him, 'Follow Me.' So he arose and followed Him" (Mark 2:13–14).

Jesus extended a public invitation to another tax collector, Zacchaeus:

Then Jesus entered and passed through Jericho. Now behold, there was a man named Zacchaeus who was a chief tax collector, and he was rich. And he sought to see who Jesus was, but could not because of the crowd, for he was of short stature. So he ran ahead and climbed up into a sycamore tree to see Him, for He was going to pass that way. And when Jesus came to the place, He looked up and saw him, and said to him, "Zacchaeus, make haste and come down, for today I must stay at your house." So he made haste and came down, and received Him joyfully. . . .

Then Zacchaeus stood and said to the Lord, "Look, Lord, I give half of my goods to the poor; and if I have taken anything from anyone by false accusation, I restore fourfold." And Jesus said to him, "Today salvation has come to this house, because he also is a son of Abraham; for the Son of Man has come to seek and to save that which was lost." (Luke 19:1–6, 8–10)

Peter Issued a Public Call to Respond to the Gospel

One of the clearest biblical examples of the extension of a public call to respond to Christ was the first sermon given in church history. The church was born on the day of Pentecost as Peter shared the gospel. On that day, after using the words of the prophet Joel and King David to explain the intricacies of Christ's death and resurrection, Peter called his hearers to repentance.

"Therefore let all the house of Israel know assuredly that God has made this Jesus, whom you crucified, both Lord and Christ."

Now when they heard this, they were cut to the heart, and said to Peter and the rest of the apostles, "Men and brethren, what shall we do?"

Then Peter said to them, "Repent, and let every one of you be baptized in the name of Jesus Christ for the remission of sins; and you shall receive the gift of the Holy Spirit. For the promise is to you and to your children, and to all who are afar off, as many as the Lord our God will call." (Acts 2:36–39)

Because they were given a public invitation, his hearers responded publicly as "those who gladly received his word were baptized and that day about three thousand souls were added to them" (Acts 2:41).

Paul Publicly Called People to Respond to Christ

When Paul spoke with the Thessalonians, he preached for a verdict. As a result many were persuaded.

Now when they had passed through Amphipolis and Apollonia, they came to Thessalonica, where there was a synagogue of the Jews. Then Paul, as his custom was, went in to them, and for three Sabbaths reasoned with them from the Scriptures, explaining and demonstrating that the

Christ had to suffer and rise again from the dead, and saying, "This Jesus whom I preach to you is the Christ." And some of them were persuaded; and a great multitude of the devout Greeks, and not a few of the leading women, joined Paul and Silas. (Acts 17:1–4)

Often the hardest challenge related to sharing Christ is *asking* for a response to the gospel. We can make friends with lost people. We can serve them with the love of Jesus. We can be proficient at memorizing various evangelism approaches. But a point comes when we need to extend an invitation to trust Christ and ask for a response.

Reasons We Don't Ask for a Response

Through the years I have heard many reasons Christians will share the gospel but fail to extend an invitation and ask for a response.

If the Person Says No, How Should I Respond?

The fear of rejection is always the most stated hesitation for not intentionally asking people to respond to the gospel message. Understandably, most people want to be liked and do not want to encounter conflict. They are somehow convinced that people are predisposed to saying no and will not listen.

This is, however, a deceptive misconception created by Satan. If the gospel is presented in a clear and loving manner by an obedient messenger, the person who says no is usually not rejecting the individual but rejecting Christ.

Therefore, if the response is no, ask why. After all, hesitation could be a simple misunderstanding. The key is the leadership of the Holy Spirit. If the person is persistent in giving a no answer, simply back away and ensure that your prayers will continue. Offer to answer any questions and to continue the conversation in the future.

Asking for a Response Seems Unnatural and Forced

People freely discuss sporting events, hobbies, or grandchildren! Unfortunately, the same is not true when it comes to intentionally asking for a response as the result of sharing one's faith. Often the witness begins to feel awkward and even weird. Such conversations may seem unnatural and pushy. But why?

Paul reminded the Ephesian Christians that we are involved in a spiritual war. "For we do not wrestle against flesh and blood, but against principalities, against powers, against the rulers of the darkness of this age, against spiritual hosts of wickedness in the heavenly places" (Eph 6:12).

The bottom line is that when a person shares Christ, the witness is being opposed by the dark forces of Satan. As the limited ruler of this earthly domain, he will not easily relinquish a soul into the hands of Christ without a desperate battle. The oppression the witness feels is often spiritual warfare.

Don't fear; the God who is in you is greater than the enemy who is in the world (see 1 John 4:4). See chapter 19 for a more detailed discussion relating to spiritual warfare.

What if I Say the Wrong Thing?

A former student named James shared with me his incident of saying the wrong thing. He had shared Jesus with a non-Christian friend and asked, "Are you ready to repent of your sin and ask Christ to save you?"

To his surprise his friend replied with a resounding yes!

For most people this would be a time of rejoicing. Not for James. He was so confused that he asked, "Are you kidding? You really don't want to do this, do you?" The non-Christian replied, "Yes, I do. I have been waiting for this all of my life. I am certain that Christ is the answer I have been looking for!"

Jesus promised that the Holy Spirit will guide you and give you the words to speak. "But when they deliver you up, do not worry about how or what you should speak. For it will be given to you in that hour what you should speak; for it is not you who speak, but the Spirit of your Father who speaks in you" (Matt 10:19–20).

What if They Ask Me a Question I Cannot Answer?

Honesty is the best policy. If someone asks a question you cannot answer, the best response is to say, "That's a good question. I will do some research and get back with you as soon as possible." The key is to be forthright and to discern between genuine questions that further the spiritual conversation as opposed to questions that may be legitimate but will take you off track and will create confusion.

What if They Get Angry?

In over 30 years of sharing Jesus, I can recall few times that someone responded with anger to the gospel. Some people will respond with indifference but not with violent anger.

Our job is to prepare through much prayer and to remember that the only stumbling block for the unsaved should be the cross, not the arrogant behavior of well-meaning Christians. We must always be careful to present the gospel with the same compassion, boldness, and understanding as Christ did.

How Do I Know Their Response Is Genuine and They Understand the Gospel?

Sharing Christ with an unsaved person should never be taken lightly. Our goal in sharing Jesus is not to gather decisions through coercing people to pray a prayer of commitment. Our goal is to "make disciples" through helping the unsaved person understand the true meaning of following Christ. We want to lead people to true conversion.

A wise witness will always be honest about the cost of becoming a disciple. I like to speak in terms of surrendering one's life under the lordship of Christ. Don't cheapen God's grace by pressing for a shallow faith that excludes a full understanding of what it means to be a sinner who is separated from a holy God.

After proclaiming the gospel of repentance and faith, if the person seems genuinely led by the Holy Spirit to receive Christ, trust the Lord and be faithful to invite the person to respond by following Christ in full submission. Trust the Holy Spirit. You are not the determining factor leading to someone's salvation.

Now What?

I love the old cartoons of the antics between Road Runner and Wile E. Coyote. Road Runner always outsmarted Coyote. That is, until the final show when by sheer luck and cunning, Wile E. Coyote caught Road Runner. In the last frame of the final cartoon, Coyote looked horrified as he held up a sign asking, "Now what do I do?"

This is what many people feel when extending an invitation in evangelism and asking for a response. The key is to be faithful to the gospel and trust the Holy Spirit to do His part by drawing lost souls to the Father. We must not ignore the opportunity to allow for an evangelistic response. While we should never be manipulative or coercive, we should always be intentional and well prepared.

As fearful as you might be when asking for a response, seek the Holy Spirit's leading and do it anyway. Keep in mind the words of Jesus spoken to His disciples in Matt 7:7–8, "Ask and it will be given to you; seek and you will find; knock and the door will be opened to you. For everyone who asks receives; he who seeks finds; and to him who knocks, the door will be opened" (NIV).

⏤ Evangelism Is . . . ⏤

1. Intentionally inviting unsaved people to surrender their lives and follow Christ.
2. Trusting the Holy Spirit to bring conviction for sin, therefore drawing lost people to the Savior.
3. Being bold!

⏤ Key Verse ⏤

"Ask and it will be given to you; seek and you will find; knock and the door will be opened to you." (Matt 7:7 NIV)

⏤ Good Quotes ⏤

If a pastor [witness] fails to invite his listeners to accept Christ, he is departing from the practice of the New Testament church.

—C. E. Autrey[1]

From beginning to end, invitations are extended in scripture. God's probing question to Adam in the garden, "Where art thou?" in Genesis 3 is something of an invitation. The final chapter of the Bible contains an invitation, "And the Spirit and the bride say, Come. And let him who heareth say, come. And let him who is athirst come. And whosoever will, let him take the water of life freely" (Rev 22:17). Holy scripture reverberates with invitations to lost humanity to turn to God for forgiveness and new life.

—Roy Fish[2]

Notes

1. Quote used in R. A. Street, *The Effective Invitation* (Grand Rapids, MI: Kregel, 2004), 17.
2. R. J. Fish, *Giving a Good Invitation* (Nashville, TN: Broadman, 1974), 11–12.

36

Volunteering

David Wheeler

You Have to Love Batman

When I was a kid, I loved Batman. My friends liked Superman, Spider-man, the Hulk, Captain America, the Green Hornet, and even Wonder Woman. Not me, I was always a fan of Batman!

It may have been his cool outfit with the black mask or his ability to climb buildings. Maybe it was the Bat Cave or the fact that he was the only superhero who drove a car, the Batmobile. Who knows, for whatever reason, I loved Batman. I have never understood the need for Robin, but I still loved Batman!

As I grew older, my passion for superheroes diminished, and I realized that you do not have to wear tights and a ridiculous suit to be superhuman. One reason I liked Batman was the fact that he was a somewhat regular guy in real life. Bruce Wayne was a millionaire who could have ignored the plight of humanity. On the contrary his response was to spend his money, to volunteer his time, and to risk his life in order to assist others. When Bruce Wayne became Batman, he was like thousands of volunteers in the church who give of themselves in order to lead hurting humanity to Christ! If you want to become a superhero, the first thing to do is to become a willing volunteer.

God Can Use a Willing Senior Adult

Nell Kerley has seen a great deal of pain in her lifetime. In fact, one of these painful experiences eventually led to her life's taking a new and exciting turn. Nell and her late husband were involved in a near fatal car accident. It was so bad that Nell had to pull her bleeding husband back into the car through the shattered front windshield. In all of the excitement, Nell cried out to God for help. He answered her prayer with the affirmation, "Don't worry, Nell. I am not done with you yet!"

That's for sure.

Today Nell is not the average senior adult. She does not own a Winnebago and has no desire to retire. In spite of having cancer, two surgically replaced knees, and a surgically replaced shoulder, she is a relentless volunteer at the local food bank and hospital. Her job is to love on the recipients while evaluating their spiritual condition. Incredibly, after over 10 years of heroic service, she has documented more than 3,000 names of people who have surrendered their lives to Christ through her witness!

That's not bad for someone who attended church for 66 years before taking her first witnessing class. She led her first person to a salvation decision three weeks into the training. As she put it, "I instantly realized that I had wasted 66 years doing religious stuff. I now understand the purpose of following Christ is to expand His kingdom by sharing His Word to a hurting world!" She further stated, "Don't be shy. We cannot afford to be silent!"[1] How about you?

God Can Use a Willing Teacher

My brother, Rick Wheeler, has been a middle school teacher for over 25 years. In that time he has been cited as the "Walmart Teacher of the Year" and regularly appeared in the national "Who's Who" directory for distinguished educators.

However, it is not the accolades that make him special. He, too, is a heroic volunteer serving with Big Brothers of Nashville, Tennessee. He also coaches students and helps with several inner-city ministries. His volunteer efforts, through working on behalf of underprivileged students, has led to numerous students' receiving college scholarships. More importantly are the number of students who eventually turned their lives to Christ because of his investment in their lives outside the classroom. As Rick said, "I am a teacher for the time being. I am His for eternity. We are His to use as He desires. The call of every Christian is to be faithful in service!"[2]

God Can Use Willing Coaches

Don Baskin and Harold Rehorn shared two common passions, Jesus Christ and baseball. While working demanding jobs, both men became local heroes to hundreds of teenagers every year through volunteering as Senior Little League baseball coaches.

They demanded hard work, commitment to team, personal excellence, and respect of authority and family. In some cases, because of divorce and abandonment, they were the primary male influence in their players' lives. This influence did not stop when the season ended.

As Coach Baskin recalled, "In 32 years of coaching, I have unwittingly served as a life coach, father, and have eventually appeared in numerous weddings several years after their playing careers ended." He continued, "God called me to this position as a volunteer coach to influence young minds for him."[3]

Coach Rehorn passed away in 2003. His influence changed my life because he believed in me and wanted the best for me. He and his wife came to hear me preach one of my first sermons when I was a young minister. Like Coach Baskin, he was much more than a baseball coach. He felt called to develop young men for the glory of God. He never hid his love for God or for his players. Both men are heroes, and one day heaven will proclaim their testimonies as "fishers of young souls."

God Can Use a Willing Young Man

Evan Roberts was a teenager when he first began to volunteer his life to pray for revival to spread across his native country of Wales. As he grew older, he became a coal miner and a volunteer at his local church. But revival consumed his life. Hour after hour, day after day, he prayed. He also surrendered his time to travel and bear testimony about the power of God.[4]

His prayers were gloriously answered in 1904 when God began to move throughout his homeland. The result was a nationwide movement of the Holy Spirit that accounted for more than 100,000 public conversions in Robert's homeland within the first six months of the revival's inception! The high point came as the movement spread throughout the world over the next few years, 1905–1907. Who would have thought that God could use an unassuming but willing coal miner like Evan Roberts to impact the world for Christ?[5]

God Can Use a Group of Willing Young Adults

An e-mail showed up in a pastor's inbox one day concerning a Haitian family who had recently moved into his community. Having grown up in the poverty-stricken land of Haiti, the family was accustomed to difficult challenges. All of this multiplied, however, when the oldest teenage daughter left a candle unattended in her bedroom. It eventually fell over, and the fire began to spread. By the time she was aware of the situation, smoke filled the dilapidated house, and the bedroom was destroyed. On top of that, the family did not have money or insurance to cover the repairs.

That is when the young adults pastor at a local church was notified. His group was always looking for ways to volunteer their time to minister through service projects. Since his group was made up of young professionals, they had resources waiting to be used. A contractor got word of the incident and offered his services as the singles raised money through weekly offerings to cover repairs and other needs for the family.

The young adults group spent several days replacing drywall, repairing electrical outlets, and laying new carpet. The team of 50 volunteers also bleached and painted the entire interior of the home. One of the volunteers said, "The family was living in the house which was filled with soot. I went in myself, and my eyes were burning and watering right away. . . . It is now a healthy living space for a family in need of a new start."[6]

In addition, the young adults group took up donations in order to provide a Thanksgiving meal for the family. They did the same a month later and filled their newly repaired home with Christmas decorations along with gifts and food. In the end God rewarded the willing heroes as the Haitian mother and several of her children responded to Christ in personal faith.

God Can Use a Willing Friend/Student

Dr. Ergun Caner is the president of Liberty Baptist Theological Seminary. He is a former Muslim who was brought to faith in Christ by a willing friend named Jerry Tackett. Jerry volunteered much of his time and energy beginning in his freshman year of high school.

As Ergun tells it, in high school he was hostile with his faith; and much like the apostle Paul before being converted, he was known to persecute well-meaning Christians. In most cases his abrasive approach made people hesitant. That's the way he liked it.

His behavior did not deter Jerry. While many of his friends thought he was crazy for taking the abuse, Jerry thought that was a price worth paying if Ergun finally came to Christ. After all, he rationalized, if Ergun was this radical as a Muslim, imagine what could happen with the help of the Holy Spirit if he became a born-again Christian.

Regardless of the constant questions and embarrassing persecution, Jerry stayed faithful. Then one night Jerry invited Ergun to an evangelistic crusade hosted by Steltzer Road Baptist Church in Gahanna, Ohio. Ergun recalls attending with the hope of being so obnoxious that Jerry and his church would not follow up and would leave him alone.

True to his word, Ergun was disrespectful and rude. Nevertheless, Jerry and his church demonstrated a loving faith in a way that shocked Ergun. He later remembered, "When I left that night, I knew that Jerry and those people had something I could never find in Islam. They had a personal relationship with a living Savior, Jesus Christ."[7] Ergun surrendered his life to Christ a few days later. It didn't take long before many of his family members followed suit.

Were Jerry's time, effort, and the abuse he took worthwhile? Consider the fact that Dr. Ergun Caner travels across the world proclaiming Christ to thousands of people each year. In addition, he is the author of 17 books and is respected as an apologist across the globe. Yes, I would say Jerry's investment was a good one! Wouldn't you?

God Used a Good Samaritan

On one occasion Jesus told a story about two men who started and ended as strangers, but one of their lives was forever changed by their encounter. The story was born as Jesus was being questioned by a teacher of the law about eternal life.

> "Teacher, what shall I do to inherit eternal life?"
>
> He said to him, "What is written in the law? What is your reading of it?"
>
> So he answered and said, "'You shall love the LORD your God with all your heart, with all your soul, with all your strength, and with all your mind,' and 'your neighbor as yourself.'" (Luke 10:25–27)

The Jewish teacher then asked a significant question, "And who is my neighbor?" (Luke 10:29). Jesus' response was to tell the story of the good Samaritan.

The story takes place on a well-traveled road between major cities. The characters were a man walking, robbers, a priest, a Levite, a Samaritan, and an innkeeper.

A Jewish traveler was walking on the dangerous road from Jerusalem to Jericho where he was attacked and robbed. The robbers took everything, even his clothes, leaving the man to die.

As he lay helplessly on the side of the road, three men passed by. The first was a priest, who saw the man on the side of the road and passed by on the other side. A second man came along, a respected Levite. When he noticed the hurting man, he too passed by on the other side of the road.

Then a third man came down the road, a Samaritan. At that time Jews looked down on Samaritans as religious and ethical half-breeds. Of all the heroes Jesus could have chosen, He took the least likely to make a point about loving one's neighbor. Notice how the Samaritan responded to the man in need.

> But a certain Samaritan, as he journeyed, came where he was. And when he saw him, he had compassion. So he went to him and bandaged his wounds, pouring on oil and wine; and he set him on his own animal, brought him to an inn, and took care of him. On the next day, when he departed, he took out two denarii, gave them to the innkeeper, and said to him, "Take care of him; and whatever more you spend, when I come again, I will repay you." (Luke 10:33–35)

Notice that the Samaritan did not check his calendar before he stopped to help the man. Obviously he was on a journey of his own, or he would not have been traveling the same road. But his needs and desires were not his focus. He reached out and *volunteered* to meet the man's needs no matter the cost in time or money.

Jesus, being a master teacher, turned and applied this story to the teacher who had asked the question, "Who is my neighbor?" "'So which of these three do you think was neighbor to him who fell among the thieves?' And he said, 'He who showed mercy on him.' Then Jesus said to him, 'Go and do likewise'" (Luke 10:36–37).

"Go and Do Likewise"

Just as the Samaritan focused on meeting the robbed man's needs without selfish considerations, we should do the same. Like the young adults who helped the Haitian family, the focus of our ministry should be to serve in hopes of pointing people to Jesus. Who receives the credit is unimportant. What counts is that Jesus is exalted and hurting people are drawn to Him.

Just as the Samaritan gave of his time to meet the hurting man's needs, we should do the same. We can easily be like the priest and the Levite mentioned in the story of the good Samaritan. We become so consumed with life and fulfilling religious duties that we pass by divine encounters without comprehending the opportunity for ministry and evangelism.

God uses willing people who will volunteer to join Him in what He is doing. The key is a surrendered heart, not special communication or administration skills. Jesus is accustomed to taking the smallest ounce of our availability and magnifying the eternal impact for His kingdom.

⟶ Evangelism Is . . . ⟵

1. Surrendering personal desires under the lordship of Christ.
2. Surrendering your schedule even when it is not convenient.
3. Turning personal interests into intentional ministries that impact the lives of hurting people.
4. Being willing to try new things.

⟶ Key Verse ⟵

"You shall love . . . your neighbor as yourself." (Luke 10:27)

⟶ Good Quotes ⟵

*If you cannot text, turn on a computer, and you think
Twitter is a nervous condition, you still have what it takes to
be a good foster parent . . . unconditional love
and a willingness to listen!*
—AN ADVERTISEMENT ON THE RADIO AIMED AT RECRUITING FOSTER PARENTS

*I instantly realized that I had wasted 66 years doing religious
stuff. . . . I now understand the purpose of following Christ is to
expand His kingdom by sharing His word to a hurting world.*
—NELL KERLEY AFTER TAKING HER FIRST EVANGELISM CLASS
AND LEADING A 14-YEAR-OLD GIRL TO CHRIST[8]

*A comfort zone can be a barrier . . . because our big dream
always lies outside our comfort zone. That means we will
have to leave [volunteer] what feels comfortable if we want
to achieve our dream [for God].*

—BRUCE WILKINSON[9]

Notes

1. Phone interview with Nell Kerley for evangelism class, May 21, 2009.
2. Phone interview with Rick Wheeler, May 22, 2009.
3. Phone interview with Don Baskin, May 22, 2009.
4. M. McDow and A. Reid, *FireFall* (Nashville, TN: B&H, 1997), 278.
5. Ibid., 280–84.
6. Interview with Michelle McCormick, member of the young adults class, April 9, 2009.
7. Phone interview with E. Caner, July 25, 2009.
8. N. Kerley interview.
9. B. Wilkinson, *The Dream Giver* (Sisters, OR: Multnomah, 2003), 89.

37 Creating Opportunities for Gospel Conversations

David Wheeler

In a day when crime is high and trust is low, busy people tend to isolate themselves from contact with others. This can make sharing the gospel challenging. While there are no easy solutions, creative thinking and subsequent approaches can open doors. Through the years I have gathered a collection of best practices of activities that create witnessing opportunities.

Creating Opportunities Through Intentional Relationships

Community Groups

Community groups are a major outreach tool at Thomas Road Baptist Church in Lynchburg, Virginia. The groups are designed to get unchurched and/or dechurched people in the church buildings for the purpose of meeting their needs and giving the gospel a chance to be heard by these people who need it most. The groups offer numerous types of educational and practical opportunities such as crafts, hunting and fishing, car repair and restoration, preparing tax returns, gourmet cooking, guitar lessons, golf, Moms of Preschoolers, and much more. The approach is a unique combination of both servant evangelism and ministry evangelism. While it is done on the church property, this effort requires incarnational intervention through the stair-step process we discussed earlier in chapter 23:

- Win the person to yourself.
- Win the person to the church.
- Win the person to Christ.

In addition, church members are encouraged to *pray* for participants, *care* for participants; and to *share* with unsaved participants. The groups meet on the church property for eight weeks, three times a year (mid-September to Thanksgiving, February through March, and May through June). Promotion of the groups and recruiting occurs in the off months. The sessions meet for one hour on Wednesday evenings, which includes a brief devotional (usually from *Our Daily Bread*).[1]

As time goes by, the aim is to look for connection points during the weeks and eventually to invite people to come for Sunday services. Church members are prayerfully intentional but careful not to rush the process.

Ministry Evangelism and Servant Evangelism

Ministry evangelism and servant evangelism are similar in many ways. Both approaches intentionally seek to meet people's needs in order to open the doors for the gospel message. However, the main difference rests in the issue of personal evangelism versus corporate outreach. In other words, the ultimate aim of servant evangelism is to mobilize *individual* Christians to engage their communities both inside and outside the corporate setting of the church while ministry evangelism mobilizes a *group* of Christians to engage the community.

Ministry evangelism usually grows out of the local church as individuals work together to meet corporate needs. For instance, feeding centers, crisis pregnancy centers, after-school tutoring, disaster relief, and English as a second language ministries are all corporately driven out of the larger church body and usually through the church facilities. These types of ministries can be extremely evangelistic and allow church members to team together to meet needs and share Christ in a more controlled setting.

Other approaches may include disabilities awareness, substance abuse, migrant workers, and medical/dental ministries. In addition, this approach can also include specialized ministries like resort and leisure ministries, truck-stop ministries, raceway ministries, and prison outreach.[2]

The SHOT Principle

The SHOT Principle was developed for the book *Friends Forever*.[3] The approach is simple yet effective. Each letter of the acrostic stands for a different relational approach to engaging an unsaved person over an extended period (preferably six weeks or less).

Somewhere. The initial aim is to invite an unsaved neighbor or friend to go *somewhere* with you—a ball game, dinner, or other places. Hopefully, this will begin the relational dialogue. The key is to be intentional but not pushy. In most cases, trust has to be acquired before spiritual conversations deepen.

Help. The next step is to ask this person to assist in a *help ministry* project, such as painting an elderly person's home or repairing the playground equipment at a local park. Believe it or not, most unsaved people are willing to assist in these types of projects. This will definitely further the relational dialogue in an atmosphere of camaraderie.

Our. The next step is to invite the person or family to your (*our*) place for a meal and more relationship building. The meal does not have to be anything fancy; the key is authenticity. People are not looking for perfection. Be real!

Trust. After establishing trust, the final step is to go to their place. If your testimony and personal faith have not already been shared through previous encounters (assuming the leadership of the Holy Spirit), this is good time to give it a "shot" and present the gospel message.[4]

Creating Opportunities Through Evangelistic Events/Ministries

Evangelistic Block Parties

Evangelistic block parties are among the easiest and most effective outreach events. They generally consist of a registration table (everyone gets registered in order to receive tickets for lunch or to win door prizes), a popcorn machine, a snow-cone machine, a cotton candy machine, helium tanks for lots of balloons, plus plenty of tables, chairs, and pop-up tents in case of bad weather. You can also use a grill for the hot dogs, hamburgers, or barbecue chicken; or you can prepare nachos, chili, or whatever is popular in your community.

Typical activities include seven to 10 simple games, moonwalks, and face painting. The block party can be held on the church campus or preferably at a local park or school. Church members usually blitz the community with invitations several times in the weeks leading up to the party and always on the morning of the event. As people arrive, smiling Christians of all ages greet them and assist in directing the families to different activities.

In many cases these simple encounters lead to divine opportunities to share a brief testimony and, in some cases, to make a gospel presentation. This is why all workers receive training ahead of time and why you plan in advance to follow up immediately (within the first three to five days) with every registered non-church member. The follow-up is a good time to combine servant-evangelism activities by taking a small gift (cookies, McDonald's gift certificates) when visiting the homes of registered guests.

An average block party will last approximately three to four hours. This is advisable for the stamina of both the workers and the participants.[5]

Sports Evangelism

One of the most effective approaches in evangelism is the process called *contextualization*. Contextualization is the adaptation of evangelistic methods into a culture without compromising the essential truths of the gospel. It is simply learning to communicate the message so that it can be understood clearly by the recipients in that culture. This usually includes obvious things such as language and dress, but in contemporary culture it should also include the avenue of sports.

Consider for a moment the power and influence of sports in American society. In many ways it is the language of contemporary culture. Almost everyone can recognize the distinctive theme tones of ESPN's Sports Center, or at least they are aware of the Super Bowl, World Series, Olympics, the Masters Tournament, or the World Cup. While sports can easily distract attention away from spiritual matters, sports has also become a cultural language that demands contextual attention.

Instead of criticizing Christians for overinvolvement in sports, maybe it is time to start commissioning them for service. What if churches teamed up with young parents who are already involved in local soccer, baseball, softball, and football leagues? Rather than instilling guilty feelings about missing Wednesday or Sunday evening services, how about commissioning these parents as missionaries to the local athletic fields.

The approach could include a time of church-based praying for the families before sending them out. The church can then keep the parents accountable through weekly contacts and encourage them to make a prayer list of team players and their families. These lists could then be sent back to the church's prayer room or dispersed among small groups for further attention and follow-up.

Congregations could also give the parents a small sum of money ($150–$200) so they can stock up on after-game snacks for the entire team. That will easily make them the most popular parents among the players. Then instruct the parents to tell the coaches that they are welcome to use church facilities for their end of the season banquet. The church may also choose to provide the meal as well as volunteers to serve the parents and the players. In the end it will be a great opportunity to demonstrate Christ's love by reaching out to young families, many of whom know little about spiritual matters or the church.

In addition, consider forsaking local church leagues in basketball, softball, or other sports. I did this one summer while serving as senior pastor of a congregation in Texas. The church invaded the local city league, and as a result they eventually assimilated several new families as well as numerous new believers. You can even provide free sodas for the other teams after the games.

The bottom line is that effective evangelism can take place in the context of sports. From church-sponsored, three-on-three basketball and dodge ball tournaments, soccer clinics, to working with Fellowship of Christian Athletes (FCA) chapters through local schools, wise Christians can easily use sports as a tool to impact their community for Christ.[6]

Seasonal and Gender-Related Events

Another effective approach in creating gospel conversations is through seasonal events such as Christmas and Easter programs, as well as July 4 celebrations and baccalaureate services. These events usually draw large audiences, thus boosting the potential impact on the kingdom.

Mother's Day celebrations and mother-daughter banquets are always effective. For men, wild game suppers (or "beast feasts"), motorcycle rallies, and car shows will always draw a crowd and provide plenty of evangelistic opportunities, especially when combined with block party-type activities. Back-to-school events and fall festivals (Halloween) are also great opportunities to impact the community for Christ. All of these approaches can be effective arenas to engage in spiritual discussions.[7]

Special-Needs Ministries

Individuals with special needs (physical or mental) and their families easily represent one of the largest unreached people groups in America. In fact, according to statistics gathered through Joni and Friends Ministries, the divorce rate of families dealing with special needs children is over 85 percent.[8] In addition, less than one out of 10 of these individuals (approximately 5 percent) or families are associated with church at any level.

Consider some other alarming statistics from Joni and Friends Ministries:

- 54 million or 20.6 percent of people in the USA live with some level of disability.
- Nationally, four million of these people are under 18 years old.
- Abuse in families with a disabled child is twice that of typical families.
- Nine out of 10 women who learn that their unborn baby has Down syndrome will abort.
- People with handicaps and their families represent the largest unreached and unchurched people group in America![9]

Local congregations who catch the vision can reach this hurting segment of the population with the gospel. According to special education teachers and those fluent in this kind of ministry, the most effective approach is family-to-family contact through genuine concern and servant-oriented ministries.

Consider several options like providing parent's-night-out opportunities, especially where the needs are chronic and demand round-the-clock care. I recently heard of a family where the parents had not been alone in over three years! No wonder the divorce rate is so high!

In some cases the situation may require securing a nurse who is trained to administer proper care. In most situations it requires a mild dose of patience, a listening ear, and a special ability to administer the love of Christ.

You might also consider shopping for groceries, preparing meals, or providing some new clothes. If they are good quality, consider offering some slightly used clothes your family members have outgrown.

Always be sensitive to special-needs situations. Don't park in spaces reserved as handicapped parking. Look around in crowded areas (malls, schools, churches, ball games) for people needing assistance. These situations can be difficult challenges for people in wheelchairs or on crutches.

Be yourself. Do not stare. People with special needs are no different from you. Everyone wants to feel accepted and loved. And according to Scripture, everyone needs a Savior.

New Wine Needs New Wine Skins

Then He spoke a parable to them: "No one puts a piece from a new garment on an old one; otherwise the new makes a tear, and also the piece that was taken out of the new does not match the old. And no one puts new wine into old wineskins; or else the new wine will burst the wineskins and be spilled, and the wineskins will be ruined. But new wine must be put into new wineskins, and both are preserved. (Luke 5:36–38)

Three of the four Gospel writers (Matthew, Mark, and Luke) recorded Jesus' teaching about new wine needing new wineskins. Jesus' point was that new wine required new wineskins; otherwise the new wine would tear the stiff old wineskins as it expanded through the process of fermentation. Likewise, we must be open to new methods that provide opportunities for life-giving ministries through sharing Jesus Christ with the lost.

The strategies described in this chapter may seem like wild, new ideas. Let's be honest, some people will read this chapter and see block parties, sports evangelism, and community groups as unbiblical and too worldly to use for evangelism. Remember these are merely new methods that have been found to be effective at creating gospel conversations with secular people. As the old saying goes, "Methods may change, but the message stays the same."

⚊ Evangelism Is . . . ⚊

1. Intentionally looking for gospel opportunities.
2. Not hiding from the world.
3. Being open to new methods.

⚊ Key Verse ⚊

"For we cannot help speaking about what we have seen and heard." (Acts 4:20 NIV)

⚊ Good Quotes ⚊

One of the keys to effective evangelism is creating opportunities for interaction that may lead to gospel conversations. . . . This is especially true in contemporary culture where trust is elusive and busy people tend to isolate themselves from human contact.

—DAVID WHEELER

*The church has too often closed itself behind
institutional walls. Evangelistic Block Parties provide
churches with a ministry of presence and visibility as the
church moves out of its building in Christ's name to feed,
teach, clothe, and evangelize.*

—TOBY FROST[10]

*If you can discover what builds trust, you are one step closer
to being able to improve your effectiveness in relational
evangelism. . . . The importance of how to build trust cannot
be overstated.*

—JACK SMITH[11]

Notes

1. Material taken from chapter 9 of *Innovate Church,* ed. Jonathan Fallwell (Nashville, TN: B&H, 2008), 141. For more information, go to www.trbc.org and search for "community groups." The concept was developed and is managed by discipleship pastor Rod Dempsey. For more on using *Our Daily Bread,* go to http://www.rbc.org/odb/odb.shtml.

2. Ibid., 140. For more information related to ministry evangelism, go to http://www.NAMB.net.

3. For much more information, see J. Smith, *Friends Forever* (Alpharetta, GA: Home Mission Board of the Southern Baptist Convention, 1994), 83–115.

4. Ibid.

5. Fallwell, *Innovate Church,* 143.

6. Ibid., 144.

7. Ibid., 145. For more information relating to the wild game feasts and sportsman outreaches, go to http://www.christiansportsman.com or http://www.legacyoutdoorministry.com.

8. Statistic provided through interview with Joni and Friends office, Knoxville, TN, October 2006.

9. Statistics taken from Joni and Friends Web site, 2006. Also see David Glover, "Disabilities Ministries Is New NAMB Consultant's Focus," January 22, 2007.

10. Quote found in T. Frost, B. Simms, and M. McWhorter, *The Evangelistic Block Party Manual* (Alpharetta, GA: North American Mission Board of the Southern Baptist Convention, 1998), 3.

11. Smith, *Friends Forever,* 27.

38

Evangelism Is . . .

Working Together

Dave Earley

I tend to be more introverted than most and am often uncomfortable talking with strangers. Therefore, one of my favorite ways of doing evangelism is with a group. This is another effective way to share the gospel.

I Became a Small Group Leader

It all started when I was 16 years old, a junior in high school. After several years of running from God, I realized the futility of trying to live life for anything other than God. So I ran to Him and was so happy to find that He accepted me. Then I started to run *for* Him.

A few weeks later my two Christian friends, with whom I ate lunch every day at our large public high school, decided that we needed to start a Bible study during the lunch period. One secured an empty music rehearsal room near the cafeteria, and we started studying the Bible and praying a few minutes each day during lunch. Within a few weeks our little group had grown to 12.

After Christmas break I returned to school to discover that their lunch period had been changed. "Who is going to lead the Bible study during my lunch hour?" I asked.

"You are," they answered. So even though I had been walking with God less than two months, I became a small-group leader.

The only lunchtime Bible study holdovers from the first semester were me and one girl. Not wanting to be the only ones, we began aggressively to pray

for and invite people to the group. Soon the room was full. By the fall of my
senior year, we had more than 100 high school kids coming to Bible study every
day. Students were coming to Christ regularly. I was addicted to leading a Bible
study that focused on helping people find their way home to God.

Together Everyone Accomplishes More

Reaching people through the power of a team is not merely practical; it is biblical. Read this story from the life of Jesus.

> One day as he was teaching, Pharisees and teachers of the law, who had
> come from every village of Galilee and from Judea and Jerusalem, were
> sitting there. And the power of the Lord was present for him to heal the
> sick. Some men came carrying a paralytic on a mat and tried to take him
> into the house to lay him before Jesus. When they could not find a way
> to do this because of the crowd, they went up on the roof and lowered
> him on his mat through the tiles into the middle of the crowd, right in
> front of Jesus.
>
> When Jesus saw their faith, he said, "Friend, your sins are forgiven."
>
> The Pharisees and the teachers of the law began thinking to
> themselves, "Who is this fellow who speaks blasphemy? Who can forgive
> sins but God alone?"
>
> Jesus knew what they were thinking and asked, "Why are you
> thinking these things in your hearts? Which is easier: to say, 'Your sins
> are forgiven,' or to say, 'Get up and walk'? But that you may know that
> the Son of Man has authority on earth to forgive sins. . . ." He said to
> the paralyzed man, "I tell you, get up, take your mat and go home."
> Immediately he stood up in front of them, took what he had been lying
> on and went home praising God. (Luke 5:17–25 NIV)

Without his friends this man would not have met Jesus. He'd still be lying
at home in grief, guilt, and depression. His life was changed because *they*
brought him to Jesus. His sins were forgiven because of *their* faith. He was
healed because *they* carried him to the house, *they* dug a hole in the roof, and
they lowered him down in front of Jesus. Without his friends this man would
not have met Jesus.

Few people come to Jesus on their own. Most of us meet Jesus because of
the invitation of a family member or friend. Eighty-five percent of the people
who meet Jesus do so because they were brought to him by a friend or family
member.[1]

Christianity 101

Cathy and I and some of our friends from Liberty University moved to a suburb of Columbus, Ohio, to start a new church. We moved in two rented trucks on Saturday and held our first church service the next morning in my basement. There were 12 of us, 11 adults and a baby. After a month of nightly prayer meetings and aggressive evangelism, we publically launched our church in a middle school with 66 people. Our church grew steadily, and eventually we owned land and built a building.

Many of the people who came to our church knew nothing about the basics of Christianity or about the Bible. So we started a group we called "Christianity 101" and invited four young couples who were spiritual seekers. We addressed basic questions such as: What is the Bible? Why trust the Bible? Who is God? Who is Jesus? What did Jesus do? How do I get to God? Being around educated people who knew so little about God but were hungry to learn was refreshing. We were also frequently reminded that lost people act . . . well, lost. For example, after a few weeks in our Christianity 101 group, a mechanical engineer named Steve raised his hand and asked, "Did I hear you say Jesus is God? Where on earth did you get an idea like that?" The next week, when I asked what he thought about the group, he had said it was "damn interesting." (We must not expect lost people to act like mature Christians.) After five or six weeks all eight of them had made a decision to follow Christ, including Steve.

We enjoyed this group experience so much that we launched a new Christianity 101 every August and January. Dozens of people came to Christ each year as a result of small-group Bible study evangelism. After completing the eight weeks of 101, they would go into a group called "Christianity 201" to learn how to grow in Christ and get involved in the church.

The Group

When my older sons were in high school, they wanted to start a group to reach unchurched students. We could not think of a good name, so we simply called it "The Group." Cathy, Daniel, Andrew, and I started with a handful of people, and it eventually grew to more than 50 high school students meeting in our house in six groups and another 20 students meeting at another home. When our younger son, Luke, reached high school, he also became a leader in The Group. The best thing about The Group is that dozens of young people who did not attend church were reached to our group and for Christ. We generally saw three or four students give their lives to Christ every month. It was one of the most fulfilling and fun groups I ever led. A few years ago a publisher asked me to write down the reasons our small group was so effective at evangelism. We were effective because we intentionally practiced 10 keys that allowed us to reach people for Christ.

10 Keys to Effective Small Group Evangelism

1. Faith

Effective evangelistic groups believe that God wants people saved even more than we do. Therefore, we have to cooperate with Him. The effective evangelistic groups I've led developed a strong expectation that if we invited people, they would come; and if we shared the gospel, they would respond. Of course not every student did, but enough responded to cause us to believe that God would honor our efforts.

2. Prayer

Evangelism is a spiritual war that is best fought on our knees. As long as the groups I've led have consistently prayed that God would save souls, He did. In our high school group a handful of students would come a half hour early and pray for God's blessing on our group meeting. Before our group events where the gospel was to be presented, we intensified our prayers as several of us would fast a few meals and pray more. God always granted a harvest.

3. Love

As we have shared previously, effective evangelism is a relational process involving three successive victories: First, we win people to ourselves. Second, we win people to our group. Third, we win people to Christ. We often fail to win people to Christ because we have not first lovingly won them to ourselves.

We found that all types of unchurched kids from the captain of the football team to a Wiccan to a drug dealer would come to our group because they felt love and acceptance there. We must never view lost people as objects or projects. Every person is someone for whom Jesus died and, therefore, valuable to God and to us.

4. Invitation

If you invite them, they might come. But if you don't invite them, they probably will never come. Unsaved people rarely just drop into a group on their own; 99.99 percent of the time, someone or several someones made the effort to invite them to come.

According to Richard Price and Pat Springer, "Experienced group leaders . . . realize that you usually have to personally invite 25 people for 15 to say they will attend. Of those 15, usually only eight to 10 will actually show up; and of those, only five to seven will be regular attenders after a month or so.[2]

This means you can grow a new group of 10 to 14 regular members in a year by inviting one new person each week! If a whole group catches the vision of inviting, a group can experience explosive growth.

If you invite enough people, some will come. When I start a new group, I invite two to five times the number of people I expect to have at the first meeting.

Some ask, "Where do I find people to invite?" There are at least four good places to look for people to invite:

- Family
- Friends
- Coworkers or fellow students
- Neighbors

5. Teamwork

The acrostic TEAM: Together Everyone Accomplishes More may be corny, but it's true. When we asked students to share how they came to our group, almost without exception they said they were invited by four or five people *before* they decided to give it a try.

Inviting is easiest when inviting is done in concert with a team of people, a lot of people in prayer, and a healthy group and church. You do not have to do everything yourself. Reaching someone for Christ is especially powerful when the person you are trying to reach already knows and likes someone else in your church or small group.

Great groups are the result of teamwork. Our entire group meetings were team productions. Several people brought and arranged snacks. Several others prayed before the group session. Others stood outside and welcomed everyone who came. Others led worship. Several others led prayer groups of four to six at the end of the night.

6. Gospel

Never underestimate the power of the gospel. Every four to six weeks we shared the story of the death, burial, and resurrection of Jesus for our sins. We also shared the plan of salvation (by admitting your sins, believing on Christ for salvation, calling on His name to save you, and committing your life to Him). Every time we shared the gospel, students responded. Many ended up coming to church.

When we had group events, we asked two or three students to share the testimony of how they were saved. Then I briefly explained the gospel using the verses of the Roman Road. Then we asked students to pray to give their lives to Christ. Without exception students responded.

7. Process

Evangelism is a process leading to an event. Few people are ready to give their lives to God the first time they are invited to a small group. Reaching a person may take weeks, months, and even years of inviting, praying, loving, and hearing the Word before the soil is ready to yield a harvest. We never made anyone feel pressured to be saved. Everyone was welcome to come along and take the next step of their spiritual journey.

8. Party

Never underestimate the power of fun, food, and a party to draw a crowd. Every two months we planned social gatherings. Among ourselves we jokingly called them "sinner dinners." (See Mark 2:15–17 for Matthew's highly effective "sinner dinner.") We discovered that we could double our attendance and get nonchurched students to come to our house if the kids invited them to a party. If we had a theme ("Squirt Gun Wars," "I Hate Winter," "Halloween Bonfire," and "Seventies Night," for example), grilled some hot dogs, and played a few corny games, we'd have a crowd. They would have a blast and then listen intently to a few of their friends share their story of how they came to a personal relationship with Jesus. We had as many as 89 kids show up and as many as a dozen make salvation decisions for Christ in one night—all because we had a party.

9. Testimony

One of the easiest ways to get attention, sustain interest, and preach the gospel without being preachy is to have someone tell how they came to Christ, preferable a testimony that somewhat mirrors the people you hope to reach. For example, in our high school group we had other high school kids share how they came to Christ. In a group Cathy and I led for adults, we reached unsaved husbands by having formerly unsaved husbands share how they came to Christ.

10. Celebration

In Luke 15 we find three stories of something lost being found—a lost sheep (vv. 1–7), a lost coin (vv. 8–10), and a lost son (vv. 11–31). In each case the event was marked by a celebration. Maybe God would give us more opportunities to win the lost if we truly rejoiced when one was found. A celebration can be as simple as cheering for and hugging new believers after they pray to receive Christ or having a special, full-blown party. *How* you celebrate is not as important as *that* you celebrate.

Start a Small Group

Maybe the best way for you to apply this book will be to start an evangelistic small group. Or possibly your application will be to turn an existing group into an evangelistic one. In any case, remember that effective evangelism is often a team effort, and small groups can be hotbeds for vibrant outreach.

⌁ Evangelism Is . . . ⌁

1. A team effort.
2. Easier with the power of a group.
3. Can be effectively accomplished in a small-group, home Bible study.
4. Enhanced by strategic parties.

⌁ Key Verse ⌁

Two are better than one, because they have a good reward for their labor. (Eccl 4:9)

⌁ Good Quote ⌁

The group aspect of cell [small-group] evangelism takes the burden off the leader and places it on everyone in the cell [small group]. It's net fishing as opposed to pole fishing. Pole fishing is done individually, while net fishing requires the help of many hands. Net fishing is a group effort and results in catching more fish, while fishing individually with a pole catches one fish at a time.

—JOEL COMISKEY[3]

Notes

1. T. Rainer, *The Unchurched Next Door* (Grand Rapids, MI: Zondervan, 2003), 24–25.

2. R. Price and P. Springer, *Rapha's Handbook for Group Leaders* (Houston, TX: Rapha, 1991), 132.

3. J. Comiskey, *The Church that Multiplies* (Moreno, CA: CCS Publishing, 2005), 80.

39

Evangelism Is . . .

A Family Affair

David Wheeler

An Honest Look at the American Family

According to statistics from the American Family Association as stated in the book *Family to Family* by Jerry Pipes and Victor Lee:

- Only 34 percent of America's families eat one meal together each day.
- The average father spends only eight to 10 minutes a day with his children. This includes television and mealtimes.
- Only 12 percent of America's families pray together.
- The average couple spends only four minutes of uninterrupted time together a day.[1]

If these statistics are accurate, no wonder the American family and the American church are being systematically dismantled. One result of this tragedy is the long-term impact on teenagers when they go off to college. According to Pipes and Lee, "88 percent of those who grow up in our evangelical churches leave at 18 and do not come back."[2]

While such statistics are alarming, there is hope for these teenagers and their parents. According to another study that is quoted in the *Family to Family* promotional video, "When parents lead their children in sharing their faith and engaging the spiritual harvest, the 88 percent fallout drops to less than 4 percent."[3]

If this is indeed the case, than families must become intently focused on a common mission that is passed to future generations. The obvious question is how.

The Need for a Mission Statement

Walk into any corporate headquarters in America, and you're likely to see a conspicuously displayed plaque or document stating that company's identity, purpose, and goals. This *mission statement* is known to everyone who works at the organization and is obvious to all who visit. Why the big deal over this creed? It provides direction and accountability to all who work there and a sense of assurance to those whom they serve.

On most days employees have little need to refer to the statement. But when a situation, decision, or proposition challenges the company's ideals, threatens its integrity, or compromises its identity, the mission statement stands like a lighthouse in a storm. "Woe to the company that loses sight of its mission statement," says one corporate help site, "for it has taken the first step on the slippery slope to failure."[4]

If a mission statement is vitally important to the growth of healthy organizations, we would do well to adapt the idea to our families. "A family mission statement will serve as a centerline and guardrails for your family on the road through life," say Jerry Pipes and Victor Lee. "When life is foggy, you will have a centerline on which to focus."[5]

Choosing the Correct Path

Staying on the road sounds like a good idea, but we must first make sure that the road we are on, the one we are leading our children down, is the right one. Proverbs 22:6 says, "Train a child in the way he should go, and when he is old he will not turn from it" (NIV). But what is "the way"? Countless books profess to know the way to go, and surely many are helpful. But for followers of Jesus Christ, the last word should be God's Word. When Jesus said, "I am the way and the truth and the life" (John 14:6 NIV), He was giving us direction through life and death.

In *Family to Family: Leaving a Lasting Legacy*, Pipes and Lee show that when we align our families with Christ, making His priorities ours, we reap two priceless rewards. First, we develop healthier, more meaningful family relationships. Second, we pass the baton of faith in Jesus Christ to our children.

Once we are on the right road, aligned with Christ, we can begin to determine what that means for our family. To whom are we accountable? How do we worship? What is our marriage model? How do we treat one another and handle conflict within the home? How do we share our faith with our children and with those outside our home? These are some of the questions the mission statement addresses. "People who live together do better when they agree on a common purpose. A family mission statement is essentially a declaration of what each member of your family agrees to live by."[6]

Joshua was clear about the mission of his family. "And if it seems evil to you to serve the LORD, choose for yourselves this day whom you will serve. . . . But as for me and my house, we will serve the Lord" (Josh 24:15).

What Is a Mission?

Joshua's mission for his family extended to the people of Israel, and they followed his lead even beyond his lifetime. Joshua 24:31 says, "Israel served the LORD all the days of Joshua, and all the days of the elders who outlived Joshua, who had known all the works of the LORD, which He had done for Israel." Despite the huge burden Joshua carried, he did not falter because he knew his purpose well, and he stuck to his mission, a mission that began at home. No success outside the home can justify failure within it. He could not have successfully led a nation to God unless he had first done the same for his family.

Joshua reminds us that the family mission begins with the parents. Deuteronomy 6:6–9 tells us:

> These commandments that I give you today are to be upon your hearts. Impress them on your children. Talk about them when you sit at home and when you walk along the road, when you lie down and when you get up. Tie them as symbols on your hands and bind them on your foreheads. Write them on the doorframes of your houses and on your gates. (NIV)

We are to impress these words on our children as we walk through life. This approach is not meant to be a "Sunday" habit but a daily expression of what it means to walk with God. The mission statement is designed to guide the family 24–7, in all areas.

The Mission and Purpose of Jesus

Pipes and Lee insist that we should begin our family mission statement by studying the mission of Jesus, which stems from His purpose. The authors identify dozens of biblical passages in which Jesus states His purpose. In

Luke 19:10 Jesus said, "For the Son of Man came to seek and to save what was lost" (NIV). This tells us in a nutshell the two parts of Jesus' mission. His first purpose was to seek. After willingly coming down from heaven, Jesus continually sought lost humankind even in the most unlikely and inhospitable places. Jesus' second purpose was to save, to offer Himself as a sacrifice for our sins.

John 18:37 reinforces Jesus' mission, saying, "For this reason I was born, and for this I came into the world, to testify to the truth" (NIV). Clearly this is a statement of His mission.

We get more insight into Jesus' purpose in Matt 20:28, where Jesus says He "did not come to be served, but to serve, and to give his life as a ransom for many" (NIV). If we are to model Christ, we need to take on this mind-set of serving others with humility, gentleness, and patience, starting at home. And although we cannot give our lives like Jesus as a ransom, we can, through our actions and words, point others to the One who did.[7]

Many other passages reveal the purposes of Jesus: to be a leader and a teacher (Matt 4:19); to fulfill the Law (5:17); to call sinners (9:13b); to separate holiness from sinfulness (10:34b); to provide rest for those who follow Him (11:28–30); to preach the good news, proclaim freedom for prisoners, give sight to the blind, release the oppressed, and proclaim the time of the Lord's favor (Luke 4:18–19); to represent man before God the Father (12:8–9); and to do the will of the Father (John 6:38).

A family mission statement will not include all of the stated purposes of Jesus. However, a deeper understanding of each purpose will provide guidelines for the document.

The Commands of Jesus

The mission and purpose of Jesus led to the commands He gave us. First among these were His commands to spread the gospel, which we recognize as the Great Commission. It's no coincidence that these commands appear in each of the four Gospels and also in Acts.

The book of Matthew contains the most comprehensive version of the Great Commission and consequently is also the most often cited. Matthew 28:18–20 reads:

> Then Jesus came to them and said, "All authority in heaven and on earth
> has been given to me. Therefore go and make disciples of all nations,
> baptizing them in the name of the Father and of the Son and of the Holy

Spirit, and teaching them to obey everything I have commanded you. And surely I am with you always, to the very end of the age" (NIV).

In Mark 16:15, Jesus told the disciples to "go into all the world and preach the good news to all creation," adding the command to "preach the good news."

Luke 24:47–48 says that "repentance and forgiveness of sins will be preached in his name to all nations, beginning at Jerusalem. You are witnesses of these things" (NIV). Luke's record adds "repentance and forgiveness of sins" to our understanding.

In John 20:21, Jesus said, "As the Father has sent me, I am sending you" (NIV). Although this version is comparatively brief, the tiny word *as* gives it considerable weight, bringing to mind how Christ was sent—in love, in sacrifice, as a substitute, and in meekness. Jesus is saying in few words to emulate Him in our mission, to go about it the same way and for the same reasons.

Acts 1:8 contains the last such command we have from Jesus, which is what makes it so important. "But you will receive power when the Holy Spirit comes on you; and you will be my witnesses in Jerusalem, and in all Judea and Samaria, and to the ends of the earth" (NIV). The last thing He said to the disciples before ascending reiterated this most critical point: *you will have the power to witness for Me worldwide.*[8]

Biblical Principles

Depending on the behaviors you wish to promote in your family, you'll find countless passages in Scripture on which to build your mission statement. The verses below, for example, deal with loving one another, encouraging one another, and sharing your faith.

"This is My commandment, that you love one another as I have loved you." (John 15:12)

Do not let any unwholesome talk come out of your mouths, but only what is helpful for building others up according to their needs, that it may benefit those who listen. (Eph 4:29 NIV)

I pray that you be active in sharing your faith, so that you will have a full understanding of every good thing we have in Christ. (Phlm 6 NIV)

Practical Application: Developing Your Family Mission Statement

Having reviewed the mission, purpose, and commands of Jesus Christ, you now have a good framework for developing your family mission statement. Remember that this is a family effort; you will want to involve all members, produce something that is meaningful to everyone, and have fun doing it.

Derrick Mueller suggests a four-step process for developing a family mission statement.[9]

Step 1: Take a Family Inventory

- What activities are we engaged in as a family?
- What motivates us?
- How would others describe our family?
- How secure are we in one another's love?
- What are our fears?
- What is lacking in our relationships?
- What is the spiritual environment of our household?
- What are our priorities?

Step 2: Consider Your Goals

- What does our family stand for?
- What values do we live by?
- How will needs be addressed and problems be solved?
- What activities will be important to our family?
- What is the desired outcome for our family?
- What Scripture summarizes our intent?

Step 3: Conceptualize the Statement

Using the questions posed in step 2, begin to draft a statement that answers those questions. For example:

> As a family, we stand for _____, living by the values of _____.
> We address needs by _____ and try to resolve problems by
> _____. As a family, we will strive to make time for _____
> and place less emphasis on _____. Our goal for the future is to
> _____ and ultimately to live together in heaven. The Scripture verses
> that guide our efforts are _____.

Step 4: Fine-tune and Personalize the Statement

Personalize the phrases in step 3 to fit your family, making sure all critical topics are covered. The final product should be appealing and meaningful to all members, something everyone can understand and embrace.

To this formula, Pipes and Lee add several guidelines.[10]

Don't Rush; Reap. When drafting your statement, do not hurry through the exercise. Take time to hear from everyone involved. Your children are much more likely to embrace something they helped create.

Use Your Heart, Not Your Head. Deuteronomy 6 reminds us that our mission statement should be something we hold in our hearts, not just our heads. Otherwise, Blackaby warns, our statements run the risk of becoming a legalistic tool.[11]

Reflect Lifestyle, Not Legalism. To our children a mission statement can seem like just another set of rules wrapped in Scripture unless we live it and show them how to live it. That means being there for the children. To carry out Deuteronomy 6, we may have to shift our priorities and/or change our schedule.

Don't Invoke; Involve. The mission statement must not be an order drafted by the parents and handed down to the children. All members of the family should be part of its development so that they can own it and embrace it.

Don't Ignore; Instill. Once drafted, the mission statement should be visible, accessible, and referred to often; use it as you would a map on a road trip.

Sample Mission Statements

Below are some examples of family mission statements as presented in *Family to Family*.

- Our family will share the love, grace and mercy of Jesus Christ with each other, our extended family, our neighbors, and our community as we go through life.
- Our family lives to be the hands and feet of Jesus Christ, sharing His mercy and offering His salvation to all who will give us the opportunity.
- This family will show love to each other through the traits of tenderness, mercy, grace, forgiveness, and gentleness. Our words will be uplifting, our tone encouraging. We will think of each other before ourselves. These characteristics will be carried outside our home as

we share the love of Jesus Christ with those around us.

- The mission of our family is to share the way of salvation through Jesus Christ with a lost and hurting world. We will do this by modeling a Christlike life first in our home, living the attitude and actions of Jesus before each other. Next, we will seek to build relationships with extended family, neighbors, and others we encounter daily. In these relationships we will model the love of Christ with the hope of earning the opportunity to share how Christ makes a difference in our lives, and how He can do the same in theirs.
- This family exists to live the great commandments and fulfill the Great Commission, beginning in our home and extending to every arena of life.
- Our family will work, play, pray, and study God's Word together with the goal of becoming Christlike and sharing the love of Jesus with all those around us.[12]

You and your family will gain peace by navigating life with a biblically inspired mission statement. "You do not want to send your family off into the wilderness of life without a compass," say Pipes and Lee. "The mission statement—based on the Word of God—is the compass."[13]

⌐ Evangelism Is . . . ⌐

1. The spiritual glue that energizes the church and families.
2. The heritage (baton) of every parent to be passed to the next generation.
3. Essential to healthy families.
4. Essential to healthy churches.
5. Bolstered by intentional mission statements.

⌐ Key Verse ⌐

"But as for me and my house, we will serve the LORD."
(Josh 24:15)

⁓ Good Quote ⁓

There are risks and costs to a program of action,
but they are far less than the long-range risks
and costs of comfortable inaction.

—JOHN F. KENNEDY[14]

Notes

1. J. Pipes and V. Lee, *Family to Family: Leaving a Lasting Legacy* (Alpharetta, GA: North American Missions Board, 1999), 1.

2. Ibid., 1.

3. Pipes and Lee, *Family to Family* promotional video.

4. http://www.missionstatement.com.

5. Pipes and Lee, *Family to Family*, 25.

6. Mennonite Brethren Web site, http://www.cdnmbconf.ca/mb/mbh3512/mueller.htm in *Family to Family*, 26.

7. Pipes and Lee, *Family to Family*, 28.

8. Ibid., 27–31.

9. Ibid., 33–34.

10. Ibid., 34–35.

11. Ibid., 34.

12. Ibid., 35–36.

13. Ibid., 33.

14. J. Pipes, *Building a Successful Family* (Lawrenceville, GA: Completeness Productions, 2002), 114.

40

Evangelism Is . . .

Leaving a Legacy

David Wheeler

A Life Defined by Christ

My dad was a master at building an outreach legacy for future generations. I will never forget the lesson he taught me at Christmas 1968. I was only seven years old.

Mom was ill with a near-fatal kidney disease. Dad was working an extra job at Western Auto to try to pay off nearly $30,000 of her medical debts. It was Christmas Eve, and I was at the store where Dad was working when I was called to the back room. He instructed me to load up our car with a large stack of toys he had received permission to take from the showroom.

A short time later I rode with Dad back home still wondering about the toys. As we arrived in our subdivision, he bypassed our road and ended up at a house on the street behind ours. I will never forget the look on our neighbor's face when Dad went to the door and informed this young mother who had recently been abused and deserted by her husband that God still cared for her family.

The look on her face was priceless. Between the tears and the chorus of "How did you know that I could not afford toys?" the young mother realized that she was not abandoned by God.

The truth is, I had more fun unloading those toys than I did opening mine the next morning. I cannot remember what I received that Christmas, but I will never forget what we gave! It was much more than a carload of toys.

Through the act of compassion, we became messengers of hope. Now that is a legacy!

A Love Defined by Ministry

I often thought my dad was old-fashioned and disconnected from the real world. I have come to realize that he did not care about being in step with the times; he cared about people! He and God seemed to have an agreement. My father would sacrificially love and serve people's needs; then eventually God would change their hearts and draw them to Himself.

He viewed life differently from most people. Who else would grow 600 tomato plants? That sounds crazy to everyone but a tomato farmer! That is, until you experienced the magic of his approach to ministry. Once the tomatoes ripened, Dad spent days visiting local ballparks and public arenas inviting people over to see his garden. In the end he was using his passion for gardening to create opportunities for ministry.

He walked miles through his garden helping others pick tomatoes and okra for free, all the while sharing about more important issues related to faith, integrity, love, and life. He even delivered boxes of tomatoes to local vegetable stands for no charge, knowing they would sell his bounty for a profit, just to share a brief word of encouragement and exemplify Christ's love in practical ways.

A Legacy Defined by Compassion

When my dad, John Wheeler, went to be with Christ in 2002, I was deeply touched by the response of the local community. Hundreds of mourners lined up for over nine hours telling outrageous stories about how he impacted their lives through living out an authentic faith. None of us ever knew that he regularly paid electric bills, purchased medical supplies, provided glasses and clothing, supplied rent, and provided groceries for hurting families.

My dad wasn't flashy, just faithful. To him God was never a celestial Santa Claus commissioned to provide his every want. On the contrary, like Christ he loved God's most precious creation—people. He once told me that if I made a new friend every week, when I died, I would be the wealthiest man in the world!

Even his passing became an answer to prayer. For over 10 years we had been praying for two specific family members to come to Christ. We had attempted every evangelistic approach. During his last 18 months Dad shared breakfast with this couple almost every morning. As always, he actively loved them by demonstrating a risen Christ through a smile, laughter, a timely word of encouragement, prayer, and genuine compassion.

In the end the exclamation point of Dad's legacy came two days after his funeral when we had the privilege of seeing this 70-year-old couple receive Christ! I remember hearing them say at the time, "There was something different about your dad." Indeed there was!

With a father like mine, it is no wonder I am an evangelism professor! Evangelism is the legacy passed on to me by my father.

The Biblical Principle

Deuteronomy 34:7 says about Moses that when he died "his eye was not dim, nor his vigor abated" (NASB). While he was never able to enter the promised land, he knew he was preparing Joshua and others who would advance God's work as representatives for righteousness. They would eventually inherit the land. Like my dad's investment in me and in others, Moses did the same for Joshua.

A few verses later Scripture tells that "Joshua the son of Nun was filled with the spirit of wisdom, for Moses laid his hands on him; and the sons of Israel listened to him and did as the LORD had commanded Moses" (v. 9 NASB).

Moses understood his calling as more than building his earthly reputation. He realized that his blessing of Joshua and investment into his life and ministry would survive as a legacy way beyond his earthly existence. This is evident when Moses passed the baton of leadership to Joshua. In doing so, God repeatedly mentioned the influence of Moses even though he had already passed on.

> "Moses My servant is dead; now therefore arise, cross this Jordan, you and all this people, to the land which I am giving to them, to the sons of Israel. Every place on which the sole of your foot treads, I have given it to you, just as I spoke to Moses. . . . No man will be able to stand before you all the days of your life. Just as I have been with Moses, I will be with you; I will not fail you or forsake you." (Josh 1:2–3, 5 NASB)

This promise is fulfilled in Joshua 6 when Joshua led the Israelites into the promised land by taking the mighty fortress of Jericho. None of this could have happened without the years of mentoring by Moses. By walking with Moses through the treacherous times in the wilderness, Joshua learned that God would always provide for His people. Just as Joshua was guided by Moses to value God's call and to trust His ways, my Father taught me. The result of Moses' leadership was Joshua's humility, faith, obedience, and deep love for others.

The legacy of a man's life has nothing to do with his possessions. Rather it is the God-given passion and influence he spreads to those under his care. It is more than being a mere example. It is living out a life that is multiplied through the attitudes and actions of generations to come! The legacy is an obsessive desire to impact the world for God!

Jesus also lived to leave a legacy. He multiplied His life in men who eventually carried His message across the world. He instructed the disciples in Matt 4:19, "Follow Me, and I will make you fishers of men." Even after His death, resurrection, and ascension back to heaven, His investment in the disciples became the evangelistic capstone of His legacy to future generations.

How to Pass on an "Evangelism Legacy"

1. Always Realize That Others Are Watching

It takes a lifetime to build a reputation and only 10 seconds to tear it down! Evangelistic legacies are born out of consistency and compassion for the unsaved. You must never allow ungodly responses and behaviors to destroy your influence with friends or family. Someone has noted, "Integrity is who we are when the lights are off and we think we are alone."

2. Legacies Are Built out of Intentionality

My dad had a keen sense of his calling as a Christian and sought to use teachable moments. As a result he modeled the kind of person he desired for me and others to be. The way he treated construction workers, waiters, coworkers, neighbors, family, and friends was amazing. He was the same with politicians and lawyers as he was with alcoholics at the rescue mission or convicts at the prison. A person's social status never dictated his mood or abated his desire to meet needs and impact lives for Christ. His greatest desire was to make a difference in his sphere of influence. That never happens by accident!

3. Do Not Just Speak the Word; Be the Word!

This goes back to being a consistent Christian influence on the people God brings into your life. People will generally not believe the truth from us until we consistently live out that truth. Assuming this is correct logic, does this not scream for us as Christians to model the life and teachings of Christ? It is one thing to speak about God's love from a biblical, informational perspective; it is even more powerful to demonstrate this love by first caring and then sharing.

4. Everyone Will Eventually Have an Eternal Legacy

Will the legacy you leave behind be positive or negative? Will your legacy be transformational to future generations, or will it be quickly forgotten?

Everyday, common people can make an eternal difference by simply modeling the life of Christ to others in their sphere of influence. The question is not what people will say about you after you are gone; that is often driven by momentary grief and temporal emotions. The real issue is whether your evangelistic passion and compassion for the unsaved will be lived out by those individuals you influence with your life.

5. Your Legacy Begins Today

Moses began mentoring Joshua early in the sojourn from Egypt to the promised land. At that time it was not evident that Joshua would be the one chosen to complete the journey after Moses' death. Still Moses was faithful to give himself away.

Our legacies are born from the daily influence we exert over the people God brings into our lives. We may never comprehend the full extent of our impact. The call is to invest ourselves selflessly into the process of multiplying disciples, and this begins within our current spheres of influence with a classmate, a student, or a friend. When you come in contact with others, your response will determine your legacy. Do they sense a passionate follower of Christ? Are you committed to live out your faith in a way that impacts the kingdom through reaching the unsaved? Will you make a difference?

6. Your Legacy Is More Caught Than Taught

My dad was a man of few words, but people wanted to be around him in order to catch his passion. He knew the gospel. More importantly, he lived the gospel. Moses represented the same for Joshua. He never lost sight of the goal (the promised land). Moses' obedience in preparing Joshua set the stage for future ministry just as my dad's investment prepared me and others for ministry.

7. Your Legacy Is Part of Everything You Do

Evangelism always thrives in the right atmosphere. The usual ingredients are compassion, love, intentionality, obedience, and the understanding that the call to evangelize is never limited by time or space. It can and will happen everywhere if you are open to divine appointments. How about tomato stands, convenience stores, ballparks, restaurants, or funeral homes? Dad was successful because he saw opportunities everywhere he went. Christians are never off duty!

8. Your Legacy Is Worth the Investment of Time and Energy

Multiplication of leaders is worth the investment. If Moses had ignored the opportunity to mentor Joshua, who would have led the Israelites into the promised land? God's work is always worth the investment of time and energy. This is especially true when it comes to the work of evangelism. Do you recall the 70-year-old couple who came to Christ days after my dad's funeral? Even though he was not present, Dad's life continued to shine. Through drawing on Dad's mentorship and ministry over the years, we merely harvested the intentional seeds of love he had planted.

Evangelism, a Lasting Legacy

My dad has been dead since 2002, yet his children, as well as many others, are carrying on his passion for ministry. In God's economy of investing into souls, I believe that every person I influence for Christ is a reflection of my dad's legacy as a mentor. Just as Joshua was the recipient of an eternal legacy that he carried in his heart every time he made a decision, the same is true for me or others who were influenced by my dad.

Our passion is not our own. It is borrowed from God but manifests itself through willing hearts of obedient servants. We stand on the shoulders of every person who has invested in our lives.

— Application —

1. Record five to 10 names of people God has placed in your life in whom you can begin to build your eternal legacy by investing your time and energy. Pray for the names every day. Follow up by creating outreach opportunities in your community in which you can include each of the people on the list. Teach them to serve, and challenge them to begin building their legacy by investing in others.
2. Go out of your way to recognize the people who invested in your life. Affirm their legacy by citing specific times in which you were blessed. Write a note, call, or make a personal visit.

⟶ Key Verse ⟵

"The things which you have heard from me in the presence of many witnesses, entrust these to faithful men who will be able to teach others also." (2 Tim 2:2 NASB)

⟶ Quote ⟵

My dad once told me that if I made a new friend every week, when I died, I would be the wealthiest man in the world!

—DAVID WHEELER

Appendix 1
Sample Methods for
Sharing Your Faith

The Romans Road to Salvation

The Romans Road to Salvation is a way of explaining the good news of salvation using verses from the book of Romans. It is a simple yet powerful method of explaining why we need salvation, how God provided salvation, how we can receive salvation, and what are the results of salvation. (We gave an example of this method in chap. 1).

1. Romans 3:23

"For all have sinned, and come short of the glory of God" (KJV).

2. Romans 6:23

"For the wages of sin is death; but the gift of God is eternal life through Jesus Christ our Lord" (KJV). The punishment that we have earned for our sins is death. Not just physical death but eternal death!

3. Romans 5:8

"But God demonstrates His own love toward us, in that while we were still sinners, Christ died for us."

4. Romans 10:9,13

"If you confess with your mouth Jesus as Lord, and believe in your heart that God raised Him from the dead, you will be saved" (NASB).

"For everyone who calls on the name of the Lord will be saved" (HCSB).

5. Romans 5:1; 8:1; 8:38–39

"Therefore, since we have been justified through faith, we have peace with God through our Lord Jesus Christ" (NIV).

"Therefore, there is now no condemnation for those who are in Christ Jesus" (NIV).

"For I am convinced that neither death nor life, neither angels nor demons, neither the present nor the future, nor any powers, neither height nor depth, nor anything else in all creation, will be able to separate us from the love of God that is in Christ Jesus our Lord" (NIV).

Other Books of the Bible to Lead a Soul to Christ[1]

	John Road	Hebrews Road	Revelation Road	1 John Road	Isaiah Road
Fact of Sinnership	3:18	10:26	21:8	1:8	53:6
Judgment of Sin	3:36	10:27–31	21:8	5:16	53:12
Christ Died for Our Sin	3:16	10:10–12	5:12	4:9	53:4–10
Accept Christ by Faith	1:12	11:1	3:20	4:15	55:6–7

Romans Seven Steps to God[2]

1. There is a God, and we are responsible to Him. (Rom 1:20; 14:12)
2. We have failed to fulfill our responsibility and have sinned. (Rom 3:10,19,23)
3. Sin separates us from God. (Rom 6:23)
4. Jesus never sinned. (Rom 5:19)
5. Jesus died to pay for our sins. (Rom 6:23)

6. He rose from the dead to prove He could offer us abundant and eternal life. (Rom 6:23)
7. We need to believe in Jesus in order to be saved. (Rom 10:9,13)

Ask the person to place themselves on one of the seven steps. If they say that they are at number 7, offer them an opportunity to believe the gospel and be saved.

God's Accounting Book[3]

Sometimes visual learners need to "see" the gospel. One way to show the gospel is by drawing two pages of a book and explaining the gospel as you explain the equation recorded on the pages. (We discussed this method in chap. 8.) God's accounting book is a way of explaining the gospel based on Rom 6:23: "For the wages of sin is death, but the gift of God is eternal life in Christ Jesus our Lord."

SIN

My righteousness	Christ's righteousness
US	
+SIN Isa 64:6; Rom 3:10; 3:23	

DEATH

My righteousness	Christ's righteousness
US	
+SIN Isa 64:6; Rom 3:10; 3:23	
DEATH Rom 6:23a	

JESUS

My righteousness	Christ's righteousness
US	JESUS
+SIN Isa 64:6; Rom 3:10; 3:23	-SIN 1 John 2:1; Heb 4:15
DEATH Rom 6:23a	

LIFE

My righteousness	Christ's righteousness
US	JESUS
+SIN Isa 64:6; Rom 3:10; 3:23	-SIN 1 John 2:1; Heb 4:15
DEATH Rom 6:23a	LIFE Rom 6:23b

FAITH

The ABCs of Salvation

When someone is clearly ready to give their lives to Christ, the ABCs are a simple way to help them understand what is necessary in order for them to cross the line of faith. (We used this method as an example in chaps. 13 and 23)

   A. Admit my need. (Luke 18:9–14)

   B. Believe completely on Christ. (John 3:16)

   C. Call upon Him to take control of my life and save me. (Rom 10:13)

   D. Do everything He asks. (Matt 7:21)

The Way of the Master[4]

The Way of the Master uses the Ten Commandments and a series of probing questions as a basis to establish "lostness" and to present Christ. The method these authors advocate for explaining the good news of salvation uses four stepping stones. The stones are represented by four letters: WDJD, which stand for "What Did Jesus Do?"

W: Would you consider yourself to be a good person?

D: Do you think you have kept the Ten Commandments?

Exodus 20:3–17

3   "You shall have no other gods before Me.

4   "You shall not make for yourself a carved image—any likeness *of anything* that *is* in heaven above, or that *is* in the earth beneath, or that *is* in the water under the earth;

5 you shall not bow down to them nor serve them. For I, the LORD your God, *am* a jealous God, visiting the iniquity of the fathers upon the children to the third and fourth *generations* of those who hate Me,

6 but showing mercy to thousands, to those who love Me and keep My commandments.

7   "You shall not take the name of the LORD your God in vain, for the LORD will not hold *him* guiltless who takes His name in vain.

8   "Remember the Sabbath day, to keep it holy.

9 Six days you shall labor and do all your work,

10 but the seventh day *is* the Sabbath of the LORD your God. *In it* you shall do no work: you, nor your son, nor your daughter, nor your male servant, nor your female servant, nor your cattle, nor your stranger who *is* within your gates.

11 For *in* six days the LORD made the heavens and the earth, the sea, and all that *is* in them, and rested the seventh day. Therefore the LORD blessed the Sabbath day and hallowed it.

12   "Honor your father and your mother, that your days may be long upon the land which the LORD your God is giving you.

13   "You shall not murder.

14   "You shall not commit adultery.

15   "You shall not steal.

16 "You shall not bear false witness against your neighbor.

17 "You shall not covet your neighbor's house; you shall not covet your neighbor's wife, nor his male servant, nor his female servant, nor his ox, nor his donkey, nor anything that *is* your neighbor's."

I normally deal first with lying, stealing, and lust because people can more easily acknowledge them as evident sins. It seems that this is what Jesus does in Luke 18:20.

J: On the day of judgment, if God judges you by the Ten Commandments, will you be innocent or guilty?

D: Destiny — Will you go to heaven or hell?

More Good Approaches to Sharing One's Faith:

Along with the evangelistic events, there are several good approaches to sharing ones faith. Some of these are:

Share Jesus Without Fear—(We discussed this method in chap. 31). A simple approach that uses a series of probing questions combined with the Bible that takes the fear out of sharing (www.sharejesuswithoutfear. com).

FAITH—An easy approach that uses the acrostic FAITH to remember the gospel presentation. It seeks to tie everything back through the Sunday school (www.lifeway.com).

Got Life—An easy outline that uses the acrostic LIFE. It has a strong apologetics application within the overall presentation (www.gotlife.org).

Evangecube—Great visual approach to sharing one's faith. Uses a small cube that is rotated to reveal a snapshot of the Gospel presentation (www.simplysharejesus.com).

God's Special Plan—A simple and well-prepared presentation of the Gospel for children (www.kidzplace.org).

Notes

1. From D. Lovett, *Jesus Is Awesome* (Springfield, MO: 21st Century Press, 2003), 248.

2. From S. J. Benninger and Dave Earley, *How to Move Believers from Membership to Maturity to Ministry* (Lynchburg, VA: CGI, 1999).

3. Ibid.

4. From K. Cameron and R. Comfort, *The Way of the Master* (Wheaton, IL: Tyndale, 2002). For more see www.thewayofthemaster.com.

Appendix 2
Ten Reasons to Plant a Church

Dave Earley

After graduating from seminary, Cathy and I led a team of four young men and their wives to Columbus, Ohio, to launch a new church. Unlike the church I served in as a 22-year-old, this new church had no building. We had no budget. Instead of 120 people, we had 12. But we had something the other church did not have; we had a vision and commitment to launch the most biblical, Spirit-led, healthy, evangelistic church we could.

Our first month in Ohio, we met nightly for one hour of corporate prayer for jobs and the new church. The second month we began to advertise and knocked on 400 doors in the community, taking a church interest survey. At the end of the second month, we went public in the music room at a middle school and were thrilled when 54 local people joined us. We grew every week for the next year and a half to an attendance of more than 200.

Our church grew every year for the first 20 years of our existence until our average attendance was nearly 2,000, with more than 100 small groups for adults and teens, plus dozens of groups for children. We owned 66 acres of property, had 70 percent of our members in ministry, and averaged more than 100 people baptized annually. We also planted four daughter churches and had several others on the way.

As a pastor, the one constant that kept me going was the never disappointing honor of working with God to help people come Christ, and the always fresh privilege of birthing a new church. This chapter is written with one purpose: to convince you and your church to get into God's nursery. I want to help motivate, stimulate, and educate you to play a much greater role in cooperating with God in His big plan to reach this world for Jesus Christ through the experience of church starting.

I am going to assume that you have already had your heart become broken by the billions of unreached people on our planet, both inside and outside our borders. I want to rekindle your passion for reaching a city and region with the gospel and touching this nation with the message of Jesus Christ. I want to motivate you prayerfully to consider planting a church. If you are a pastor or hope to be a pastor, I want to spur you to consider leading a church to become what I call "a multiplication center" by starting churches that will subsequently plant other churches in North America. Our continent is, in fact, starving for the hope of the gospel of Christ.

Let's examine 10 critical reasons you must prayerfully consider being a part of a church-starting effort.

1. North America Desperately Needs More Churches

The questions are common: Why plant churches in North America when so many churches are dead or dying? Shouldn't the focus be on returning struggling churches to health? Why plant churches in North America when so many churches have so many empty seats? Shouldn't churches work to fill all those seats before we start other churches? Is it worth the time, money, and effort to train church planters? Are new churches really needed?

The answer to the last two questions is a resounding, "Yes!" Let's examine some data that shows just how much America needs new churches. As unbelievable as it may seem, recent research indicates that there are now more than 200 million nonchurched people in America, making our nation one of the largest unchurched countries in the world. Author Justice Anderson has stated, "The American church is in the midst of one of the largest mission fields in the world today. Only three other nations—China, India and Indonesia—have more lost people."[1]

Did you know that in 1987 the number of evangelicals in Asia surpassed the number of evangelicals in North America? And did you know that in 1991 the number of evangelicals in Asia surpassed the number of evangelicals *in the entire Western world?*[2]

In spite of the rise of American megachurches, no county in our nation has a greater churched population than it did 10 years ago.[3] During the last 10 years, combined communicant membership of all Protestant denominations declined by 9.5 percent (4,498,242), while the national population increased by 11.4 percent (24,153,000).[4]

In 1990 20.4 percent of Americans attended church on any given Sunday. By the year 2000 only 18.7 percent attended church. This percentage is still in decline, and if this trend is not turned around, it will not be long before only 6 percent of Americans attend church each week. According to Dave Olson's research, the recent increase in the number of churches is only about one-eighth of what is needed to keep up with population growth.[5]

As a result, even though America has more people, it has fewer churches per person than at any time in its history. And while the number of churches in America has increased by 50 percent in the last century, the population has increased a staggering 300 percent.[6] There are now nearly 60 percent fewer churches per 10,000 Americans than there were in 1920!

Table 1: Number of Churches per Americans[7]

1920	27 churches existed for every 10,000 Americans.
1950	17 churches existed for every 10,000 Americans.
1996	11 churches existed for every 10,000 Americans.

2. North America Is Rapidly Becoming a Post-Christian Nation

A couple of years ago, my youngest son came home from his first day of high school in a suburb of Columbus, Ohio. I asked him who was at his lunch table. "It was interesting, Dad," he said. "There was a Muslim, a Buddhist, a Mormon, a Catholic, a Jew, a Christian friend, and some kids that don't consider themselves anything." Thirty years ago he might have answered, "A Methodist, a Presbyterian, a Catholic, a Baptist, and a kid whose dad works on Sundays." Times have certainly changed, even in the Midwest. For Americans my age and even somewhat younger, the America we grew up in is not the America in which we now live.

Any student of the American culture knows that, in spite of vast amounts of time, energy, and money spent to influence the political process, Christian values are quickly disappearing from our culture. Honesty, morality, and integrity are concepts that have been either redefined or completely discounted. And as our culture has become increasingly less welcoming to the Judeo-Christian principles that are the bedrock of our nation, many in our nation have simultaneously become more hostile to evangelical Christianity. One of the key reasons for this is that we have proportionately less evangelical Christians in our culture.

Dr. Aubrey Malphurs, professor of pastoral ministries at Dallas Theological Seminary and head of the Malphurs Group, has made a wise observation on this culture shift. "Essentially," he says, "what was a churched, supposedly Christian culture has become an unchurched, post-Christian culture. People in our culture are not antichurch; they simply view the church as irrelevant to their lives."[8] It is evident that we must plant churches so that Americans will once again see the church as relevant to their lives and families.

As America increasingly moves from a Christian to a post-Christian, post-modern culture, it will become increasingly important to plant new churches to present the timeless truths of the gospel in a new and timely manner. We must put new wine in new wineskins. A new army of well-trained, effectively taught church planters is essential to win back the North American continent for Christ in the twenty-first century.

Longtime church growth expert Lyle Schaller observes, "There is not a congregation that possesses the ability and the financial resources to attract, reach, and respond to the needs of all the residents of the community."[9] What many evangelicals fail to realize is that there exists a flawed understanding that the United States and Canada are already evangelized. While there is abundant access to Christian information, many unchurched persons in North America are amazingly untouched by the evangelical culture (or maybe subculture) because the Christian community is too often incapable of providing a culturally relevant gospel witness.[10]

3. "The Single Most Effective Evangelistic Methodology Under Heaven Is Planting New Churches"

The above statement was made several decades ago by Peter Wagner, president of the Global Harvest Ministries. I believe the statement is as true today as it has ever been. For example, one American denomination recently found that 80 percent of its converts came to Christ in churches less than two years old.[11] Further, baptism rates for new churches are three- to ten-times higher than existing churches.

New churches reach lost people more effectively than existing churches. Churches that are more than 15 years of age win an average of only three people to Christ per year for every 100 church members. Churches between three and 15 years old conversely win an average of five people to Christ per year for every 100 church members. But churches less than three years of age win an average of 10 people to Christ per year for every 100 church members.[12] Truly, when the church exhales churches it inhales converts.

New churches reach new people; existing churches reach existing people. This is true because most new churches are focused as "missional" entities, meaning they typically concentrate on reaching the lost and fulfilling the Great Commission. But too many existing churches have turned inward and have forgotten why they exist. New Christians reach lost people; established Christians fellowship with Christian friends. After a person gets saved, they generally have a network of unchurched friends they want to evangelize. But after they have been saved a few years, they have either reached their lost friends, or they no longer spend much time with them. Their ability to reach people through friendships drastically declines.

America needs new churches if the Great Commission is to be fulfilled because new churches are noticeably more effective at reaching lost people than existing churches. Church growth expert Win Arn states,

> Today, of the approximately 350,000 churches in America, four out of five are either plateaued or declining. . . . Many churches begin a plateau or slow decline about their fifteenth to eighteenth year. Eighty to 85 percent of the churches in America are on the downside of this cycle. Of the 15 percent that are growing, 14 percent are growing from transfer, rather than conversion growth.[13]

This means that only 1 percent of the churches in our nation are making a significant impact regarding our responsibility to reach lost people for Jesus Christ. It is painfully clear that we need more new churches.

4. "It Is Easier to Give Birth Than to Raise the Dead"

This statement was a trumpet call of the great church-planting efforts of the Baptist Bible Fellowship of the 1950s. This great theme prompted a young graduate of Baptist Bible College named Jerry Falwell to start Thomas Road Baptist Church in his hometown in 1956, along with a handful of believers. It also is the theme that motivated me to launch New Life Church in Gahanna/Columbus, Ohio, when I was just 26 years old and a recent graduate of Liberty University and Liberty Baptist Theological Seminary. I understood that I did not have the experience, wisdom, wiring, or patience to lead an existing church in its retooling efforts to reach the lost members of my generation. So I started a new church that was better designed to speak the language of the unchurched.

While we started out being smaller than most of the existing churches in our suburb, we quickly outgrew and reached more lost people than all of them. I say this not to brag but to show how new churches can uniquely impact a community. At this new church we had no traditional barriers to hurdle, no mind-set strongholds to tear down, no committees to please, and no inward focus to circumvent. We could simply focus on the task at hand: wining the lost at any cost.

Maybe your calling is to be what I call a "transitioner" at an existing church. In this I mean you are attempting to shift old assumptions regarding evangelism so that you can reach out to your community in new ways. If that is the case, may God bless you! I hope you are able to lead your church in becoming a true multiplication center that is also dedicated to launching new churches all over the world. However, it is important to note that incredible amounts of time, energy, and effort can be expended trying to transition existing churches, and some have done so with great success. While it can sometimes be done, we need to accept the fact that it is indeed easier to give birth than to raise the dead.

5. "The Great Commission Is Church Planting"

You cannot fully follow the "Great Commission" without ending up planting churches. Any Great Commission initiative that does not result in the forming of new churches misses the mark. Let me explain. After Jesus rose from the dead, He laid out for His followers the desires He most deeply longed for them to fulfill. Repeatedly, Jesus gave a command that has become known as the Great Commission. The writers of the Gospels record Jesus giving His Great Commission five times. The fullest statement is found in Matthew 28.

> Then Jesus came to them and said, "All authority in heaven and on earth has been given to me. Therefore go and make disciples of all nations, baptizing them in the name of the Father and of the Son and of the Holy Spirit, and teaching them to obey everything I have commanded you. And surely I am with you always, to the very end of the age." (Matt 28:18–20; see also Mark 16:15–16; Luke 24:46–48; John 20:21; Acts 1:8)

After examining the Great Commission, the question that begs to be answered is: How does God expect His followers to implement it? The obvious answer is: by planting churches. Church planting involves all the elements of fulfilling the Great Commission. New churches are the result of Christians invading a culture, preaching the gospel, baptizing believers, and training them to live for Christ.

After the disciples heard the five offerings of the Great Commission, what did they do to obey it? The book of Acts reveals that they started new churches.

Ed Stetzer, director of LifeWay Research, has planted churches in New York, Pennsylvania, and Georgia and transitioned declining churches in Indiana and Georgia. He writes, "New Testament Christians acted out these commands as any spiritually healthy, obedient believers would; they planted more New Testament churches."[14] He concludes, "The Great Commission *is* church planting."[15]

The way the first followers of Jesus carried out the Great Commission directly resulted in the planting of churches. Peter (and others) preached the gospel (Acts 2:14–36), the people were baptized (Acts 2:37–41), and the baptized believers were immediately incorporated into the life of obeying what Jesus had taught (Acts 2:42–47). The ultimate fulfillment of the Great Commission was, is, and always will be church planting. This is how I can say that your church is not fulfilling the Great Commission until it is actively involved in starting new churches.

6. Church Planting Expands the Kingdom of God

Jesus told us that the top priority on our lives was to be God's kingdom (Matt 6:33). He taught us to pray for the coming of God's kingdom (Matt 6:9–10). He said that unless someone is born again, he cannot even see the kingdom of God (John 3:3–7). God's passion is that His kingdom spread to all peoples. His plan is that His kingdom increases through church planting.

Fred Herron makes this case following a careful study of the Word of God:

> God's heart for the expansion of his kingdom is revealed throughout
> the Old and New Testament. God intends the church to proclaim and
> demonstrate the kingdom so that his kingdom will spread to every
> people group on the earth. The passion in God's heart for the expansion
> of his kingdom is a desire for all nations to glorify God the eternal
> King. He has given the church a kingly commission to go into the entire
> world and make disciples who are loyal worshippers of the King. The
> heart of God for kingdom expansion is the foundation for planting new
> churches.[16]

Authors David W. Shrenk and Ervin R. Stutzman also see the kingdom link with church planting. They have written, "Church planting is thus the most urgent business of humankind. It is through the creation (or planting) of churches that God's kingdom is extended into communities which have not been touched by the precious surprise of the presence of the kingdom of God in their midst."[17]

Every time we start a new church in a new community we are being a part of the answer to that prayer. Every time a new church reaches a person for Christ, a new citizen has been added to the kingdom of heaven. I fear that there are too many pastors in our nation that have allowed a passion for church growth to supersede a passion for the kingdom of God. It is refreshing to know, however, that many pastors and church leaders are more excited about building God's kingdom than building their own kingdoms.

7. Church Planting Is Being on a Mission with God

Missio Dei is a Latin phrase that has been helpful in reminding the church that its mission is not the invention, responsibility, or program of human origin but flows from the character and purposes of God.[18] Historically, the term *mission* was used to describe the acts of God rather than the activities of churches. Mission is not something the church does for God; it is rather the church getting in sync with the heart of God and cooperating with the activity of God.

According to noted church planting coach and professor Tom Jones:

> God's nature is at the root of mission. The living God portrayed in the Bible is a sending God. He sends because of His love for the world (John 3:16). He sent Abraham from his home into the unknown, promising to bless the world through him if he obeyed (Genesis 12:1–3). God sent Joseph into Egypt to help preserve God's people during a time of famine (Genesis 45:4–8). When the time had fully come, God sent His son. Later, the Father and the Son sent the Spirit on Pentecost (Galatians 4:4–6; John 14:26; 15:26; 16:7; Acts 2:33). Finally Christ sends His church (Matthew 28:19–20).[19]

Jones adds, "The most efficient way to fulfill the total mission of a sent church is the multiplication of local churches. . . . Every local church should consider itself a center for world mission."[20]

The late Swiss theologian Emil Brunner has memorably stated, "The Church exists by mission, just as fire exists by burning."[21] The church of God is to be on mission with God. When a church ceases to be on this mission, in a real sense, it ceases. David Bosch concurs, stating, "It is impossible to talk about church without at the same time talking about mission. Because God is a missionary God, God's people are missionary people. The church's mission is not secondary to its being: the church exists in being sent and building up itself for its mission."[22]

Our God is the Missionary who sent His Word, His Son, and His Spirit into the world. God is the One who defines, directs, energizes, and accomplishes mission here in our midst. Therefore, God is the originator, catalyst, architect, and engineer of church planting. Church planting is merely cooperating with Him in fulfilling His global mission initiative.

8. Church Planting Brings the Hands and Heart of Jesus into the Lives of Needy People

Two thousand years ago the miraculous act of God's incarnation (taking human flesh) did not merely reveal Him as a man; it also served to model evangelism to mankind. When the Word became flesh, believers learned the importance of enfolding proclamation into incarnation. It is not enough merely to tell the gospel; it must be lived out with and before people in Christian communities.

The New Testament way of "living Jesus" with, and before, hurting people was and still is through His body, the church. A healthy church is the body of Christ on earth. Establishing a new church brings the hands and heart of Jesus into the lives of needy people.

In 2003, Roscoe and Maryanna Lilly moved to Clifton Park, New York, and began serving the community by washing car windows in the mall parking lot and cleaning public restrooms without charge. As a result, the Northstar Church was born with a handful of people. They are passionate about being the hands and feet of Jesus, making Him relevant to their community. They exist to show God's love in such a way that people will exchange ordinary living for an extraordinary life through the power of Jesus Christ. Last year, the young and growing congregation clocked more than 1,600 community service hours. They say their ministry embodies a formula they call SALT, which is:

Seeing people the way Jesus saw them.

Accepting people the way Jesus accepted them.

Loving people the way Jesus loved them.

Touching people the way Jesus touched them.

9. "Be Fruitful and Multiply!"

The first command in the Bible is "be fruitful and multiply" (Gen 1:22). For plants this commandment meant they must reproduce plants. For Adam and Eve, it meant they should bear children. And for churches, this command means to plant new churches.

Dr. Elmer Towns, who is involved in the Innovate Church project, and Douglas Porter write,

> The Church is a living body. Just as everything that's alive will grow and reproduce, so your church should be growing and reproducing itself by starting another new church. Just as God originally created all living things to reproduce, that is, 'according to its kind' (Genesis 1:11–12,21), so your church can double its ministry by planting another church.[23]

Some time ago there was a display at the Museum of Science and Industry in Chicago. It featured a checkerboard with one grain of wheat on the first square, two grains on the second square, four on the third, then eight, sixteen, thirty-two, sixty-four, and so on. At the end of the board, there were so many grains of wheat on one square they were spilling over into neighboring squares. And here the demonstration stopped. Above the checkerboard display was a question: "At this rate of doubling every square, how much grain would be on the checkerboards by the sixty-fourth square?" To find the answer to this riddle, you punched a button on the console in front of you, and the answer flashed on a little screen above the board: "Enough to cover the entire subcontinent of India 50 feet deep."[24]

The problem in North America is that we have been working hard to *add* converts when we should have been investing our energy and effort into *multiplying* churches. The population grows through multiplication, but we have focused on addition. If we have any hope of turning the tide, we must invest our lives in multiplying churches. The *slow* process of multiplying churches is the *fastest* way to fulfill the Great Commission.

Multiplication may be costly, and in the initial stages much slower than addition, but in the long run it is the most effective way of accomplishing Christ's Great Commission. In fact, it is the *only* way. Your church cannot call itself a Great Commission church until it becomes a church multiplication center.

10. "Storm the Gates!"

Too many Christians and churches have gone on into hiding. We have retreated to our Christian ghettos, going to our Christian schools, listening to our Christian radio stations, and hanging out with only our Christian friends. As the culture moves further from biblical values, we retreat further from the culture. And it breaks Jesus' heart.

In Matthew 16, Jesus was giving His disciples an opportunity to grasp a deep understanding of His identity and, thereby, a clearer comprehension of their destiny. In verse 18, He gives a statement which has become known as the Great Promise: "I tell you that you are Peter, and on this rock I will build my church, and the gates of Hades will not overcome it" (NIV).

This promise clearly states that, because Jesus is the church builder, the church is an unstoppable force that must storm the gates of hell! We are not to be passive cowards who are hunkered down in fear of the world around us. We are to be a militant, aggressive army on the offensive for God, working to rescue captives from hell.

Nothing causes the enemy to sit up and take notice as much as the start of a new church that is willing to penetrate the culture, identify with the captives, and kick down the very gates of hell, if that is what it takes. Every church planter I know has come face-to-face with severe spiritual warfare. But they also tell me that the trials they have faced have been small prices to pay in exchange for the great joy of seeing souls set free.

Two Questions

If you can read half of these 10 reasons without being deeply stirred about getting more involved in church planting, you may be spiritually asleep or even dead. I want to conclude this appendix by asking you two important questions about starting new churches:

If not you, who?
If not now, when?

Notes

1. J. Anderson, in *Missiology: An Introduction to the Foundations, History and Strategies of Word Missions*, ed. John Mark Terry, Ebbie Smith, Justice Anderson (Nashville: Broadman & Holman, 1998), 243.

2. W. Craig, *Reasonable Faith*, "Subject: Molinism, the Unevangelized, and Cultural Chauvinism" http://www.reasonablefaith.org/site/News2?page=NewsArticle&id=5681 (accessed January 21, 2008).

3. R. Sylvia, *High Definition Church Planting* (Ocala, FL: High Definition Resources, 2004), 26.

4. T. Clegg, "How to Plant a Church for the 21st Century," seminar materials, 1997, author's collection, Gahanna, Ohio.

5. D. Olsen, http://www.theamericanchurch.org.

6. B. Easum, "The Easum Report," March 2003, http://www.easum.com/church.htm.

7. T. Clegg and T. Bird, *Lost in America* (Loveland, CO: Group Publishing, 2001), 30.

8. A. Malphurs, *Planting Growing Churches for the Twenty-first Century* (Grand Rapids: Baker, 1992), 27.

9. L. Schaller, *44 Questions for Church Planters* (Nashville, TN: Abingdon Press, 1991), 43.

10. E. Stetzer, *Planting New Churches in a Postmodern Age* (Nashville, TN: Broadman & Holman, 2003), 9.

11. R. Moore, *Starting New Churches* (Ventura, CA: Regal Book, 2002), 3.

12. B. McNichol, quoted in "Churches Die with Dignity," *Christianity Today*, 14 January 1991, 69.

13. W. C. Arn, *How to Reach the Unchurched Families in Your Community* (Monrovia, CA: Church Growth, n.d.), 41, 43.

14. Stetzer, *Planting New Churches*, 37.

15. Ibid., 35.

16. F. Herron, *Expanding God's Kingdom Through Church Planting* (Lincoln, NE: iUniverse, 2003), 19.

17. D. W. Shrenk and E. R. Stutzman, *Creating Communities of the Kingdom* (Scottsdale, PA: Herald Press, 1988), 23.

18. A. Murray, *Abide in Christ* (Springdale, PA: Whitaker House, 1979), 39.

19. T. Jones, *Church Planting from the Ground Up* (Joplin, MO: College Press, 2004), 10.

20. Ibid., 16.

21. W. R. Shenk, *Write the Vision* (Harrisburg, PA: Trinity Press, 1995), 87.

22. D. J. Borsch, *Believing in the Future* (Harrisburg, PA: Trinity Press, 1995), 32.

23. E. L. Towns and Douglas Porter, *Churches That Multiply* (Kansas City, MO: Beacon Hill Press, 2003), 7.

24. W. Henrichsen, *Disciples Are Made, Not Born* (Wheaton, IL: Victor Books), 143.

Appendix 3
Evangelism in the Early Church

David Wheeler

A few years ago, I was challenged by a close friend to read slowly through the book of Acts with no agenda except to ask the simple question, "Where are we missing it in the modern American Church?" After several weeks of deep study and prayer, I was shocked how far we had strayed from God's ideal for His Church and His people as revealed through the ministry of the apostles in the early church.

There are at least five basic characteristics of the New Testament Church revealed in Acts 1–4. Each of these principles should serve as a foundation for future generations to follow.

1. The Early Church Ministered Through *Constant Presence* (Acts 2:46-47)

Even a quick reading of the first few chapters of Acts reveals that the early church did not hide or run from the community they were called to serve. They engaged the culture.

> Every day they [the early church] continued to meet together in the
> temple courts. They broke bread in their homes and ate together with
> glad and sincere hearts, praising God and enjoying the favor of all the
> people. And the Lord added to their number daily those who were being
> saved. (Acts 2:46–47 NIV)

Unlike many contemporary believers who seem afraid of mingling with the unsaved world, the early church was out in the community on a daily basis, thus creating a constant presence for the purpose of spreading the gospel. As a result, God added to the Church "daily."

Understanding this dynamic requires that we understand the church as an *organism* rather than a mere *organization*.[1] How does our culture normally explain the idea of church? Usually as a location, a building, something you do, or somewhere you go.

If we view a church as existing in a separate location from which we live, then it becomes easy to ignore ethical mandates and especially Great Commission responsibilities relating to outreach. However, if we genuinely understand that we are the church in flesh, our neighborhoods and workplaces become mission fields in which we share Christ in both words and action. In addition, if a congregation is defined as primarily an organization, it will usually go from one event/program to another in evangelism, rather than developing a completely biblical strategy centered on the principles of the harvest.

Ultimately an organization mind-set breeds a mentality of addition over biblical multiplication. If this is not recognized and corrected, the driving force of ministry becomes a stressful numbers game that is more interested in the "bottom line" than it is in creating disciples. In turn, this bottom-line mentality can easily become a source of arrogance that has little to do with expanding the kingdom and creating a movement of God and much more to do with building up the ego and reputation of the organization's leader.

Perhaps this is one reason it is so difficult to get church leaders to surrender members to plant new congregations. Much of this mentality goes back to an unbiblical model of church. In reality, the church must always be driven by the desire to multiply at every level of ministry and to give it away to the glory of Christ, not man.

Sadly, even with the establishment of the new covenant, we often practice church in more of an Old Testament than a New Testament expression. We typically treat church as a temple in which we worship, not as a body of believers. Much like the Pharisees, we also tend to worship our rules and preferences, even if it is driving people away from Christ, rather than attracting people to Him. The sad part is that God has much more for the church to experience than simply hanging on to grace and mercy from an Old Testament model.

Even the phrase we hear so much in prayer — "thank you God for bringing us to your house today" — is not really a proper New Testament understanding of the church. In the new covenant, God dwells within His people, not in brick and mortar. A deeper understanding of this will radically transform us and change how we go about living out our faith and doing outreach in daily life.

Why should God bless us when we refuse to become what He has called us to be? What matters to Him is not our preferences or procedures but reaching the hearts and minds of unsaved people!

2. The Early Church Depended on a *Consuming Power* (Acts 1:8; 4:8)

From the beginning of Acts, it is evident that the consuming power of the early church is the Holy Spirit as manifested in the lives of committed believers. Jesus spoke to the disciples shortly before ascending into heaven: "But you will receive power when the Holy Spirit comes on you; and you will be my witnesses in Jerusalem, and in all Judea and Samaria, and to the ends of the earth" (Acts 1:8).

This passage restates the Great Commission, as shared by Christ in Matthew 28, and also expresses the theme for the book of Acts and the establishment of the early church. That the Holy Spirit is the motivating power of the early Christians is evident in the first four chapters of Acts. According to Acts 2, various individuals were "filled with the Holy Spirit." The key person was the apostle Peter, who preached to the multitudes at Pentecost

> "Brothers, I can tell you confidently that the patriarch David died and was buried, and his tomb is here to this day. But he was a prophet and knew that God had promised him on oath that he would place one of his descendants on his throne. Seeing what was ahead, he spoke of the resurrection of the Christ, that he was not abandoned to the grave, nor did his body see decay. God has raised this Jesus to life, and we are all witnesses of the fact. Exalted to the right hand of God, he has received from the Father the promised Holy Spirit and has poured out what you now see and hear." (Acts 2:29-33 NIV)

A similar theme is repeated in Acts 4:8 where it states that Peter was "filled with the Holy Spirit" as he defended himself and John before the religious leaders. The consuming power spreads further according to Acts 4:31, where the whole church was "filled with the Holy Spirit and spoke the word of God boldly" (NIV).

3. The Early Church Shared a *Consistent Message* (Acts 2; 3; 4:12)

A close reading of Acts chapters 2 and 3 reveals that the early apostles never compromised the integrity of the gospel message. Even in the face of intimidation and possible death in front of the religious leaders, Peter refuses to back down.

> "Rulers and elders of the people! If we are being called to account today for an act of kindness shown to a cripple and are asked how he was healed, then know this, you and all the people of Israel: It is by the name of Jesus Christ of Nazareth, whom you crucified but whom God raised from the dead, that this man stands before you healed. He is 'the stone you builders rejected, which has become the capstone. Salvation is found in no one else, for there is no other name under heaven given to men by which we must be saved." (Acts 4:8–12 NIV)

It is obvious that the death, burial, resurrection, and exclusive claims of Christ's deity were central to the message of the early apostles. Christ is not merely the best choice for salvation; He is, rather, our only hope.

4. The Early Church Possessed a *Convicting Boldness* (Acts 4:31)

With this in mind, consider what Scripture says in Acts 4:31–33:

> After they prayed, the place where they were meeting was shaken. And they were all filled with the Holy Spirit and spoke the word of God boldly. All the believers were one in heart and mind. . . . With great power the apostles continued to testify to the resurrection of the Lord Jesus, and much grace was upon them all.

Obviously the early believers and the apostles were not afraid to speak the message of Christ with boldness regardless of the repercussions. This was not, however, a testimony to human *brashness* that depends upon possessing an aggressive personality. On the contrary, the boldness of the early church was the fruit of a lifestyle of prayer and dependence on the Holy Spirit.

The early church was defined not by fancy programs or Hollywood style presentations but by a relentless *power* that *boldly* testified "to the resurrection of the Lord Jesus."

5. The Early Church Consistently Displayed a *Contagious Courage* (Acts 4:18-20)

The earliest Christians fully realized that life is disposable and can be taken away at any moment. They were not driven by the fear of death. A good example of this occurs when Peter and John face the religious leaders in Acts 4:18–20. After sending them out of the court in order to discuss their fate, the religious leaders "called them in again and commanded them not to speak or teach at all in the name of Jesus. But Peter and John replied, "Judge for yourselves whether it is right in God's sight to obey you rather than God. For we cannot help speaking about what we have seen and heard."

It took amazing *courage* to stand in the face of certain death and refuse to be silent. This characteristic, above all else, is the greatest difference between the early apostles and the modern American church. *Sadly, while the early church was willing to die courageously for their faith, contemporary believers are not willing to live for that same faith!* In order for the church to be the church, Thom Rainer has stated: "In the postmodern culture of the twenty-first-century America, Christians may as well accept that the criticisms of intolerance will continue. The greater concern is that many Christians are unwilling to take a narrow view because they do not want to be regarded as intolerant."[2]

If the modern church is to enjoy the effectiveness of the early church, we must follow in the footsteps of the apostles, who were totally different in their approach.

1. The apostles did not spend their time trying to keep church members happy.
2. In fact, the apostles did not seem to value or push church membership.
3. The apostles did, however, expect every believer to participate in evangelism.
4. The apostles proclaimed the truth regardless of how it was received.
5. Overall, the apostles were more concerned with multiplying disciples and growing God's kingdom than they were building individual ministries.

Notes

1. For more information, see G. Bulley, "What Is Church," in *Introduction to Church Planting* (Alpharetta, GA: North American Mission Board, 2000).
2. T. S. Rainer, *The Unchurched Next Door* (Grand Rapids, MI: Zondervan, 2003), 225.

Scripture Index